*Léon Walras*

# THE EVOLUTIONIST ECONOMICS OF LÉON WALRAS

This book offers an overview of Walras's pure, applied and social economics. It is based on a newly constructed taxonomy which considers Walras's ideas on philosophy and philosophy of science. These ideas were recently discovered through the author's archival research at the University of Lausanne.

Walras's work is placed in a broader context by stressing the nineteenth-century cultural and historical background in which Walras lived and worked. In particular, the book shows that the influence of Saint-Simonism and Auguste Walras were decisive factors in Léon Walras's economics.

Hence, a new perspective on Walras's work as well as new insights into the making of neoclassical economics is obtained. Walras's work is presented as an important thread between the Romanticism of the early nineteenth century and logical positivism in the twentieth century.

**Albert Jolink** is a Research Fellow at the Tinbergen Institute and Assistant Professor of Economic Methodology at the Erasmus University Rotterdam. He is co-author of *The Equilibrium Economics of Léon Walras* (1993) and has published several articles on Walras. He is currently working on an intellectual biography of Jan Tinbergen.

# ROUTLEDGE STUDIES IN THE HISTORY OF ECONOMICS

1 ECONOMICS AS LITERATURE
*Willie Henderson*

2 SOCIALISM AND MARGINALISM IN ECONOMICS 1870–1930
*Edited by Ian Steedman*

3 HAVEK'S POLITICAL ECONOMY
The socio-economics of order
*Steve Fleetwood*

4 ON THE ORIGINS OF CLASSICAL ECONOMICS
Distribution and value from William Petty to Adam Smith
*Tony Aspromourgos*

5 THE ECONOMICS OF JOAN ROBINSON
*Edited by Maria Cristina Marcuzzo, Luigi Pasinetti and Alesandro Roncaglia*

6 THE EVOLUTIONIST ECONOMICS OF LÉON WALRAS
*Albert Jolink*

# THE EVOLUTIONIST ECONOMICS OF LÉON WALRAS

*Albert Jolink*

ROUTLEDGE

London and New York

First published 1996
by Routledge
11 New Fetter Lane, London EC4P 4EE

Simultaneously published in the USA and Canada
by Routledge
29 West 35th Street, New York, NY 10001



Typeset in Garamond by
J&L Composition Ltd, Filey, North Yorkshire.
Printed and bound in Great Britain by
TJ Press (Padstow) Ltd, Padstow, Cornwall



*British Library Cataloguing in Publication Data*
A catalogue record for this book is available from the British Library

*Library of Congress Cataloguing in Publication Data*
Jolink, Albert, 1962–
The evolutionist economics of Léon Walras/Albert Jolink.
(Routledge studies in the history of economics
Includes bibliographical references and index.
1. Walras, Léon. 2. Evolutionary economics. I. Title. II. Series.
HB105.W3J638 1996
330.15′7–dc20 95–33628
CIP

ISBN 0–415–09824–6

*To Nina and Floortje*

# CONTENTS


*List of figures* ix
*Preface* x
*List of abbreviations* xii
INTRODUCTION 1

1 EVOLUTION AND PROGRESS 9
*Evolution defined* 9
*Stages in the history of economics* 11
*From natural order to social construct* 16

2 THE WORLD ACCORDING TO WALRAS 25
*The Walrasian dream* 25
*Social views* 28
*Political views* 30

3 INDICATIONS OF PHILOSOPHY 35
*The Romantic touch* 35
*Philosophia prima* 37
*Philosophy of science* 42
*Methodological procedures* 46
*'The social perspective'* 48

4 INDICATIONS OF HISTORY 53
*The Saint-Simonian seduction* 53
*A Walrasian stages theory* 55
*The 'social question'* 60
*Theoretical consequences* 64

5 INDICATIONS OF SCIENCE 67
*A general theory of society* 67
*'Classified' facts* 70

*Towards a philosophy of economics* 73
*The economic sciences* 76

6 THE ELEMENTS 81
*Elements of exchange* 81
*The elements of society* 97

7 THE APPLIED 105
*Organizing free competition* 105
*The property of taxation* 114

8 ECONOMICS OF TRANSITION 123
*Savings and capital formation* 123
*Economic progress and monetary reform* 131

9 FROM ROMANTICISM TO LOGICAL POSITIVISM 139
*Enlightenment and Romanticism* 139
*The evolution of society and evolutionist economics* 142
*In the arms of positivism* 145

*Notes* 151
*Bibliography* 179
*Index* 193

# FIGURES


| | | |
|---|---|---|
| 1.1 | A typology of progressivist and evolutionist theories | 21 |
| 5.1 | The Walrasian research programme | 68 |
| 5.2 | The Walrasian classification of sciences | 73 |
| 5.3 | Walras's economics 'classified' | 78 |
| 5.4 | Walras's economics 'filed' | 79 |
| 6.1 | Production and exchange | 91 |
| 6.2 | Capital formation, production and exchange | 93 |

# PREFACE

During the last decade the literature on Léon Walras has expanded enormously and, if the signs are right, there is more to come. Undoubtedly, the increased attention for the work of Walras has a lot to do with the increased accessibility of the work through the publication of the collected works by the Centre Walras at the University of Lyon and the archival work at the Centre Walras & Pareto at the University of Lausanne.

When I first began to 'research Walras' in 1987, the accessibility was not at its present state and most of the information I obtained was through my own plodding through the archives at the University of Lausanne, with the kind assistance of the archivists. I also had the pleasure of meeting some of the members of the Centre Walras at Lyon, who kindly led me through some of the Walras labyrinths. Their help made my annual pilgrimage to Walras territories both useful and pleasant.

I met Jan van Daal in 1986. He first introduced me to Walras when I started to write my Ph.D. thesis. Jan van Daal's Walrasian expertise, his mathematical eloquence and, above all, his enthusiasm for the Walras project made him into a very pleasant co-author of the articles and books we wrote or edited together during the last years. The working together on *The Equilibrium Economics of Léon Walras* at Jan van Daal's cottage behind the dike will remain a wonderful memory (he sold the house) but has also led to a better understanding of the need of formalism in economics. He also kindly supervised my thesis, which I finished in 1991. All I have to offer is thanks.

Most of the material in this book draws heavily on the 1991 thesis although my personal feeling was that I was working on a new and very different book. In retrospect this feeling can probably be motivated by the fact that in van Daal and Jolink (1993) we concentrated on 'equilibrium', in Jolink (1991) I expanded on the unity of Walras's work whereas here I tried to add a pinch of 'whodunit'. In particular, Chapters 2, 5 and 10 were written to emphasize the new direction in which I was heading. Other chapters were customized (or thrown out) to serve the purpose. In most of the Walras references I used my own translation of the French texts. In the case of Walras's *Eléments d'économie politique pure* I read the French texts but used, with a few exceptions, the Jaffé translation in the chapters.

In the process of reshaping Walras I was supported, strengthened and stimulated (the 3 S's) by what now seems an incredible number of people. Although it is impossible to name each and every one I would like to thank Mark Blaug, Pascal Bridel, Neil De Marchi, Pierre Dockès, Rien Dullaart, Philippe Fontaine, Claude Hébert, Bruna Ingrao, Vincent Lhuillier, Uskali Mäki, Philip Mirowski, Mary Morgan, Claude Mouchot, Jean-Pierre Potier, Margaret Schabas, Jean-Michel Servet, Jan Tinbergen, Cor van Eijk, Rudi Verburg, Jack Vromen and Jan Zuidema. Despite all the help, all errors and specific views remain my own responsibility.

I also thank Alan Jarvis of Routledge, London, for his interest . . . and patience. My deepest thanks are to Nelly, Nina and Floortje who have borne with me in the daily process of writing a book.

# ABBREVIATIONS

The following is a list of abbreviations used for the major works cited in this book.

| | |
|---|---|
| *EES* | *Etudes d'économie sociale* |
| *EPA* | *Etudes d'économie politique appliquée* |
| *EPE* | *Eléments d'économie politique pure* |
| *EPJ* | *L'économie politique et la justice* |
| *MEPS* | *Mélanges d'économie politique et sociale* |
| *PA* | *Philosophie de l'art* |

# INTRODUCTION

— This book is about Léon Walras.
— About . . . Walras?
— Yes, about Walras.
— Why would anyone be interested in a book about Walras? Isn't it just general equilibrium economics we are interested in?
— Your question reminds me of my mathematical economics professor, who, after a decade, or so, of teaching general equilibrium theory, nevertheless started wondering 'who was behind all this?'. Out of simple curiosity he started reading Walras's *Elements of Pure Economics*. But simple curiosity is hardly ever without consequences.
— What happened?
— After reading Walras's *Elements* he began discovering discrepancies between 'his' GET literature and the original sources. And, what is more, he started putting more and more Walras into his lectures.
— Now, surely, there is nothing wrong with quoting 'authorities' in our specific field? Not only do the quotes exemplify what it is that we mean but they also add some strength to our argument.
— But doesn't this presume that we know what it is that our quotes say?
— And do we know?
— Right! (long pause) I must admit there is no simple answer to 'what it was that Walras said'. Let's put it this way: in my view modern interpretations of Walras's theory can be divided into at least four broad groupings. In the first place, one can distinguish the group of interpretations which presents Walras's pure economics, as contained in the *Elements*, as the only complete theory produced by Walras. The presentation of Walras's theory by this

interpretation, then, consists of a detailed review of the general equilibrium model, in which marginal utility and equilibrium concepts are considered to be the central features. This interpretation can frequently be found in textbooks on economics, but also in an authoritative interpretation of the history of economic thought such as Blaug's *Economic Theory in Retrospect*, which restricts its analysis of Walras's theory to the mathematical model of the *Elements*, described as an 'abstract model of how actual markets move to equilibrium' though 'thin in substance, stressing form at the expense of content'.

— So in most cases these interpretations are only concerned with Walras's contribution to modern economics?

— Right. A second group of interpretations of Walras's theory that can be distinguished also concentrates on the pure economics, i.e. the *Elements*, though they do take pains to justify the exclusion of Walras's studies on applied and social economics. Walras's latter studies are rejected, either because of their relatively minor influence on latter-day economists, or because they are considered as relatively uninteresting from the point of view of the interpreter. The presentation of Walras's theory, then, consists of an overemphasis on the *Elements* at the expense of both *Etudes*. One of the most pronounced examples of this type of interpretation can be found in Schumpeter's *History of Economic Analysis*. Praising Walras as an economist 'as far as pure theory is concerned', Schumpeter opposes 'his [Walras's] questionable philosophies about social justice, his land-nationalization scheme, his projects of monetary management, and other things that have nothing to do with his superb achievement in pure theory'. Others, such as Hicks, Patinkin or Morishima, have built their own myths around Walras's theory from which the applied and social economics were excluded.

— So you are saying there is more than just the *Elements* we should look at?

— Not really. What I am saying is that some tend to select between the different texts Walras supplied. This also applies to the third group. This third group of interpretations of Walras's theory concentrates on his social economics, stressing the element of social reform. One could think of Boson (1951) or Cirillo (1984). In particular Walras's ideas on social justice and his emphasis on land nationalization are taken from their context and placed in a more practical, political light. This interpretation mostly ignores the relation with Walras's theoretical pure natural economics suggesting an isolated contribution to political economy. As such, Walras's work is mainly examined on its practical relevance for the alleviation of social problems.

— So, in a sense, they are saying the same thing as this second group but tend to prefer other texts?

— That's it. The different texts are taken as separate contributions which happen to have the same author.

— Is that wrong?

— I don't know. I can see the difference between looking at texts on the one hand, and taking the work as a whole on the other. This latter point of view can be seen as the characterization of a fourth group. This fourth group of interpretations of Walras's theory stresses the importance of all parts, the pure economics on the one hand, and the applied and social economics on the other.

— In these types of interpretations, though, stressing the relevance of both parts is question-begging: is there an interdependence of pure, applied and social economics?

— Well, an important representative of this group of interpretations is William Jaffé. In several of his writings, Jaffé emphasizes the influence of specific social circumstances in Walras's day on the economic theory which he then produced. In addition, Jaffé is well aware of Walras's ambition to reform society in order to propel it towards a predetermined ideal. Jaffé tried to solve this problem of linking the different parts by reading a notion of justice, i.e. commutative justice, into the *Elements*. Another important representative of this group is Donald Walker, who puts a lot of effort into looking into the market-mechanism in Walras's theory and the way it could be linked to the real world.

— But what about the discrepancy between Walras's static pure theory and his dynamic applied and social economics?

— Yes, there is a problem there. Some authors, such as Morishima or Van Witteloostuijn and Maks, have attempted to offer a dynamic interpretation of the *Elements*, but this solution seems to do more justice to the creativity of the authors than to the original idea in Walras's pure economics.

— And then, in this fourth group, you would need to find some satisfactory way of linking the normative applied and social economics to the supposedly positive pure theory.

— You are right all the way. In my view, if you want this trick to work you would need to get away from the charm of the elegance

of Walras's general equilibrium theory, by not putting the *Elements* at the centre of the discussion all the time.
— So we're back to discussing the relative importance of the different texts again?
— No. It is not a matter of relative importance. It is matter of piecing the puzzle together.
— Oh, but that presupposes that there is a puzzle; I mean, that the work as whole has significance.
— Do you expect that the work as a whole has no significance?
— No, no, no, that's not fair. What I am saying is, that you may be constructing something that won't hold together.
— OK. I think I can answer that one. In my 1991 thesis on Walras, I tried to position Walras's *Elements* in his entire work, knowing that there was more to Walras than just this one book. In this thesis I presented a taxonomy of Walras's work which would not only give a different emphasis to the *Elements* but would also allow for a different interpretation of his entire work. In this view the *Elements* is only part of a much larger whole in which the arguments which suffice to link the pure economics to the applied and social economics are primarily found outside those restricted segments.
— You mean a taxonomy of Walras solves all our problems?
— Well maybe not all our problems; and maybe only the problem of there being no such taxonomy, to my knowledge, at that time. It is only recently that scholars of the Centre Walras at Lyon (Potier) and the Centre Walras et Pareto at Lausanne (Baranzini) started working on this. But then you also need to read this rather inaccessible *Elements* in a broader context. In Van Daal and Jolink (1993) we have given an interpretation of Walras's *Elements* and how this could be extended to a more general framework.
— And that's it?
— Oh no. I realized I had only scratched the surface and that I would need to understand more about the actual debates during Walras's life time to understand the ground for Walras's work. But this clearly requires a systematic research into concepts and ideas that may cross the ordinary boundaries of disciplines and, for that matter, of time.
— On the other hand, a detailed study of certain elements would certainly enrich the literature on Walras further.
— Certainly. In this respect, one could think of at least four areas in which one could envisage an extension of the literature on Walras. In the first place, an investigation into the origins and

sources of Walras's philosophical ideas. This is what I have done to some extent in Chapter 3. In this chapter some of Walras's early influences of, and ideas on, philosophy will be reviewed. This chapter will, however, primarily supply the building blocks (concepts, definitions) for the subsequent chapters. A separate study of the philosophical material by Walras, such as Lhuillier (1992), could reveal that Walras had provided a full justification for the assumptions he made in what I call his pure natural and pure moral economics.

— I didn't know that. What's the second?

— In the second place, an examination of the historical setting would be useful. I have taken this historical setting as a point of reference for the theoretical reconstruction, mainly in Chapters 2 and 4 but also throughout the other chapters. I concentrated on the theoretical construction rather than on the setting itself, but a study of the accuracy of the reflection of the conditions of time and place in Walras's theory could clarify the social elements in his economic science.

— So History really matters?

— Actually you are right twice. History matters here as a point of reference but also, as I set out in Chapter 4, the concept of History, or actually the concept of historical change matters. At least according to me.

— Are you trying to tell me that History was a source of inspiration for Walras?

— Not just History. There are several sources of inspiration for Walras. As I have set out in Chapter 4 Saint-Simonism plays a role but also his father's influence is important. The latter's influence deserves special attention for it could reveal large sections of a prototype Walrasian structure. Chapters 5, 6 and 7 give some insights into this structure.

— How about the relation between the Walrasian legacy and the modern 'Walrasian' economics? Is this the fourth area you explored?

— Frankly, I didn't go into this relationship but it certainly would be a very interesting study. Others, such as Donald Walker and Pascal Bridel, are working on this. The reason I didn't has everything to do with the fact that modern 'Walrasian' economics is rooted in the *Elements* and I wasn't going to pay exclusive attention to the *Elements*. No, the fourth area I hinted at has to do with Walras's place in cultural history. If we restrict cultural history to major movements in arts and sciences it is clear that Walras was born in the late-Romanticist era and died just before (logical) positivism caught on. The more I read about Walras the more I realize that this has been an era of remarkable changes. This fourth area is rather broad, but in Chapter 9 I tried to give an idea on how Walras could fit in this transitional period.

— So now Walras is a romantic?

— No, that's not what I said. But it would be interesting to know if traces of romanticist ideas can be found in Walras's work. And I say they can.

— You mean Walras and his work has to be seen in its own context?

— Well, it is my impression that Walras was, if not engaged, at least inspired by the problems of his own time. As I see it now, these problems were according to Walras mainly caused by a gradually changing society, or, as I have denoted it, by the evolution of society. This book is therefore also about Léon Walras and 'evolution'.

— Come on. Walras and evolution?

— Yes I agree. This may seem at first sight to be a contradiction in terms: the work of Walras is generally considered as a static representation of a general equilibrium model. Evolution, on the other hand, is by definition non-static and seems incomprehensible in a Walrasian context. The endeavour to bring both worlds together in one book, therefore, may appear as a courageous though impossible mission.

— Is this where you try to discourage the potential reader?

— No, I don't think potential readers are that easily discouraged. So, in the remainder of the book I will elaborate on the thesis that Walras's work was inspired, and shaped, by his conception of an evolving society, in the transition from the agricultural stage to the industrial stage. What I say is that Walras's conception was motivated by his observations of the social problems of mid-nineteenth-century France and I will demonstrate that Walras's solution to the social problems is above all the scientific formulation of the social arrangements of the new economic order. As I will set out, Walras's general equilibrium economics is but one step in the formulation of these social arrangements.

— But is this 'evolution' or simply 'change'?

— This is exactly why I need Chapter 1. In this chapter I will first go into the definition of evolution as used in the subsequent chapters, followed by the implications this definition may have on the outlook on history and what it represents in terms of a social order. This leads to a Walrasian stages theory. As you will see, I will adopt the distinction between 'evolutionary' and 'evolutionist'.

— And how does this relate to Walras's static models?

— As we go through the static models to Walras's applied economics it gradually becomes clear that the static models have a function: they supply the fundamental exchange relations in an industrial and commercial society. At least, this is what Walras says. These fundamental relations also refer to a tendency of prices in the short and long run. In Chapter 8, I will set out Walras's accompanying ideas on a process of transition which will comprise both short-term and long-term economic progress. In particular, the process of capital formation will display business cycles in the short run and long waves in the long run. By then we will have left the strict models of the *Elements* and move into a more verbal economics which I call Walras's evolutionist economics.

— Well, this all sounds very interesting but is it science or just academic day-dreaming?

— I would say it has elements of both. In the end, I would say, we are dealing with the 'Walrasian dream', as I call it in Chapter 2: the goal set by both Auguste Walras, the father, and Léon Walras, the son. This Walrasian dream is placed in the political discussion, between rather fuzzy conceptions of liberalism and socialism, and in the philosophical discussion, between rather esoteric conceptions of reality and ideal. In a sense, it is interesting to see how this type of 'day-dreaming' has become part of our profession. But as I said before: *this* book is about Walras.

# 1

# EVOLUTION AND PROGRESS

## EVOLUTION DEFINED

The idea of evolution in modern economics is generally regarded as a derivative of the biological analogy. To some extent this is too specific. Although the entry 'evolution' in *The New Palgrave* is connected to 'natural selection', this is only to indicate the adaptive traits of the idea of evolution. In this respect, 'evolution' may set a framework for conceptualization of 'adaptations' and need not be confined to the specific objective of biology.

The idea of evolution as a general concept, rather than as its biological specification, is widely used in economic, social, philosophical and historical literature. In most cases, however, 'evolution' is used in a mixed composition of different elements. The elements which can frequently be observed, and which can be placed in a hierarchy (Lewontin 1968) are: change, order, direction, progress and perfectibility.

The hierarchy, here, can be seen as one of an increasing degree of moral intention. In the elementary stage, the concept of evolution merely implies 'change'. The differentiation that is made in this case is between a static world view and an evolutionary world view. In European social history prior to the eighteenth century the world view was considered to be mainly static. Society and the relations within it were characterized by fixity and, to some extent, stability. As the influence of industrial or bourgeois revolutions amended the conditions in society, 'change' became the rule. Evolution, then, implied the idea of continual change possibly following fixed laws.

A second element to be included is the idea of 'order'. While the concept of evolution above embraces continual change, change itself does not necessarily imply the concept of evolution. Following this line of thought, the idea of evolution is further specified by including the premiss that change leads to a transformation of what existed before. In the case of a social organization, the evolutionary process leads to the transformation of the existing society into a new social organization. Whether this new social organization be a rearrangement, or a redistribution, of existing social components or something completely new remains undefined. In any case, the assumed outcome of the evolutionary process is order rather than chaos.

Once the transformation premiss is accepted, the question about the direction in which the transformation takes place follows naturally. By stressing the direction, the evolution of, say, a social organization describes the history of that society. As such, one could think of evolution as passing through successive stages, or a 'changeful sequence' (Lotka 1956). Each consecutive stage is related to earlier stages from which it has evolved. When and how one stage transforms into a next stage is thereby subordinate to the question of direction. As will be explained in the next section, the evolution of society in terms of a change from a stage of hunting and gathering to a stage of agriculture, and from a stage of agriculture to a stage of industry, stresses the direction of the evolution rather than the actual process of transformation.

A derivative from the matter of direction is whether the direction is reversible or irreversible. In the reversible case, it would be possible to imagine evolution as a process of continual change in which the transformation could give rise to an earlier variety. At this point of defining evolution one could speak of a reversal rather than regression or degeneration, as we shall see below. It therefore seems quite a dramatic step to define evolution as an *ir*reversible process of continual change. In this irreversible case the transformation is a uni-directional one in which, say, the new social organization cannot be transformed into an earlier or older social organization.

Only in the presence of the idea of evolution as an irreversible change it seems possible to speak of progress. With the introduction of the element of progress, however, a moralistic undertone is brought in. This moralistic undertone is manifested in the question whether the change in the evolutionary process has led to an improved state. The improvement could apply both to the individual or to the collectivity. In an eighteenth-century society, in which a man from modest descent could improve his social status, change may even be conflated with progress. Evolution in this context is regarded as a process of improvement and, to some degree, natural selection.

A final element in the process towards defining evolution is the element of 'perfectibility'. The element of perfectibility adds the end terms towards which the evolution is likely to proceed. The continual change, therefore, is not only an improvement but could ultimately lead to an utopian state. In my definition of perfectibility, I will add an element of 'intention': perfectibility implies a deliberate intention, through human intervention, to change the object to be perfected. In the case of a society, 'perfectibility' refers to deliberate human actions intended to improve their surroundings. As we will elaborate in the following sections and in Chapters 2 and 3, the element of perfectibility will play a dominant role in the understanding of the context of Walras's work. In its connection to Walras's work we will therefore define evolution as a process of continual, progressive change leading to predetermined, though often utopian, end terms. In this definition of evolution, several stages in the development of society can be described. These stages in the history of civilization are neither fact nor theory, but merely organize the concept of evolution in terms of progressive change. We will refer to an 'evolutionist' theory rather than evolutionary theory when history is regarded 'as development, as progress, as a succession of stages of increasing complexity or perfection' (van Parijs 1981, p. 51). We will therefore leave references to evolutionary theories aside.

## STAGES IN THE HISTORY OF ECONOMICS

With evolution defined as a succession of stages of increasing perfection the fundamental thought is that of 'history in stages'. If we deal with the history of societies or of civilization, as in the remainder of the book, societies are assumed to go through different stages with different characteristics. It is inadequate to describe this evolution of societies, however, when the process has no scale of reference. Thus, it seems meaningless to describe the successive stages of the history of civilization without indicating which common element varies. In this section we will elaborate on a scale of reference that will characterize the conception of stages in the history of economics.

In his history of economics Meek (1976) has given an elaborate framework of the conception of history of eighteenth-century economists which had, as he claims, remained unnoticed by modern historians of economics. This framework, which Meek labelled 'the four stages' theory, seems to voice a longstanding tradition in looking for laws in history which originates in the thinking of the Enlightenment.

The basic idea underlying the four stages theory is that the successive stages are founded on different economic modes of subsistence. On the basis of these modes of subsistence, such as hunting or agriculture, several stages in the history of civilization can be formed. The important point here is the economic scale of reference, which, as we shall see, has a tradition in economic science which lasts until far into the nineteenth century. Although several examples can be found in the literature on the evolution of societies which cite either more refined or less detailed categories, the general idea of successive stages on an economic basis remains the same.

The search for laws in history was inspired by the preoccupation of Cartesian science with laws and uniformities in an apparently chaotic world. This search was partly based on inferences drawn from cultural differences among the different continents. In particular the Indians of 'the Americas' and the conditions they lived in aroused the fantasy of historians and philosophers stressing the cultural similarities between the modern 'savages' and the primitive ancestors of the civilized world.

Meek (1976) distinguishes three 'streams of thought' giving rise to the four stages theory entering economics, one through Smith and the other two through Turgot. The first stream is the Grotius-Pufendorf-Locke stream, which mainly goes into the historical origins of property. The idea here is that changes in the mode of subsistence are the chief cause of changes in property rights and are therefore also the chief cause of changes in society. Meek argues that Adam Smith can be placed in this tradition. The second 'stream of thought' is represented by those works that emphasize the role of God in the making of history. Its major representative is J. B. Bossuet who wrote his *Discours sur l'histoire universelle* in 1681. In the *Discours* Bossuet distinguished twelve successive cultural or religious epochs. The third stream distinguished by Meek focused on the progressiveness of philosophy, literature, and arts and sciences since the classical times. One could mention Fontenelle's *The Origin of Fables* in this respect. According to Meek, Turgot was mainly influenced by the second and third 'streams of thought'. As set out by Pesciarelli (1978) the four stages theory was not at all confined to Britain and France. Representatives of the four stages theory in Italy, such as Giambattista Vico, already published their ideas in the early eighteenth century. My concern in this book, however, is not so much the prehistory of the four stages theory but the framework of stadial types the four stages could provide and what the consequences of this framework could be, in particular for the economics of Walras. It therefore seems worthwhile to go into Turgot's and Smith's framework of the four stages theory in some more detail.

According to Du Pont de Nemours, Turgot paid Bossuet the honour that seemed appropriate to the quality of the work, although Turgot regretted that the *Discours sur l'histoire universelle* lacked original views, reason and true knowledge. Bossuet's historical importance is therefore suggested to lay in his role as whipping-boy for Turgot and other *philosophes.* There are major differences between Bossuet's and Turgot's stadial theories which made the latter's version more acceptable from a scientific point of view. In the first place, Turgot preferred to give a secular account of the historical developments as opposed to the biblical version in Bossuet. In the second place, and of greater concern for this book, Turgot emphasized progress rather than simply temporal sequence. Both elements entered into Turgot's *Plan de deux discours sur l'histoire universelle.*

In his *Plan*, Turgot unfolds a four stages theory. Starting from the beginning, 'without provision, in the middle of the forest', man can do little more than to try to survive. Since the wild fruits will prove to be insufficient man will have to hunt animals to survive. Hence, small groups of people, dispersed over the earth will each have their own territory to hunt. This is what Turgot calls the hunting stage. After a lapse of time man will find it much more convenient to group certain animals in herds and domesticate them rather to run after wild animals. This will be the pastoral stage. The shepherds and their families will find themselves assured in their subsistence and their number will grow. The shepherds living on fertile lands and aided by draught-animals will start to cultivate the land. This is what Turgot calls the stage of (agricultural) labourers.

The hunters who are deprived of either fertile land or animals will remain hunters.

According to Turgot the labour in agriculture will create a surplus value. Because of this surplus value only a few agrarians will be able to supply the food to a larger group. Others will therefore be able to specialize in other trades and live in villages and towns. In this manner commerce can arise and the first signs of inequality among men will become apparent.

In Turgot's *Plan* small nations will grow into larger nations and the first discord between groups will arise leading them into wars and conquering. Through their activities the land-labourers are richer than other people and will therefore have to defend themselves against violence. Turgot believes governments have an important function here.

Turgot's formulation of the four stages theory in his *Plan* serves above all to explain the formation of nations and governments. The modes of subsistence described in Turgot's four stages theory explain why certain political constitutions reign at one stage and why this political constitution is adjusted in a different stage. The discussion, therefore, mainly takes place on a national, or macro-economic, level.

In Smith's version of the four stages theory the discussion centres around the origin of property rights. From the beginning, with '10 or 12 persons of different sexes settled in an uninhabited island', man will pick wild fruits and hunt animals for his support. This is Smith's age of hunters. However, when the number of people has increased, hunting may exhaust the available animals, so man will try to tame some of the animals in order to secure a living. Smith calls this the age of shepherds. As society evolves the amount of people will grow; in the end, however, their herds will be insufficient to support the population. Man will therefore turn to agriculture and society will gradually advance into the age of agriculture. In this process of evolution a specialization of arts will take place giving rise to a surplus. Because of this specialization people will produce more than necessary for their own support and will exchange the surplus for other commodities they needed but did not produce themselves. 'Thus', Smith concludes, 'at last the Age of Commerce arises.'

In Smith's four stages theory the framework serves to explain the changes in the laws and regulations with regard to property. In this account the role of the government is an important one, but, as it seems, only to secure the individual's property rights and thus enable further progress.

> Laws and government may be considered in this and indeed in every case as a combination of the rich to oppress the poor, and preserve to themselves the inequality of the goods which would otherwise be soon destroyed by the attacks of the poor, who if not hindered by the government would soon reduce the others to an equality with themselves by open violence.
>
> (A. Smith 1762, quoted by Meek 1976, p. 123)

As set out by Meek (1976), the four stages theory in economics gradually changed its character as time went by. As economic science gradually retreated from the sociological and historical areas, the four stages theory was recast into a backward projection of the capital accumulation process. In the late eighteenth century and early nineteenth century, the four stages were classified according to the use of, and access to, capital. The resulting historical outlook arose out of a Whiggish attitude, in which the commercial stage arose out of a gradual increase over time in the division of labour, exchange and capital accumulation. The economic activities of the commercial stage were thus confirmed by the developments of the pre-commercial stages.

In the mid-nineteenth century, the four stages theory usually took the form of a theory of development, although by then the stadial descriptions were only subordinate parts of the theoretical works. Partly, this was due to a concentration on the workings of the commercial society; for the other part, the differentiation of the various stages was often inapplicable in reality. Simultaneously, the concentration on the modes of subsistence gave way to an array of criticisms on the question of property and property rights. The criticism opened the way for any suggestion of political, economic, or social reform which would remedy the detected imperfections of society.

The four stages theory, as developed in the works of Turgot and Smith, thus, displayed similarities but also differences as time went by. In terms of the definition of evolution given above, both versions of the four stages theory embraced the elements of 'change', 'order' and 'direction'. The difference in emphasis, already between Turgot and Smith appears to be manifested in the elements of 'progress' and 'perfectibility'. The question whether the four stages theory may or may not include an element of improvement will be discussed in the next section.

## FROM NATURAL ORDER TO SOCIAL CONSTRUCT

It may be argued that the four stages theory is completely compatible with 'progress', or even 'perfectibility'. This statement, however, requires substantial refinement. At the risk of pretending to give an exhaustive overview of Western eighteenth-century social orderings, which is not my intention, it may be useful to provide the reader with a rough mapping of evolutionist theories, with Turgot and Smith as founding fathers, which may serve to position Walras's social order. In this mapping of social orders one may place on opposite sides the 'natural order' and the artificial construct, respectively. The ambiguity of both terms may justify a brief detour.

In the history of economics, the 'natural order' is associated to the physiocratic doctrine (i.e. the 'doctrine of the natural order') of Quesnay and fellow '*économistes*' but can also be found in Adam Smith. The content of the term 'natural order' is not straightforward though most modern commentators would describe it as an agricultural-based, idealized society.

The ideas about the natural order, at least in France, may be placed in the eighteenth-century discussion in natural law philosophy and are embedded in the more general tendency of the social rising of the bourgeois class. The increasing economic influence of this social class gave rise to a demand for greater freedom; at the same time it required a removal of privileges and acquired rights of the establishment, which could frustrate further economic changes. By claiming rights which followed from the nature of things, and not depending on man, the bourgeois class sought indisputable grounds for their claim of free disposition of property (see Droz 1983).

A natural order, then, would be the society which would 'evidently' be the most advantageous for humankind at all times. In this respect, the natural order could diverge from 'the state of nature', where property rights were not defined. Similarly, the natural order could diverge from 'natural laws', in terms of physical laws, when these laws would be disadvantageous to humankind. Whether this natural order would have divine origins[1] or whether it would find its cause in universal harmony would seem less relevant here.

Since man is not the author of society, it was claimed, it would be his task to find the arrangements of the natural order. If the natural order did not prevail, the criteria for a natural order would have to originate from elsewhere. According to the Physiocrats, the criteria would follow from the evidence revealed to men of reason. Hence, not observations but the 'nature of things' would unveil the natural order. This suggests that the natural order has an element of universality and immutability since it applies to all men and at all times. It does not imply, however, that once the principles of the natural order were found man would be subjected to a deterministic society in which the liberty of man would be seriously curtailed. Nor does it imply that only one natural order exists.

It has often been observed that the Physiocrats claimed that the natural order of society is a society based on agriculture. This may have given the impression in later literature, particularly those inspired by Adam Smith's observations, that an agricultural-based natural order should be considered isolated and is, as such, unrealistic:

> That system which represents the produce of land as the sole source of the revenue and wealth of every country has, so far as I know, never been adopted by any nation, and it at present exists only in the speculations of a few men of great learning and ingenuity in France.
>
> (A. Smith 1976: Book IV, Ch. 10)

Meek (1976), however, has shown that the agricultural state was only part of the Physiocrat doctrine. In particular Du Pont de Nemours, in *Table Raisonnée des Principes de l'Economie Politique*, attempted to demonstrate that society evolves through four distinct natural states culminating in a natural state in which agriculture prevails. The reason for society to change is then found in man's changing needs, rights, and duties. At the same time, Meek (1976) observes that Du Pont's natural state based on agriculture reveals similarities with what other authors denoted as 'commerce'. My point here is that the natural order is not one, fixed arrangement of society but an arrangement which may change over time based on the prevailing mode of subsistence. The order is then called 'natural' because it represents the best means for a given end.

Neither the work of Turgot nor the work of Smith seems to conform to the static notion of a natural order, often accredited to the Physiocrats. On the other hand, neither Turgot nor Smith seems to be able to leave the idea of a natural order entirely behind. In the case of Turgot, there appears to be an idea of a 'natural ordering' in which the interaction of the constant physical laws and the gradually progressing ideas of mankind, lead to a universal, chronological ordering of societies. In Turgot's *Plan*, the relevant history focuses on the development of mankind but the eventual outcomes are natural orders at different stages. In the case of Smith, this same idea of a 'natural ordering' of a progressing society can be found:

> According to the natural course of things, therefore, the greater part of the capital of every growing society is, first, directed to agriculture, afterwards to manufactures, and last of all to foreign commerce. This order of things is so very natural, that in every society that had any territory, it has always, I believe, been in some degree, observed.
>
> (Smith 1976: Book I, Ch. 1)

For Smith the natural ordering is even stronger than for Turgot, because the order itself follows from the habits and customs of man:

> That order of things which necessity imposes in general, though not in every particular country, is, in every particular country, promoted by the natural inclinations of man.
>
> (Smith 1976: Book I, Ch. 1)

Hence, Turgot and Smith regard society in terms of a progressive process.

This conclusion may be slightly revised whenever the element of 'perfectibility' is inserted. The element of perfectibility presumes the element of progress; simultaneously, the process of change may reach a state of 'perfection'. 'Perfectibility' expresses a capacity for improvement. It is here that Smith's four stages theory deviates from Turgot's. In Smith's work the four stages theory only serves to demonstrate that the natural ordering of societies may not always be followed in real life. In particular the European economies, Smith observed, followed this 'unnatural' course.

> But though this natural course must have taken place in some

> degree in every such society, it has, in all the modern states of Europe, been, in many respects, entirely inverted. The foreign commerce of some of their cities has introduced all their finer manufactures, such as were fit for distant sale; and manufactures and foreign commerce together, have given birth to the principal improvement of agriculture. The manners and customs which the nature of their original government introduced, and which remained after that government was greatly altered, necessarily forced them into this unnatural and retrograde order.
>
> (Smith 1976: Book III, Ch. 1)

According to Smith, the disturbance of this natural ordering has had serious consequences for the workings of a progressive economy.

> This order, however, being contrary to the natural course of things, is necessarily both slow and uncertain.
>
> (Smith 1976: Book III, Ch. 4)

The main reasons, according to Smith, for this 'retrograde order' were to be found in the disturbing influences of human institutions:

> Had human institutions, therefore, never disturbed the natural course of things, the progressive wealth and increase of the towns would, in every political society, be consequential, and in proportion to the improvement and cultivation of the territory or of the country.
>
> (Smith 1976: Book III, Ch. 1)

Hence, the main implication of Smith's four stages theory is to illustrate the hindrance of certain human institutions and the necessity to return to the natural course of things. In Smith's four stages theory, therefore, the element of 'progress' may be thought of in theory but certainly not in practice. Smith's four stages theory seems to demonstrate that society is optimal when left to its natural course and that it may be 'the result of human action, but not of human design' (A. Ferguson). It is above all the ordering of the various stages which makes the natural course progressive rather than a capacity of improvement at each stage. Hence, 'perfectibility', in these terms, is not an element of Smith's four stages theory. I, therefore, would not denote Smith's theory as an evolutionist theory.

In Turgot's case it is quite a different matter. For Turgot the four stages theory does not represent the necessary course of societies, which may or may not be met in a real life situation; instead, for Turgot, the understanding of history, and the stages within history, would enable the 'philosophe' to make a prediction of the direction in which society should be moving:

> *Universal history* embraces the consideration of successive progress of mankind and of the details of the causes that have contributed to it. The origins of man; the formation and merging of nations; the origins and revolutions of governments; the progress of languages, of physics, of ethics, of habits, of sciences and arts; the revolutions which make empires succeed by empires, nations by nations, religions by religions; mankind always in commotion, as the sea during a storm, and ever marching towards its perfection. Unveiling the influence of general and necessary causes, of particular causes and actions of great men, in relation to man's own condition; to demonstrate the motives and the mechanism of moral causes by their effects: this is history seen through the eyes of a philosopher.
>
> (Turgot 1751)[2]

By stressing the mechanisms in society and the forces leading to a law-governed progress, Turgot seems to translate some of the Physiocratic traits in his own progressive framework. Progress, however, will take place because of, and through, a better understanding of reality by means of an improvement of man's senses. Underlying this universal history, therefore, is a notion that progress will finally lead to perfection of society through the perfectibility of man.

We may now return to our former question and give a first approximate typology of evolutionist theories. The question that may underlie this mapping is whether the evolutionist theories were, or were not, written as models for societal progress. The theories that were not written as models for societal progress need not concern us here any further. As for the theories of Smith and Turgot I believe that both were written for societal progress: Smith's four stages theory illustrated how the natural course of societies diverged from the actual, historical course, and why the human institutions need to be changed in order to correct the retrograde course; Turgot's four stages theory described the mechanisms which underlie the progress of societies and in which direction this would lead.

The differences between Smith's and Turgot's four stages theories may serve as a second division in the mapping of evolutionist theories. The distinguishing feature here is whether the element of perfectibility is accounted for. As has been set out above, the element of perfectibility is accounted for by Turgot's four stages theory but not by Smith's version.

A final division may be based on the manner in which societal progress takes place. In the case of Smith, societal progress would take place by changing the societal arrangements; in the case of Turgot, societal progress takes place by a change of individual men. Both features, i.e. changing societal arrangements and a change of individual men, are present in both theories, although the causes and effect in the former are reversed in the latter.

These three distinguishing features give rise to the scheme outlined in Figure 1.1.

In Figure 1.1, the divisions are displayed. In this figure, only those types of theories that describe progress are specified. A subdivision of those theories that presume societal progress is achieved by distinguishing those theories that emphasize a natural course of progress, and those that include elements of perfectibility. As we have seen in the two cases above, Smith would satisfy the

| | | | |
|---|---|---|---|
| Societal progress | Natural course | Changing individual men | 'Natural-order based progressivist theory' |
| | | Changing social arrangements | |
| | Perfectibility | Changing individual men | 'Liberty-orientated evolutionist theory' |
| | | Changing social arrangements | 'Justice - orientated evolutionist theory' |
| Societal regress / steady state | | (not specified) | |

*Figure 1.1* A typology of progressivist and evolutionist theories

former, whereas Turgot would satisfy the latter. A final subdivision is achieved by distinguishing between those theories in which progress is achieved by changing ideas of man, and those in which progress is achieved by changing the social arrangements. It seems this subdivision would be applicable to both the 'natural course' case and to the 'perfectibility' case. One may, in this case for expository purposes only, denominate the various categories according to either their basis, i.e. natural order, or to their orientation, i.e. individual liberty or social justice, respectively. On the basis of this subdivision I have distinguished three broad categories of theories: 'natural order-*based* progressivist theory', 'liberty-*orientated* evolutionist theory', and 'justice-*orientated* evolutionist theory'.

The 'natural order-based progressivist theory' stresses the natural course of societal progress, which can take place either by changing ideas of man or through a change in the societal arrangements. In the case of Smith and the Physiocrats, and as we shall see later on also for J. B. Say, the actual situation diverges from a preconceived natural order. Since, in general, the natural order is believed to be superior to any artificial construct and, therefore, an adaptation may take place to conform to the natural order.

The 'liberty-orientated evolutionist theory' is directed towards a description of the attainment of a greater freedom of individuals, which may take place by a subsequent replacement of new, and better, ideas. The perfectibility of man creates the possibility to, deliberately, change society towards perfection. In the case of Turgot the improvement of the individual is the key for evolution of society. In the extreme case, this type of theory coincides with Hansot's definition of a classical utopia:

> Classical utopian criticism addressed itself first and foremost to changing individuals and concerned itself only secondarily with the societal arrangements in which men live.
>
> (Hansot 1974, p. 9)

The 'justice-orientated evolutionist theory' emphasizes the process towards a greater equality in society, which may take place by changing certain social arrangements.

> Modern utopias address themselves primarily to changing the arrangements of society and are only indirectly concerned with changing man.
>
> (Hansot 1974, p. 9)

Hence, by changing the social arrangements the evolution of society is guided along these new lines towards perfection. This type of social engineering theory is typically a product of the mid-nineteenth century and, as we shall see, will find Walras among its practitioners. In the extreme case we find here Hansot's definition of a modern utopia. The above classification will serve, and this is the only claim I will have, to give a better understanding of the debate in which I will position Walras. I will therefore make references to these categories in the next chapters.

# 2

# THE WORLD ACCORDING TO WALRAS

## THE WALRASIAN DREAM

The story of 'Walrasian' economic theory started around 1850. At that time, Auguste Walras, father of Léon Walras and an economist, had already published several essays on the theory of exchange value in which he had introduced his ideas, which deviated from Smithian economic theory. Convinced of the relevance of his own work, Auguste Walras insisted on joining forces with his son. Léon Walras, at a much later stage, would briefly recount this event to a younger economist as follows:

> I was almost your age [22] when my father had completely initiated me into his theory of exchange value and into his theory of property . . . when I realized, by a clear and quick intuition, the truth of his system, and I decided to devote my life to establish the necessary deductions to link *his principles* of pure economics to *his conclusions* of social economics.
>
> (Jaffé 1965)[1]

The Walrases clearly believed they had a message for the world. It could be argued, as some tend to do,[2] that of the two Walrases, Auguste Walras was even somewhat more the economist, but in the end it was the combination of father and son.

Auguste Walras, originally interested in questions of law and society, launched himself into political economy to support his ideas on property.[3] Amazed by the disharmony in economic science he decided to look into the matters himself. The results were published in *De la nature de la richesse et de l'origine de la valeur* (1831) and *Théorie de la richesse sociale, ou résumé des principes fondamentaux de l'économie politique* (1849). Auguste Walras's ideas mainly concerned an alternative approach to the theory of value in economics combined with a social reformist theory of property. The perceived labour theory of value in nineteenth-century France was rejected by Auguste Walras, who instead suggested the introduction of a notion based on scarcity and utility. The theory of property proposed by Walras-père was intended to address the social distribution of the factors of production on a natural law-basis which, in fact, would imply the reconstitution of society itself. Auguste Walras's only problem was that his professional position in a rather unstable political climate would not allow agitating, let alone anti-clerical, writings. The few publications by Auguste Walras were enough for his superiors to 'excommunicate' him through an appointment as Inspecteur d'Académie at the town of Pau, in the South-West of France.

From the letters Léon received from his father after this event, images arise of an encaged person placed behind bars by the political climate, by his wife and, above all, by his own restless mind. From his 'imprisonment', Auguste Walras prompted the ideas to his son which he himself would have liked to have put into practice: notions of how to change the social order by changing the tax system.

Clearly enchanted by his father's ideas and willing to disseminate them, Léon Walras first started to work for the *Journal des Economistes* in the last months of 1859. In the meantime, however, he tried to find employment with *La Presse*, a newspaper of liberal signature. Echoing his father's words, Léon wrote to the editor-in-chief of *La Presse*, Adolph Guéroult:

> I need a Journal, a newspaper, where I can develop scientific truths. But I only find ideological or commercial outlets. I cannot give up my goal before having tried everything and this is why I am writing you, who may be the only one left to see journalism as an instrument of progress and as a refuge for ideas rather than notices.
>
> (Jaffé 1965)[4]

He was employed at *La Presse* from June 1860 until February 1861. In this short period of time Walras succeeded in bringing the fury of the French economic establishment upon his head. His new ideas clearly diverged from the ideas expounded by the school of J.-B. Say. The journalist A. Nefftzer stigmatized Walras's ideas as '*diablement socialistes*' referring to the sketchy ideas on agrarian reform put forward by both father and son Walras.

Ironically, Léon Walras himself repudiated socialist doctrine as presented in all of its varieties in nineteenth-century France. A clear illustration, in this respect, was Walras's *L'économie politique et la justice* (*EPJ*), which was published in 1860. This essay was presented as a refutation of the economic doctrine of P.-J. Proudhon although it mainly consisted of the reiteration of Auguste Walras's thesis on agrarian reform combined with some fragmentary arguments for unproven results[5], and cut down Proudhon's ideas in passing. More in general, however, Léon Walras's critique was aimed at the 'empirical' methodological principles advocated by socialist studies. The lukewarm reactions to *EPJ* stressed the lack of topicality of the subjects discussed though acknowledged simultaneously the importance of the contribution of a young economist.

In July 1860, Walras attended a conference on taxes in Lausanne, which turned out to be decisive for his career. During this conference, which featured a contest for the best essay, Walras presented a work entitled 'Théorie critique de l'impôt'. The essay was, as appears from the correspondence with his father, mainly based on the unpublished manuscripts of Auguste Walras. As it turned out, the contest was won by Proudhon and Léon Walras came fourth. Ten years later, by virtue of the impressions he had left at the conference, Walras was appointed as a professor at the Academy of Lausanne.

The Walrasian Dream was therefore a dream shared by Auguste and Léon Walras. The Dream was a perspective on a future society based on scientific grounds. Auguste Walras's suggestions for reform addressed both theoretical as well as practical matters. These same ideas were 'inherited' by Léon Walras. From the very start, therefore, Léon Walras's affinity to his father's ideas would result in a conflict with the most influential liberal economists of the time, i.e. the school of J.-B. Say, as well as with the French 'students of society', i.e. the heterogeneous group of 'socialistes':

> *My father and I have devoted our lives to the elaboration of a pure and social economics which differs substantially from the prevailing one, with respect to both the starting point and the conclusions, either economic or moral.*
>
> (Jaffé 1965)[6]

## SOCIAL VIEWS

The ongoing industrialization in France from the first half of the nineteenth century onwards exhibited some of the characteristics of an 'industrial revolution', in particular in terms of the consequences: the creation and impoverishment of a growing industrial working class in a previously agrarian society. This part of the population sank to a minimum in working conditions, salary and housing as well as in morality, which even then was described as being unworthy of mankind. The slums encircling Paris, such as Saint-Denis and La Villette, housed masses of potential workers willing to offer their services for a minimum of payment, although at the same time they were hotbeds of social disorder.

In February 1848, the social abuses eventually led to what is now known as the Revolution of 1848. The revolt meant the end of the reign of Louis-Philippe, and the beginning of the Second Republic with Louis Bonaparte[7] as president. On 2 December 1851, a *coup d'état* elevated Louis Bonaparte to his investiture as Emperor Napoléon III, which in practice implied a period of repression. It is these events that served as a background[8] to Walras's upbringing and the emergence of his ideas, as he himself wrote:

> I was thus one of these young men united through the Revolution of [1848] by heads and hearts in a movement, on which the *coup d'état* of December 1851 fell so brutally.
>
> (Jaffé 1965)[9]

The 'February revolution' was an important sign of the struggle against pauperism among the labouring class. Cournot, in his *Revue sommaire des doctrines économiques* (1877), attributed the pauperism in France to a combination of, first, a reversal in the demographic trend, which after a prolonged period of a falling population showed a marked increase at the beginning of the nineteenth century, and second, a strong tendency towards industrialization and mechanization of production.[10]

The attitude of the '*philosophes*' and politicians towards the 'social injustices' was inherently connected to the ideological conception of the perfectibility of society. At one end of the ideological continuum one encountered those who simply ignored the 'social question' and at the other those who were preoccupied with it. It is obvious that Léon Walras should be classified among this latter group. Walras's ideological conception of the perfectibility of society, however, was not entangled with any particular prevailing political dogma. The political and societal turbulence of the Revolution of 1848 had led him to renounce the practices of the traditional parties. As a young and enthusiastic novelist, he wrote in '*L'art et la démocratie*':

> But I speak of those who, endowed with a keen intelligence and an honest heart, have promised to be worthy of the role that has been given to them. They declare: We don't accept the traditions of any party. We dislike even the name 'party'. Greed that one wants to gratify, vengeance that one wants to savour, emotions which constitute the motivation and the reason for the existence of parties, we know of nothing. Bloody combat, fracticidal struggles, and everything which they glorify, fill us with horror. No revolution can give to the people the equivalent of what it will cost them in blood and tears. Let those who are concerned with the future prepare for it through science and art.
>
> (Jaffé 1984)[11]

Unlike those who proclaimed the need for a complete renewal of society, either by violent means or otherwise, in order to overcome the social problems, Walras favoured a different approach. According to him, a gradual change in the organization of society could, eventually, lead to a more durable result. The main idea underlying this approach was the determined belief in progress, as affirmed in the preface to *Francis Sauveur*:

> And believing, as I do, in humanity, in eternal progress, the causes will be found in the development of human progress.
>
> (Walras 1858a)[12]

In this sense, the revolutions as experienced by eighteenth- and nineteenth-century France did not lead to the optimal path towards a progressive society. The continual breakdown of the social organization and its subsequent reconstruction from scratch, was, according to Walras, not the solution for the social malaise.

The natural course of progress, however, did not guarantee an optimal solution to the 'social injustices' either. The active process of perfecting society, then, first required a detailed study of society and its possible developments. In this sense, his social views and the attempt to address the social injustices 'through science and art' marked the beginning of Walras's career. For Walras, therefore, the economic reform of society and the solution for the social problems demanded a scientific approach prior to the practical implementation of policy. This scientific approach would contemplate, rationally, the alternatives. This was affirmed in Walras's *EPJ*:

> The improvement and perfecting of our present social state, i.e. the extinction of pauperism, the founding of taxes, and the definitive organization of labour and property, imply the theoretical knowledge of normal economic conditions of an ideal society, and, generally, they imply the rational study of all social conditions, civil, political, etc.
>
> (Walras 1860a)[13]

For Walras, therefore, the factual circumstances would have to be translated into theory, which brings us to the relation between reality and ideal.

## POLITICAL VIEWS

Walras's 'scientific' approach to the social problems was intended to displace the 'unscientific' solutions put forward by the French 'socialists'. These 'socialists', according to Walras, combined an exclusively empirical approach with an involvement of highly personal and emotional factors, and as such, their approach could be characterized as 'unscientific'. What Walras proposed instead, was an objective, or 'positivist', attitude to the problems in society.

In this respect, Walras distinguished between those matters that belonged to *factual* reality and those that belonged to the world of ideas;[14] in other words, between 'real' and 'ideal'. This distinction between real and ideal was, in fact, inspired by E. Vacherot's[15] *La métaphysique et la science* (1858), a book in which Vacherot attempted to reconcile positivism and metaphysics, an endeavour which strongly appealed to Walras. Like Vacherot, Walras used the distinction between real and ideal to create two separate, though linked, worlds. The world of the ideal represented in Walras's words the 'perfection or the absolute'.[16] Every ideal is, by definition, perfect and every perfection is ideal. On the other hand, one encounters in Walras's writings a world of reality which represented the 'imperfection or the relative'. When introducing this distinction, Walras reasoned that the perfectibility of society implied both an imperfect reality (the present state) and a perfect ideal. If the 'present social state' is taken to represent an imperfect reality, two questions remained to be answered. In the first place, how reality is to be changed in order to obtain the ideal, and in the second place, what the contours of this (perfect) ideal would, or could, be.

In Walras's conception, (factual) reality was not an inevitable yoke but could be changed by policy-makers in a practical environment.[17] As such, factual reality belonged to the arena of practice, i.e. politics. On the other hand, ideals were defined as abstractions from reality which were formulated in theory. Ideals, and ideas, therefore belonged to the domain of theory and science. In this sense, any improvement in the social situation, or solution to the 'social injustices', implied the deployment of both scientific and political concepts.

The 'scientific' approach to the social problems thus first demanded a thorough study of ideals which would then be followed by the necessary policy measures in reality. Science would, in this respect, provide the guiding principle for the desirable reforms in practice:

> We are apt to believe that the time has come to scientifically prepare the most desirable and most fruitful economic reforms, to discuss them freely, calmly and without rage, and to execute them with prudence and conviction.
>
> (Walras 1866)[18]

Science is therefore, in Walras's words, the idealization of reality. It precedes politics which, in this same scheme, is the realization of the ideal and therefore succeeds science. It is through politics, in an imperfect reality, that Walras postulated a gravitation towards the perfect, ideal organization of society.[19]

The differentiation between reality and ideal forced Walras to choose sides in the nitty-gritty of the political arena, as exemplified by the polemic with Edmond Scherer[20] on the question of Socialism versus Liberalism. Scherer, a liberal, had written a severe critique of Adolphe Guéroult's Saint-Simonian approach to the social situation. In an attempt to reconcile both socialism and liberalism, Walras compromised that both authors were right and both were wrong, depending on whether they were discussing science or politics. He explained that both socialism and liberalism agreed on a certain degree of perfectibility of society. Their means to achieve this, however, differed fundamentally. Assuming some sort of 'common denominator' in socialism, Walras explained that the socialists' approach to science consisted of a formulation of a doctrine based on a thorough study of society. The implementation of their doctrines in practice, or their politics, consisted mainly in imposing their doctrines through a strong State, described by Walras as 'despotic'. The liberals, in general, turned this order of science and politics around. The liberal politician considered the individual's spontaneous activity to be the main driving force which was directed towards realizing the perfectibility of society and a *laissez-faire* policy consequently prevailed. Science, in the liberal sense, was restricted to critical observation which was itself incapable of formulating rules.

Since science, Walras reasoned, should deal with ideals and ideas, the liberals' approach to science was considered to be inappropriate because it only dealt with observational facts, rather than the formulation of fully fledged doctrines. Instead, Walras claimed, the manner in which socialism tends to proceed in science is much more legitimate, for it deals with the development of ideas which enable the formulation of ideals. This rather crude classification led Walras to conclude that 'as far as science is concerned, I am a socialist.'[21]

Turning to politics, Walras argued that it should take account of, and deal with, imperfect reality. Politics in the socialist sense, Walras claimed, did not take account of reality but instead imposed its doctrine on the existing situation. In this context, although a narrow one, 'socialist policy', in Walras's eyes, is not the desired policy. Instead Walras advocated liberal policy since it takes reality as its starting point and regards the individual's liberty as a policy instrument. It is in this sense that Walras concluded: 'as far as policy is concerned I am entirely a liberal.'[22]

The discussion on Liberalism and Socialism illustrates the essential distinction between reality and ideal, although it does not discuss the dichotomy between reality and ideal itself.[23] Walras's own characterization of his work as *Scientific Socialism* was in that sense no more than a pleonasm. It represented the 'scientific' answer to the social problems or, in other words, the theoretical preparation for practical reforms.

Walras remained faithful to his *Scientific Socialism* throughout his career. In 1905, he summarized this approach in the following conclusions:

> I have . . . held this double conviction throughout my life: firstly, that one should make *reforms* rather than have *revolutions*; secondly, that each reform must be prepared and reconsidered thoroughly by *science* before it is effectuated by *politics*.
>
> (Jaffé 1965)[24]

The reformist approach implied gradual improvement, or perfection, of society and required theoretical insights of possible consequences of reform:

> This [social] organization should not be destroyed nor entirely be reconstructed: it should simply be perfected according to the indications of history, of economics, of philosophy, of the sciences.
>
> (Walras 1860)[25]

What these indications of philosophy, of history, of the sciences and of economics were remained enigmatic at the time but can be deduced from his later writings. We will elaborate on this in the subsequent chapters.

# 3

# INDICATIONS OF PHILOSOPHY

> Our role is to distinguish the goal, the character and the method of science rather than to assert the subject of science.
>
> (Walras 1987)[1]

## THE ROMANTIC TOUCH

Léon Walras grew up in a family of four children. His first years were spent in Evreux (1834–6), in Paris (1836–9) and in Lille (1839–40). At the age of six, Léon Walras accompanied his family in a move to Caen (Normandy) where he attended the college from 1844 to 1850. At the age of sixteen Léon Walras entered the Lycée in Douai and was awarded the degree of *bachelier-ès-lettres* a year later, in 1851. Two years later, having attended courses in mathematics, he was awarded the degree of *bachelier-ès-sciences.*

In 1853 Léon Walras applied for admission to the prestigious Ecole Polytechnique but failed to pass the admission examinations twice. Instead, on the instigation of his father, Léon entered the Ecole des Mines de Paris in 1854 as '*élève externe*'. His stay at the Ecole des Mines was not much of a success and as it seems he was student in name only. Presumably he spent only two years at the Ecole although his parents were given a different idea. In a letter dated February 1858 from Auguste Walras to his son, we read:

> We strongly hope, your mother and I, that this year you will finish your courses at the Ecoles des Mines, and our dearest wish is that you will finish them properly, reaping at the end of the education you have received and which you are still

> receiving, the degrees, certificates and diplomas which may recommend you to those who will need you and who will make an appeal to your knowledge. You will disappoint our expectations cruelly if you leave from there as a sort of dry fruit, and, while losing sight of your initial goal, you would dream of another way of living than one of the careers for which you have been preparing yourself during the last four years.
>
> (A. Walras 1912)[2]

While his parents thought that Walras was building up a career as a mining engineer, in reality he was attending the social events of Paris and writing his novel, *Francis Sauveur.* In his novel, Walras describes the life of a young student in Paris in the 1850s, which seems oddly to coincide with his own experiences.[3] As such, we read:

> During my second winter in Paris the world had made its advances, which it dissipates indistinctively to all young people, and I conceded to it without always renouncing my working habit and my regular life. To employ the common expression to designate this pursuit, *I went out into the world.*
>
> (Walras 1858a)[4]

This world in which he entered was a world of dreams, imaginations, aspirations and enthusiasm.

> Little by little, the enthusiasm to know invades this candid soul. The vivid imaginations smooth in rose the accidents of a slightly bohemian life.
>
> (Walras 1858a)[5]

At this time, the revolution of 1848 and the *coup d'état* of 1851 were echoing through in the intellectual milieu and were greatly influencing Léon Walras's generation. Clearly, ideas of a future ideal society were emerging in the minds of many a young man, among whom we find Walras. According to Walras, society required the reordering of sentiments at least as far as the moral side was concerned. These sentiments, or the 'facts of the world inside'[6] could easily be exhibited by works of art, such as painting, poetry, music or literature. In terms of literature, Walras acknowledged the contribution of what he called 'the romantics', whose work would describe mainly the impressions of the exterior world; what was needed now, according to Walras, was the description of sentiments and morals of individuals in society such as the work of the writers of the 1830s, including Walras's all-time favourite *Le Père Goriot* of Balzac. The stories that would result would subsequently have to moralize the actual circumstances of the world following the Walrasian egalitarian ethics:

> morality is nothing else but the equilibrium and the harmony of individual interest and general interest. . . . We have characterized the goal towards which we should proceed, and the way which we should take, as social equality.[7]

For Walras, his novel *Francis Sauveur* was meant to contribute to this 'healthy morale'. The novel was a dramatic story of two friends showing affection for the same woman and in which romance and tragedy were driven to their extremes. Despite Walras's characterization, the subject of the novel as well as the style clearly exhibit 'a touch of romanticism' in his writing. Between the lines, Walras expressed his feelings of social discomfort and the desire for improvement of the real world. The writing of the novel seemed to him just one of the means by which to improve the world around him.[8] The moral that would eventually follow from *Francis Sauveur* implied that society would support and protect each individual in proportion to his contribution to society. The novel was directed to the younger generation of the working class, marked as the 'generation of 1848', who would be interested in the improvement of society through science and arts.

The criticism of *Francis Sauveur* by Auguste Walras was annihilating. According to Léon's father, the book lacked both the temperament and the originality so urgently needed to change the social situation in France. It is quite clear from the letters which Léon Walras received from his father from this particular time onwards that Auguste Walras's influence on the 'economist' Léon Walras is decisive and led Léon Walras to turn away from his literary work *Francis Sauveur*.

## PHILOSOPHIA PRIMA

In the late 1850s, Walras directed his attention towards philosophy and art, and found his new destination in the philosophy of art. The guidelines set out by his father's daydreams led Walras to embark on a book on aesthetics. This book, to be entitled *Philosophie de l'Art*, was intended to continue a long-standing dispute on the representation of reality and ideal in the arts. The artist, in this sense, would have to translate contemporary ideas into a material representation. The dispute centred on the question of whether this 'artistic' representation of reality would have to reflect reality itself or an idealized version of it. The problems attached to the concepts of reality and ideal induced Walras to venture into the realm of philosophical ideas, which he then employed in *Philosophie de l'Art*.

According to the manuscripts,[9] *Philosophie de l'Art* was to have been divided into three parts, although only the first two chapters of part one were actually written. In order to arrive at the 'general aesthetics' in part two and the 'literary aesthetics' in part three, the first part was entirely devoted to the 'existence of reality', or ontology, and its relation to the ideal in the arts.

> If there is in the subject of art not a larger and finer question than that of the Real and Ideal, there is not one that is also so complex and vexed. It takes its origin from the womb of Metaphysics and that is where I will look for it. I will pass through the *ontology* to arrive at *Aesthetics*.
>
> (Walras 1858b)[10]

The first chapter on ontology, entitled, '*Synthèse du fait ontologique*' (Synthesis of the ontological fact), was primarily to be directed towards an examination of 'reality'; the second chapter, entitled '*Phénomènes physiques et moraux*' (Physical and moral phenomena), was to build on the definitions of the first chapter with the addition of a dichotomy based on the differentiation between human and other, non-human, beings. Neither chapter, however, reflects a very original philosophical mind and both consist, in fact, of a pot-pourri of continental European philosophical thought.[11] In search of authorities who could disguise his lack of philosophical originality, Walras clung to the first thinker he came across. In this sense, Walras was as eclectic in the choice of his philosophical theories as he was in the choice of his philosophers. As for Jouffroy, Walras wrote in 1859, 'I am an eclectic with Jouffroy, whose authority has convinced me',[12] though some years later he referred to himself as a follower of Vacherot:

> it is enough that I have mentioned the name of the master [Vacherot] of whom . . . I am a follower.
>
> (Walras 1896)[13]

After reading Etienne Vacherot's *La métaphysique et la science*

(1858) at the end of its year of publication, Léon Walras abandoned his plans to continue his ontological essay, which, with Vacherot's book, had become obsolete.[14] His earlier writings on ontology and aesthetics, however, served him well in his efforts to develop a methodological structure for his ideas on science. At the beginning of 1859, Walras wrote to the editor-in-chief of *La Presse*[15] to explain his plans for a philosophical exposition:

> To proceed in the correct order, one should investigate a Theory of Reality which could serve as a basis for a Theory of Science in general, far from the religious prejudices which impede the progress of social ideas in the domain of nineteenth century Metaphysics.
>
> (Jaffé 1965)[16]

This '*Théorie de la Réalité*', as expounded in the *Philosophie de l'Art*, was primarily concerned with a metaphysical description of 'reality'. Following Aristotelian tradition, Walras reasoned that before one could describe 'reality' one would have to have an idea about its existence and its substance.

In his theory of reality Walras strove for the synthesis of the ontological, that is, the synthesis of materialism[17] and spiritualism.[18] Following Vacherot, Walras echoed that

> independently of the purely sensitive element in our external perceptions, through the exercise of our sense, there is in these perceptions also another, subjective, element, i.e. the unity which our mind gives to it . . . if our internal perceptions do not have a sensitive element, due to the exercise of the conscience, they nevertheless have, as a subjective element, the unity given to them by our imagination or the faculty which our mind has to synthesize the intuitions of experience.
>
> (Walras 1898)[19]

Hence, the conceptualization of the ontological fact also implied the acceptance of the functions of both the senses and conscience and the synthesizing function of reason. In this context, the senses reveal exterior phenomena and the conscience reveals the interior phenomena. Subsequently, reason will perceive that there is an external phenomenon, related to an object, and an interior phenomenon, related to a subject (the self) and that object and subject form 'substance'. All three perceptions, exterior, interior and rational, can be summarized as 'idea'.

Subsequently, the idea of what 'existed' was called 'substance' in a primary sense; that is, prior to being anything else, something is 'substance'.[20] The idea of 'substantial existence' necessarily implied an idea of Space and Time, or in other words, of extent and duration. Only in Space and in Time could an idea of existence be defined and everything that exists has, thus, an extent and a duration. In Walras's construction, the senses would perceive the extent and reason would perceive Space; analogously, conscience would grasp duration and reason would perceive Time. In this respect, Walras only copied a combination of Kantian ideas and the ideas of Auguste Walras.[21]

In this same tradition, Walras unfolded an 'idealistic world' which he opposed to a corresponding 'realistic world'. In order to analyze the realistic concepts, Walras argued that one would need aprioristic ideas. Walras divided the idea of 'substantial existence' into two categories, by defining 'matter' as the 'substance which extends' and 'force' as 'the substance which endures'. On the one hand, he posited an idea of 'material existence' associated with the idea of extent, and on the other, an idea of 'virtual existence' associated with the idea of duration.[22] The entities in the realistic world would have their transcendental phenomenon in the world of ideas.

'Reality', therefore, could in principle be thought as being represented by a material and virtual existence, that is, by an idea of 'real existence'. By consequence, an idea of reality existed *because of* the combination of matter and force.[23] Walras called matter and force the 'hypothetical causes of real existence' in order to indicate that both constituents were mere abstractions and not observable in reality.

For the manifestations of substance in reality, Walras introduced another set of definitions. As such, Walras defined 'individual' as the only real and concrete existence of substance, which appeared in an indefinite number in reality. The 'individuals' could be distinguished from one another through the presence of different 'qualities'. As in the case of the world of ideas, in which one could distinguish the ideas of 'matter' and 'force' within the idea of substance, the real and concrete individual could also be conceived of as being a composite entity. Thus, by abstracting from the element of duration, Walras obtained the (abstract) concept of 'corporeal entity' or 'the individual described in terms of extent.' Likewise, by abstracting from the element of extent, Walras obtained the concept of 'phenomenon', or 'the individual described in terms of duration'. Both corporeal entity and phenomenon are, by definition, intimately united in reality, as explicitly implied by the combination of matter and force. Walras called, in this respect, 'matter' the cause of corporeal entities and 'force' the cause of phenomena.

Since 'quality' was the distinguishing aspect of the 'individual', a distinction was made by Walras between the 'quality' relating to a corporeal entity, or 'property', and the 'quality' relating to a phenomenon, or 'circumstance'. Walras concluded that only reason will be able to synthesize that:

> *There is a reality or a unity of individuals, in Space and Time, in extent and duration, through the combination of force and matter, as corporeal entities subject to phenomena or as phenomena ruling corporeal entities.*
>
> (Walras 1858b)[24]

In the presence of reality, these individuals would have their particular specificities, in extent and in duration. Simultaneously, these individuals would have properties and circumstances which could be observed among all individuals. Hence, one could see the individuals as manifestations of general facts. Corporeal entities would thus be individual manifestations, in terms of extent, of general facts; similarly, phenomena could be regarded as individual manifestations, in terms of duration, of general facts. According to Walras, individual corporeal entities and individual phenomena were of an ephemeral nature and would undoubtedly go by whereas general facts were enduring. Walras, hence, concluded:

> The true consequences of reality are thus the general facts, which are also the only ones which allow a fruitful study.
>
> (Walras 1858b)[25]

By combining the above ideas Walras was neither being very original nor claiming to be so. In fact, Walras was merely following a trajectory through which the eclectic philosophers of his day were wont to pass.

While Walras felt that Vacherot's book had resolved the ontological question, the dispute on the representation of reality and ideal in the arts, i.e. the aesthetic question, remained open. This latter question was dealt with in an unpublished article by Walras entitled '*Du sens esthétique; de l'art, et des opinions en matière d'art*'.[26] In this article, Walras placed 'art' in a much larger context within which human beings were examined in a social context. 'Art' was then but a single aspect of the observation of reality in that it appealed to the human 'senses'. These senses, together with other human faculties, such as 'Will' or 'Reason', were the means by which human beings would have to find their way in society. In this respect, 'art' could contribute to human destiny by reflecting, and representing, reality rather than some idealized version of it. Although the work of art, conceived in the mind of the artist, could never represent reality exactly, it would, nevertheless, inevitably remain recognizable by virtue of its human context. Exact knowledge, however, could only be acquired through scientific investigation, as Walras was at pains to explain in this same article. The concept of 'art', then, which in the first instance had been related to the 'fine arts', was gradually transformed into a late-nineteenth-century conception of 'art', whereby 'art' acquired a function in the process of transforming theory into practice, albeit in a normative connotation.[27]

At the time, Auguste Walras wrote to his son:

> I see you have put your *Philosophie de l'Art* a bit aside and I cannot say I disapprove of the wise decision you have taken on this. One should prepare oneself through numerous researches, through a vast amount of literature and through serious reflections. It will come little by little, and the more one waits the more one procures oneself the chance to make a solid and durable book. I think you have foreseen all these thoughts and I have no further wish to insist on this.
>
> (A. Walras 1912)[28]

During the latter months of 1858, Walras's interest in aesthetics gradually faded in favour of science. The 'indications of philosophy' were used by Walras in a later period of his career in which his philosophy of science and his methodology played an essential role. We shall therefore turn to these subjects next.

## PHILOSOPHY OF SCIENCE

> Man should not only know individuals but he should also know the relations of order and causalities of the phenomena.
>
> (Walras 1860b)[29]

In 1860, Walras published an article entitled '*Que le sens commun n'est point le critérium de la science en générale, ni en particulier celui de l'économie politique.*'[30] The piece was intended to be the first in a series of six articles, grouped together under the heading of '*Paradoxes Economiques*', which were to be published in the *Journal des Economistes.*[31] This series of '*Paradoxes Economiques*', as envisaged by Walras, would have to conform to a style described as '*économie politique 'amusante' à la façon de Bastiat*'.[32] At the same time it would contribute to his scientific reputation, something which he seemed less likely to achieve in his daily work as a journalist with *La Presse.* Unfortunately, at least for Walras, his plans were frustrated after the first '*Paradoxe*', the difficulty being, as Walras reported, 'differences of opinion' with the editor of the *Journal des Economistes.*[33] Subsequent instalments of the '*Paradoxes*' were consequently rejected by the editor. Two of these rejected instalments of the '*Paradoxes*', can be found in manuscript in the archives of the Fonds Walras (Lausanne).

The first, and the only, published article discussed several practical matters, such as free trade and taxation, though in the final analysis it amounted to a refutation of the methodology of Jouffroy and other 'common-sense philosophers'. In the article, which is written in the form of a dialogue, a businessman and an economist engage in a discourse on the role of common sense in contributing to the achievements of science in general and of economics in particular. The eventual outcome was the establishment of the poverty of common sense as a useful criterion in science. After the establishment of the 'existence of reality' in his *Philosophie de l'Art* and the possibility of describing some of its features, Walras applied himself to a scientific approach of individual observations. In the *Journal des Economistes* of 1860, he published an article entitled 'Philosophie des sciences économiques' in which some preliminary thoughts were presented on what a 'science' would look like and which type of questions would properly be asked. According to Walras, this type of activity was clearly of a philosophical nature, and, in that respect, his ontological ideas could serve as a starting point.

> It is comprehensible that a Theory of Science in general is indispensable to compose the theory of social science, the theory of political economy, or the theory of any other particular science. In the absence of a both experimental and rational *philosophy of science*, which, to be honest, does not yet

> exist, it is undoubtedly allowed to sketch some of its traits in a given case.
>
> (Walras 1860b)[34]

A first aspect in Walras's scientific approach towards individual observations was the idea that science would concern itself with the *phenomena* rather than with the related corporeal entities. Although in reality phenomena and corporeal entities were considered to be inseparably linked,[35] one and the same corporeal entity could be envisaged from different points of view, presenting different phenomena. As such, each science should study a corporeal entity from one point of view, thereby studying the related phenomena.

A second feature in Walras's interpretation of science, is that science was considered as the study of enduring, general, phenomena. The scientific mind, according to Walras, would search for common 'qualities' thereby abstracting 'species' and, at a higher level, 'genres' until irreducible, general facts, could be determined. In this sense, no science of individuals could exist. This approach is, in fact, based on Platonic philosophy, as affirmed by Walras:

> A truth long ago demonstrated by the Platonic philosophy is that science does not study corporeal entities but universals of which these entities are manifestations.
>
> (Walras 1988)[36]

The discussion on 'universalia' contra 'particularia' had gradually evolved through time since the Greek philosophers. For Walras, the 'universals' were represented by the general facts, as abstractions from reality. The general phenomena for Walras were universal and permanent, that is, they applied to all times and in all places.[37] Science, then, in studying general facts, would not necessarily relate to reality but to generalizations of individual manifestations. In this sense, as we have seen in the discussion about reality versus the ideal, each individual manifestation of reality was not the subject matter to be dealt with in science. Since the phenomena, according to Walras's ontological exposition, were 'caused' by the idea of 'force', the nature of a science also depended on the 'forces' involved. In this respect, Walras distinguished two main types of forces, i.e. 'forces of nature' and 'forces of the human will', according to which facts could be classified:

> We may divide the facts of our universe into two categories:

> those which result from the play of the blind and ineluctable forces of nature and those which result from the exercise of the human will.
>
> (Walras 1988)[38]

The main distinction between these two forces was the element of liberty, which subsequently characterized the human will as 'free and cognitive'. The phenomena, then, resulting from the 'forces of the human will' were called 'human phenomena'; likewise, the phenomena which are the result of the 'forces of nature' were called 'natural phenomena'.

The corporeal entities, related to these phenomena, were consequently also divided on the basis of the concept of liberty. Hence, '[w]hatsoever is not conscious of itself and not master of itself is a thing'[39] and '[w]hatsoever is conscious of itself and master of itself is a person.'[40] The only 'person', in fact, in Walras's classification appeared to be 'man'; all other corporeal entities, such as minerals, plants and animals, were simply 'things'.

This classification of 'persons' and 'things' was an idea which Walras, apparently uncritically, borrowed from Jouffroy's work, as can be inferred from Walras's unpublished manuscripts related to the second chapter on ontology in the *Philosophie de l'Art.* In these manuscripts 'corporeal entities', in his ontological sense, were classified according to their degree of 'organization' or 'aggregation'. Minerals were, in this respect, considered as least 'organized' and human beings as most 'organized'.

An implication of this distinction in Walras's theory is related to the *destiny* of individuals. Each 'individual' in reality, in terms of a particular corporeal entity subjected to particular phenomena, was considered by Walras to have a 'destiny', a term which comprised both the idea of means as well as of an end. The question addressed by Walras was whether these means were generated by the 'blind and ineluctable forces of nature' or by the 'forces of the free human will of man'. As such, one would have to differentiate the distinct destinies according to the distinction in forces. Walras, subsequently, considered those destinies of 'individuals' caused by the forces of nature, i.e. of 'things', inferior to the destiny of 'persons', or man. A person is responsible for the pursuit of his ends and for the fulfilment of his destiny, because he is self-conscious and self-directing. A thing, because it is neither self-conscious nor self-directing, has no such responsibility. Persons, therefore, do not only have the moral power, but also the duty to subordinate the purpose of things to their own purpose, according to Walras.

> If it were useful and possible for us to perforate the earth through and through, to drain the ocean, to bring our planet closer to the sun, that would be permitted if not commanded by the only fact that it is both our right and our duty to subject the destiny of things to our own.
>
> (Walras 1860a)[41]

Where the interpersonal relations between men were concerned, Walras asserted that every man is as much a person as anyone else, and it is, therefore, the right and duty of all men to co-ordinate their common destinies.

Although Walras was aware that 'man' may not be as self-conscious and self-directing as he supposes himself to be; as a criterion it is sufficient to suppose 'man' to be self-conscious and self-directing *within certain limits.* By drawing this distinction Walras followed what he thought to be the Kantian doctrine that persons are ends in themselves.[42] The implication of the distinction between persons and things and the necessity of persons to co-ordinate their destinies will play an important role, as we shall see when moral considerations in Walras's economics are under discussion.

Walras's contribution to the philosophy of science can, at most, be characterized as modest and is, in fact, primarily in the domain of the economic sciences. Developing a philosophy of science was for Walras not a goal in itself anymore but had become an intermediate phase. His own interpretation does, however, highlight a number of features which clarify his scientific approach. We will first discuss the methodological features.

## METHODOLOGICAL PROCEDURES

Walras's concern for the development of a philosophy of science and methodological procedures in order to establish a scientific approach to the social question, was above all a reaction to the empirical socialists of his time. For Walras, the approaches advocated by the socialists as solutions to the social question were characterized by ignorance and arbitrariness. His reproach was, in fact, that the socialists relied exclusively on their personal experience.

> I have said that the socialists have affirmed, with reason, the social question, but that they pretended, unjustly, to resolve it far from scientific results and with only recourse to their personal experience, that is, to the empirical method.
>
> (Jaffé 1965)[43]

Science, as envisaged by Walras, should not exclude empirical observation but neither be restricted to it. To this end, each science should formulate, at least five questions to enable the study of the phenomena. The first question involved examination of the *nature* of a phenomenon. Subsequently, the origin or *cause* of the phenomenon was to be investigated. A third question concerned the *number* of species of the phenomenon that could be detected. A fourth question asked whether the phenomenon appeared according to regularities or '*laws*'. Finally, Walras suggested that the consequences or *effects* of the phenomena should be investigated. These questions were related to, what Walras called, 'methodological procedures':

> *Observation*, *experience*, *induction*, *hypothesis* . . . these are the principle procedures that lead to the answer to the questions posed.
>
> (Walras 1860b)[44]

In an untitled and unpublished manuscript stored in the archives at Lausanne,[45] Walras explains in detail how he envisaged these 'methodological procedures'. In this respect, 'observation' and 'experience' merely comprised the identification of the object of study, in particular the identification of the individual 'qualities'. 'Experience' was regarded by Walras as 'experimentation' and in that sense 'auxiliary to observation'. Empirical insights are not excluded as long as they lead to theorizing and science.

The procedure of 'induction' was only added by Walras in his later publication[46] and replaced a combination of what he had earlier named 'analysis' and 'synthesis'. In the 'analysis', as defined by Walras, all observed individuals were analysed according to their 'qualities'. This was succeeded by the 'synthesis' in which, by abstraction, common elements were generalized into general phenomena. Using different terms in the *Elements*, though referring to the same procedure, Walras defined induction as the procedure in which observations were translated into 'real-type' concepts. These 'real-type' concepts were subsequently translated into, so called, 'ideal-type' concepts, which would capture the 'nature' of the phenomenon. The hypothesis procedure was intended to generate explanations and statements of causal relations. In this respect, one could speak of causality between two phenomena, according to Walras, when one phenomenon always followed upon another and when the consequence was always in a certain proportion. Hypotheses, by definition, related to general phenomena and were based on the rules of logic. New observations, however, could reveal new insights and could result in one hypothesis being replaced by another:

> Observation and Experience continue to work, and day by day an increasing amount of individual manifestations of general phenomena penetrate science through a more conscientious study and a better knowledge. Once the knowledge of them improves, the general phenomena demand still more precise explanations. Hypotheses succeed hypotheses.
>
> (Walras ca. 1860)[47]

The final stage in scientific endeavour is to transmit completed results to those engaged in the practical application in view of the attainment of a given end. The interesting point here, is that the confrontation with practice is not intended as a test with which to confirm the conclusions but rather as a means of applying them. This, indeed, seems to raise doubts about Walras's interest in 'verification'. As pointed out by Pokorný,[48] the concept of 'truth' seems to be absent in Walras's approach to science. As we shall see in Chapter 9, it is exactly this hypothesis procedure which changes in the middle of the nineteenth century in the debate on philosophy of science. The criticism of Walrasian economics can, to some extent, be addressed to this methodological chain, as we shall see below.

## 'THE SOCIAL PERSPECTIVE'

In '*Paradoxe Economique II*', entitled '*Que le point de vue économique est le point de vue social par excellence*', Walras presented an outline of how 'individuals' in 'reality', that is, 'persons' and 'things', could be studied from an economic point of view. The general idea was to examine the relation between economics and moral philosophy.[49] As such, economic science was seen as the study of the aggregate of individuals from an economic perspective, and was thus considered by Walras as only a part of a more general theory of society.

Intervening in a discussion between 'materialists' and 'spiritualists' on the nature of human destiny, Walras argued that human destiny could neither be seen as the exclusive satisfaction of physical wants, nor as the exclusive exercise of the individual free will, but would, in fact, contain elements of both. In addition, Walras asserted that human destinies were not independent, as was claimed by the spiritualists who referred to the individual free will of human beings. Instead, free will itself was, according to Walras, influenced by social necessities through which human destinies would find themselves related in a social activity and, as such, would form 'society':

> All individual destinies find themselves directly related to one another. They are the proper object of social activity, as they are the elements of the general phenomenon *Society*.
>
> (Walras 1896a)[50]

The social activity referred to by Walras, was differentiated into, on the one hand, relations between persons on an *economic* basis, and, on the other, relations between persons on a *moral* basis. Both 'points of view', however, were seen as inseparably forming the 'social perspective'.

The *economic* relations between men were, according to Walras, based on the natural fact that man's wants always surpass his own abilities to fulfil them. The only way to satisfy his wants, then, is to specialize in a certain occupation and to create, and exchange, a surplus of produce with others in society. Economic relations were, thus, based on the division of labour in which all men were in contact with each other as specialized workers. In this sense, the division of labour was the *condition* of human destiny in society, in which Robinson Crusoe-like situations were excluded: either languish in isolation or prosper in, and through, society. The only motive in, what could be called, 'economic' society was considered to be 'social interest'. By adopting this position, Walras questioned the idea that society could be considered as a '*contrat social*' of commitments on a voluntary basis by emphasizing the inevitability of the division of labour.

On the other hand, *moral* relations were based on the fact that men tend to voluntarily arrange the results of their efforts in regulation of property and taxation, or in civil and political agreements. In this sense, all men find themselves in contact with each other as moral persons in an arrangement which could be called 'moral' society. The motive, in this case, was considered to be 'justice', which, as such, characterized the *nature* of human destiny.

By virtue of its combination of economic and moral relations, Walras considered society to be a necessary phenomenon. Not only would man be able to satisfy his wants through the division of labour, in and through society, but he could moreover only exist as a moral person in, and through, society.

By drawing this double distinction, Walras apparently believed that he was departing from the 'naturalistic' viewpoint of the Physiocrats whose position, in his opinion, had been taken over by the school of J.-B. Say. According to Walras, the school of J.-B. Say had characterized the study of society (i.e the social phenomenon) as a natural science:

> Such a viewpoint was particularly useful to them [the school of J.-B. Say] in their controversy with the socialists. Every proposal to reorganize production, every proposal to redistribute property was rejected *a priori* and practically without discussion, not on the grounds that such plans were contrary to economic well-being or to social justice, but simply because they were artificial arrangements designed to replace what was natural.
>
> (Walras 1988)[51]

The distinguishing feature in Walras's conception of society would lie in the fact that, though he considered it to be a necessary phenomenon, society was nevertheless not seen as being immutable in view of man's adaptive capacities:[52]

> Man is a creature endowed with reason and freedom, and possessed of a capacity for initiative and progress.
>
> (Walras 1988)[53]

This interaction of man and society, either in economic or moral relations, was considered by Walras to constitute an entirely new conception of human destiny which had previously been dominated by conceptions belonging to the individualistic tradition. Walras claimed that this new conception of human destiny would create the possibility of deducing the conception of a new social ideal based on the double perspective. Hence, implicitly referring to the social question, Walras wrote in the early 1860s:

To criticize the actual organization, and to establish the rational and ideal theory of society, the author must continuously keep this double perspective of the good and the useful in mind, that is, of moral philosophy and political economy.

(Walras 1960f)[54]

# 4

# INDICATIONS OF HISTORY

## THE SAINT-SIMONIAN SEDUCTION

The encounter between Léon Walras and the Saint-Simonian sectarians of the late 1850s was short-lived but provided a second anchorhold for Walras's theory. The Saint-Simonian movement had lived through several scissions in the 1830s and 1840s, and in the 1850s regrouped to unite the Saint-Simonian family.[1] In the late 1850s several adherents of the Saint-Simonian leader Enfantin tried to recruit young people to renew the movement.

Among the few recorded encounters between Léon Walras and the Saint-Simonians a crucial discussion took place around 1860 with Charles-Joseph Lambert, alias Lambert-Bey,[2] *polytechnicien* and graduate of the Ecole des Mines.[3] As reported by Walras in the *EPA* with seeming precision:

> Once my book [*EPJ*] was published, I presented a copy to Lambert-Bey, a Saint-Simonian with whom I had become acquainted and who saw in me a disciple to recruit. Some time later I paid Lambert-Bey a visit at the rue de Tournon, at the house of the publisher Douniol . . . he had read my work with care and vigorously criticized it.
>
> (Walras 1898a)[4]

As it seemed Lambert-Bey had taunted Walras for lacking a proof of the optimality of *laissez-faire*. While Walras acknowledged he was unable to provide any form of proof at the time, the Saint-Simonist had unintentionally set Walras on a track to work on this proof.

During another occasion with Saint-Simonists, the seduction of the doctrine came close, as reported several decades later by Walras. In a letter to the journalist and politician Henri Fouquier, dated 9 June 1883, Walras wrote:

> I don't know if you remember that, around 1860, we met one evening at Georges Le Roy's home, rue de la Ferme des Mathurins. There were the six of us: Le Roy, Habenack, and you on one side; my friend Gustave Maugin, Dr. Thulié and I on the other. It was your intention to convert us to the Saint-Simonian doctrine. The discussion lasted until one o'clock in the morning. We came out, my two comrades and I, without being affected. I must say, as for myself, I could not be converted since I had already received in trust the germ of a social doctrine to which I have remained attached and to the development of which I have devoted my life.
>
> (Jaffé 1965)[5]

In early 1860, Léon Walras had started a thorough study of Saint-Simon,[6] though it seemed that an intervention by his father had, for the time being, kept Léon Walras away from the Saint-Simonian doctrine. From the correspondence with his father it becomes obvious that at this time Auguste Walras had set the record straight: despite the attraction the Saint-Simonian doctrine may have, it proved to fall to pieces at some essential points. In a letter, dated 1 April 1860, Auguste Walras wrote to his son:

> I see that you have been persuaded by the Saint-Simonians. I trust that you will not abandon yourself to their sweet talk. It is one of those sects which I know best, because I have studied the doctrines, and on which I could give you some advice. I do not know whether you have noticed that, in my work on Mr. Thiers's book on property, I have professed my faith on the Saint-Simonian school. In any case, I believe I will be able to recall the points that have always refrained me from agreeing completely with the Saint-Simonian school.
>
> (A. Walras 1912)[7]

The points Auguste Walras referred to mainly related to the theoretical originality in the domain of political economy the Saint-Simonian doctrine seemed to lack.

At the end of his life, and at the death of Henri Fouquier, Léon Walras confessed that the Saint-Simonian ideas had not entirely left him unaffected. To his 'fellow-victim' and good friend Gustave Maugin Walras wrote:

> The death of Henri Fouquier reminded me these days of a recollection of ours of a different nature: the one of the

> evening we spent at the house of Georges Le Roy, Mrs Du Camps's nephew, at the rue des Mathurins. There, Roy, Ch. Habenack, and Fouquier were to convert us, Thulié, you and me, to the Saint-Simonian doctrine, but we left safe and sound around one o'clock in the morning. I say safe and sound, but without the pretence, however, that as for myself I have borrowed nothing from the Saint-Simonians.
>
> (Jaffé 1965)[8]

The question remains what it was that Walras had 'borrowed' from the Saint-Simonians. From other correspondence related to this short period it appears that the subjects Léon Walras did agree upon with the Saint-Simonians were to be found in the areas of history and social economics.[9]

In the Saint-Simonian doctrine, history was the science of progress, which revealed the secrets of the future. Progress, in this sense, was the process towards the fulfilment of an ideal society and hence highly deterministic. For the Saint-Simonians history was the history of civilization, developing over the centuries through several stages following the law of progress. It was believed that Saint-Simon's contribution could be seen in the tradition of history and human perfectibility proposed by Vico, Turgot, Kant, Herder and Condorcet.[10] In the Saint-Simonian doctrine periods characterized by harmony were followed by transition periods of disharmony which, finally, would result in an harmonious 'industrial state of universal association'.

In Léon Walras's early manuscripts elements of Saint-Simonian views on history are given air,[11] among which the interpretations of the sequence of revolutions in the post-1789 era.[12] The main difference, as it seems, became Walras's emphasis on economics as a science. In a letter, composed much later, he wrote:

> I make a great case out of history; but I believe that by itself, and without the assistance of pure economics, history will not suffice for application nor for practice.
>
> (Jaffé 1965)[13]

## A WALRASIAN STAGES THEORY

In the summer of 1858, Léon Walras had been summoned to Pau to speak to his father. In his autobiography, Walras described, full of nostalgia, a summer evening stroll in a valley near Pau. During the conversation Auguste Walras had explained to his son that there were two more tasks to fulfil for the nineteenth century: to finish the creation of a History of Civilization, and to engage in the creation of a social science.[14] The choice of words indicated that the writing of a History of Civilization had already been started but needed a finishing touch, whereas a social science would have to be started from scratch.

On 16 December 1860, Auguste Walras returned to the subject in a letter to his son indicating the various alternatives Léon Walras could work on. As appears from the letter, Léon Walras had expressed a strong desire to write a work of several volumes that would set his career on a right track. Among the works that Léon Walras had in mind appeared rather fashionable subjects such as 'On property and taxes' and 'The history of the committee of public safety' ('*Histoire du Comité du salut public*').[15] Auguste Walras, conversely, suggested a *Traité d'Economie politique* in four to five volumes, in which he was quite willing to assist to draw out a set-up of the work. Auguste admitted that the *Traité* would be a rather laborious task but as it seems Léon Walras did take the suggestion seriously.[16]

In the same letter Auguste Walras returned to his 'History of Civilization':

> I could have suggested to you another subject which has preoccupied me for some time, but which is still harder than the previous one [the '*Traité d'Economie politique*'], and which requires quite some effort and research. I would like to talk about a history of *economic regimes* in societies. I drafted an abstract of the subject when I gave my lectures on political economy at Evreux in 1832.[17] Just as there are three states of aggregation for bodies in physics, the *solid* state, the *liquid* state, and the *gaseous* state, I conceived of 5 modes of subsistence, or 5 economic regimes, for human societies. These are: the *hunting* Stage, the *pastoral* Stage, the *agricultural* Stage, the *industrial* Stage, and the *commercial* Stage. I have defined each of these stages and I have given examples of them. Consequently I have gone into their causes and their effects. I have observed the conditions which prevail at their establishment. And finally, which is the most serious and important part but also the most instructive and the most striking part, I have tried to study the

> effects of these different regimes on the population, on its welfare, on its knowledge, on its habits, on peace, on war, on legislation, on the forms of government, etc., etc.
>
> (A. Walras 1912)[18]

Although the subject of a universal history could hardly be considered as original, Auguste Walras believed that one of his contributions would lie in the addition of an industrial and commercial stage. Most authors until then, according to Auguste, had only stressed the first three stages, up to the agricultural stage. But agriculture could hardly be the last word of civilization, so he claimed, and thus two new stages were defined. As we have seen above,[19] however, this claim of originality could hardly be sustained with the works of Smith and Turgot in mind.

What seemed to be more of a contribution by Auguste, however, was his distinction between history and political economy. The definitions and descriptions of the different stages of societies, as Auguste Walras presented them in his 1832 lectures[20] were part of a broader discussion on the classification of sciences and the role of history and economics therein. Reverting to the ancient Greek theme, Auguste Walras distinguished two classes of facts: facts subjected to change and constant facts. The former facts would have a certain duration and would be replaced by similar facts after a lapse of time. This, according to Auguste, would be the domain of history. The constant facts would remain the same for ever and would be repeated without alteration. These would supply the domain for the sciences.

The class of constant facts, however, could again be partitioned into two classes: constant facts relating to nature, and therefore 'necessarily' constant, and constant facts relating to society, and therefore constant 'by free will'. Hence,

> Necessity, Liberty, and Progress; these are the three facets of this unique fact which forms in its primitive simplicity the whole of this universe that we call truth. Natural science, moral philosophy, and history will thus be the three principal divisions of the universal science
>
> (A. Walras 1990)[21]

With respect to political economy it was claimed that it was a natural science. This resulted from the supposition that political economy was based on a constant fact. Although wealth was generally considered as a variable fact, Auguste argued that wealth in terms of the possession of value is a constant fact. This, again, followed from the supposition that value was a constant fact as opposed to utility, which was considered as a variable fact. This nineteenth-century type of limbo-dancing was only arranged to differentiate political economy from history and to conclude that political economy remained separate from history.

> I admit that wealth considered from its true point of view, true wealth if you wish, is a progressive fact, that the opulence of nations is a necessary element in their general civilization, and that this opulence increases or decreases, just as a multitude of other facts which are part of that civilization. But I deny that wealth from that point of view would be the object of political economy. Voilà how I have escaped the contradiction into which I seemed to have fallen. Political economy is the science of value; there is an enormous gap between wealth and value. Value is not a progressive fact and political economy remains independent of history.
>
> (A. Walras 1990)[22]

As such, the 'Walrasian stages theory' represented a body of knowledge in which change and progress were viewed from an economic perspective but which was separated from political economy. The five stages were considered to give an impression of the ascending line of human civilization, in which the constant facts of political economy reappeared without alteration and variable facts showed improvement:

> The five stages described above form without doubt an ascending series of progress and perfection. They can serve to trace the development of civilization.
>
> (A. Walras 1990)[23]

In the literature on the works of Léon Walras, the 'indications of history' have somehow remained neglected. In the manuscripts kept at the Fonds Walras at the University of Lausanne, however, several traces of the Walrasian stages theory can be found. Lesson 2 of the manuscript entitled '*Theorie de la production et de la richesse sociale*' is in this respect revealing. It is entitled 'The five economic regimes – Their causes and effects' (*Les cinq régimes économiques – Leurs causes et leurs conséquences*) and is almost a literal transcription of Auguste Walras's 1832 lectures.[24] This lesson, as it appears, formed part of the courses on applied economics Léon Walras taught at the University of Lausanne.[25]

Referring to historical evidence, Léon Walras also distinguished five 'economic regimes' or stages in human civilization. The first stage in human civilization was the *uncultivated stage* (*'état sauvage'*) in which man lived exclusively from hunting and fishing, and from gathering a selection of wild plants and fruits. What seemed to characterize man at this stage was that he relied more on nature than on his own personal faculties. In the second stage, the *pastoral stage* (*'état pastoral'*), man fed and clothed himself with the products of his animal husbandry. Man seemed to rely more on the raising of his stock than on the produce freely available in his natural surroundings. The *agricultural stage* (*'état agricole'*) did not exclude either of the first two activities, but hunting, fishing, and raising animals became specialized operations in the more general whole of agrarian activities. In addition to hunting, fishing and raising animals, man began to apply his efforts to the land. The fourth stage was the *industrial stage* (*'état industriel'*). Housing and luxuries become increasingly important and a new class of men emerges: the industrial entrepreneur. The fifth and last stage was the *commercial stage* (*'état commercial'*). Alongside the agriculturalists and industrial entrepreneurs, a class of merchants appeared, people who engaged in domestic or international trade of products. According to Walras, this latter stage, the commercial stage, was the most advanced and most complex of all stages.

Although a civilization would not necessarily have to pass through each consecutive stage, nor would it have to start or end at any particular phase,[26] the character of each regime as such does imply certain consequences for a society. One of the main factors that Walras seemed to be stressing, is the relative importance of capital, and of land in particular. As Walras explained in his '*Théorie de la Propriété*',[27] ownership of land was changing throughout the different stages. In both the uncultivated stage as well as in the pastoral stage the land was the property of the community, in which each member would claim an equal right to the use of the land. As society evolved towards the agricultural stage, the land would, according to Walras, be divided among the individuals due to the degree of specialization inherent in individual agricultural production. This private ownership of land, then, would continue to exist in the industrial and commercial society. This process of privatization of land, as we shall see, will be the starting point of a disharmonious transition period with inequality of conditions. One of the 'indications of history', therefore, was the so-called 'Social Question'.

## THE 'SOCIAL QUESTION'

In the unpublished '*Des Réformes Economiques*', written in 1861,[28] Walras argued that the revolutionary movements of the eighteenth and nineteenth centuries emerged from two distinct impulses. The first impulse was effective in the direction of civil and political freedom and originated from the philosophical and moral ideas of the eighteenth century. The second impulse was directed towards a more rational economic order of society and could, according to Walras, only have originated from nineteenth-century metaphysics and the social theories which were elaborated on during the late 1840s. Although attention had focused primarily on the first impulse, Walras's main concern was the latter impulse because it explained the actual social circumstances in which the French found themselves.

Discussing the dissatisfaction in France with the failure to accomplish the goals the French Revolution of 1789 had set itself, Walras explained that this dissatisfaction could not be attributed to the absence of reformist impulses. In fact, Walras argued, the French Revolution had provided the impulses towards civil and political freedom, in the sense that it had cast away the feudal system and obtained universal suffrage and certain property rights.[29] The failure to achieve economic equality, that is, equality in the conditions of production and distribution,[30] could be explained by the fact that, before the impulse of the first order had been allowed to exhaust itself, France had experienced an impulse of the second order. In that sense, economic reform was still going on, a fact which could actually be observed in reality, according to Walras, and therefore there was little reason for despair. The nineteenth century would in this sense be characterized by the movement towards the accomplishment of civil and political freedom. Walras prophesied that the twentieth century would show a tendency towards a more rational economic order and, thus, provide a solution to what was called 'the social question'.

Walras's first book on economics, *L'économie politique et la justice* (*EPJ*), opened with an extensive discussion of the 'social question'.

In it he described the miserable existence of the Parisian workers and possible explanations for their strained circumstances. Like most writers concerned with social problems, Walras was convinced that no satisfactory solution had yet been found. At the same time, he declared to set himself the task of finding this solution.[31]

As pointed out by Jaffé,[32] the 'social question' in nineteenth-century France was in Walras's work attributed to the outcome of an entangled conflict relating to social, political, economic and ideological matters. But even then, Walras's interpretation of the social question underwent some degree of modification during the fifty years in which the issue was being addressed by him.

During the early 1860s, the social question was mainly related to the social position of the labourers, who, through the existing system of distribution, were forced to live a life of poverty. This issue was discussed by Léon Walras in *L'économie politique et la justice* but also appeared in several of his newspaper contributions at that time.[33] Later, in 1880, Walras published the newspaper article '*La Question Sociale*'[34] in which the argument mainly concentrated on the proper social conditions for society. As such, the social question was elevated to the level of the macroeconomic order at which questions involving production as well as distribution needed to be solved simultaneously.

In 1909, the issue was once again slightly reformulated as follows:

> The new political economy has completely enlightened the old problem of 'population and subsistence' . . . which may be posed as follows: 'How can an *increasing* population in a *limited* territory, having arrived at the industrial and commercial State, be given a rising standard of living?'
>
> (Walras 1987)[35]

Although the social question in Walras's work was reformulated several times, the core of the issue never changed: the changes in society. As observed by Walras:

> We know that in the present era, due to the railways, we are leaving the pure agricultural state and entering into the industrial and commercial state which is also a financial one.
>
> (Walras 1896)[36]

The social question, then, was placed in the context of the gradual reform of society in which the economic conditions for both production and distribution would require proper adjustment. With this long-term vision of gradual reform, Walras fits into the French evolutionist tradition that, according to Barrault,[37] starts with Condorcet and was followed by Comte. Evolutionist thought in economics started, in this respect, with Saint-Simon and the Saint-Simonian doctrine but was later also adopted by other schools. The general idea embraced the thought that societies experience gradual changes in which revolutions are accidental events. This same idea can be found in Cournot's work:

> The conditions of society slowly change in the course of centuries, due to internal and general causes. In this respect, one can distinguish the movements among the events in history from the erratic shocks, also called revolutions, which have a limited and incidental cause and a local impact of varying extent.
>
> (Cournot 1872)[38]

This evolutionist idea can also be found in Walras's theory, with respect to the social problems. As he described in the *EPJ*, progress would follow its natural course, which in the Saint-Simonian tradition he called 'organic', and thus avert the self-destruction of society:

> We must accept our social state, which may at times appear quite defective, without revolt because it is necessary, without regrets, and because it embraces the indestructible principle for its own, normal improvement.
>
> (Walras 1860a)[39]

Thus, for Walras, the 'social question' was merely the indication of a transition in society. The industrialization of 'agricultural' nineteenth-century France was gradually changing the economic relations in society, and, as such, induced strained conditions in the economy. This evolution of the economic relations in society, then, required a socially acceptable restructuring of the economic conditions:

> the establishment itself of the industrial and commercial stage requires the solution to the social question.
>
> (Walras 1896a)[40]

The different conditions of production and distribution, then, which were appropriate to the economic organization in the agricultural stage, required an adaptation of these conditions for the organization of the industrial and commercial stage.

> To resolve the social question, we need to implement great progress in the conditions of production and distribution.
>
> (Walras 1896a)[41]

This interpretation of the 'social question' was closely connected to Walras's evolutionist ideas of history and to social economics.

A reform of the economic organization would find its justification in a direct confrontation with other forms of organization. Free competition, as a form of organization, was considered by Walras as the outcome of a historical process of organizational progress in which the conditions for material well-being and justice had gradually improved.[42] Walras believed that a 'socialist' organization of society had not experienced this historical evolution although it could, in principle, be evaluated on the same grounds of interest and justice in matters of industry and trade:

> Man has progressed from a system of guilds, trade regulations and price fixing to a system of freedom of industry and trade, i.e. to a system of *laissez-faire, laissez-passer* . . . The superiority of the later forms of organization over the earlier forms lies . . . in their closer conformity with material well-being and justice. The proof of such conformity is the only justification for adhering to a policy of *laissez-faire, laissez-passer*. Moreover, socialistic forms of organization should be rejected if it can indeed be shown that they are inconsistent with material well-being and justice.
>
> (Walras 1988)[43]

In this debate, *L'Economie politique et la justice* propagated free competition along the lines set out by Auguste Walras though larded with Saint-Simonian rhetoric. As the natural course of progress could guarantee an optimal solution to the 'social question', accepting free competition as this natural economic mechanism *a priori*, Walras was obliged to examine the necessary conditions under which this mechanism would procure an optimal result. In this respect, by concentrating on the conditions governing the efficacy of free competition, Walras not only examined its limits, but also tried to draw attention to the ill-conceived applications of '*laissez-faire*' policy proposed by orthodox economists in France.

Only by knowing how the mechanism of free competition worked under certain conditions would it be possible to formulate a specific policy. The active process of perfecting society, then, first required a detailed study of society and its possible developments. In addition, it entailed the description of a situation which did not yet exist but which could be realized. According to Walras this would be the task of science: to find the conditions of an ideal society which has just entered the industrial and commercial stage, based on principles of social justice and individual interest. One of the offsprings of this approach, so it seemed, was the consequences it had for existing economic theory.

## THEORETICAL CONSEQUENCES

Walras's 'indications of history' should not be confused with, what may be called, the 'historical method' of the nineteenth-century historical school. Nevertheless, there were lessons to be learned from history which could have theoretical implications.

As indicated by Walras in the '*Cours d'économie politique et sociale*', history could supply the relevant definitions and concepts for economics. As such, history would be one of the theoretical benchmarks for economics but only when viewed from an economic point of view. Unfortunately, so Walras claimed, there were very few examples of this:

> One must admit, however, that few histories have been studied from an economic point of view. There are above all histories of wars and of conquests; there are histories of governments and of political revolutions; but one has neglected the history of labour and of agricultural, industrial and commercial production. This kind of history can above all be found in the works of the Germans which go by the name of works on political economy.
>
> (Walras forthcoming)[44]

Hence, the work of the German Historical School supplied Walras the 'relevant' kind of history.

The Historical School supplied facts, though subject to change, which were characteristic for an industrial and commercial stage to come and could be regarded as economic ideal-types for that stage.

> As has been noted by the masters of the historical school themselves, our economic types of *markets*, of *products*, of *services*, of *entrepreneurs*, of *landowners*, of *workers*, of *capitalists*, of *current prices*, of *rents*, of *salaries*, of *interests*, refer to the industrial and commercial stage and not to the agricultural stage, to the future and not to the past.
>
> (Walras 1898)[45]

The conclusion for Walras to be drawn from this was that the empirical observations revealed that society was entering the industrial and commercial stage. This claim was certainly unfounded since it only served as a self-reference: the economic stages were defined by their economic types so Walras's conclusion would be tautological. However, Walras's message was clear: a new era required new theoretical concepts which could serve in the study of constants facts in science. The historical facts and figures as such, however, were not sufficient to be labelled 'economics'. Walras rejected the exclusively inductive method he recognized in the work of the Historical School. In that sense, Léon Walras adopted the same distinction his father had made between facts subject to change and constant facts, in which only the latter supplied a domain for science.

In this respect, Walras's reference to the type 'entrepreneur' or the types 'products and services' not only revealed the part of his own plans but also revealed the area in which most of the discrepancies with physiocratic and classical economics would lie.[46] The 'indications of history' thus led to the indications of science.

# 5

# INDICATIONS OF SCIENCE

## A GENERAL THEORY OF SOCIETY

Towards the end of 1861, Walras had apparently planned to write nine new '*Paradoxes Economiques*'[1] though he changed his strategy by communicating the subjects of his '*Paradoxes*' to the editor prior to writing an entire article.[2] As far as we know, only one was drafted.[3] In this third surviving '*Paradoxe Economique*', entitled '*De la richesse naturelle ou gratuite – De la richesse sociale ou économique – De la richesse intellectuelle*', the discussion, started in the first article,[4] was continued. Common sense, as a methodology, merely appeared to represent an approach of empirical observation and was in itself inadequate for science, according to Walras. In this article, the businessman and the economist once more discussed methodology. Falling back on his earlier ideas about ontology and methodology, Walras argued that each science studied phenomena from a certain perspective, but each (social) science was also rooted in the same general theory of society. At the time, however, Walras had not yet arrived at a fully elaborated theory of society. From his published and unpublished material it can be inferred that a draft of a 'Walrasian research programme' would at that time have been organized in the manner as depicted in Figure 5.1.

The *Théorie générale de la société*, as it had come to be named, had developed during the 1860s out of the idea of the '*Paradoxes Economiques*'. The initial articles on the concepts of materialism and spiritualism were eventually presented in an extended form as public lectures in Paris (1867), and later as Part I of the *EES*. At the time, Walras's reasons for developing such a theory had everything to do with the lack of a satisfactory theory of landownership, and the fact that the distribution of this factor was fundamental to

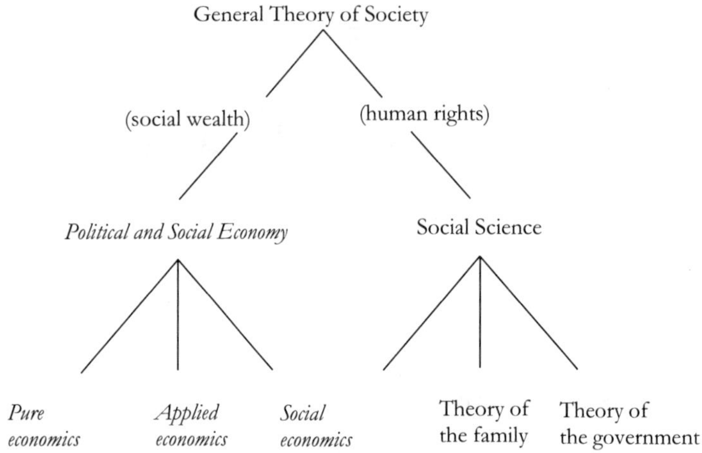


*Figure 5.1* The Walrasian research programme

the solution to the social question. Walras's critique was directed towards both J.-B. Say, who was regarded as a *utilitarian*, as well as to F. Bastiat, who was associated with the *moralists*. Having rejected their exclusively individualistic philosophy,[5] Walras's prime objections remained the predominance in the respective theories of the consideration of interest (utilitarians) and of justice (moralists). In Walras's *Théorie générale de la société*, instead, the considerations of interest and justice entered simultaneously.

The article '*Que le point de vue économique est le point de vue social par excellence*'[6] served as a first draft for Walras's *Théorie générale de la société*. In this article, Walras argued that political economy had so far only played a minor role in the social and political arena. Provocatively he asked:

> What has political economy been until now? — Nothing.
> What should it be from now on? — Everything.
>
> (Walras 1860f)[7]

What Walras seemed to suggest was that society was primarily based on the division of labour. In this respect, the point of view of production and distribution was an essential and fundamental vantage point from which to study man and society. As such, all considerations on society would have to take account of economic considerations as well. The 'economic perspective' was, therefore, the 'social perspective par excellence' in that it stressed the necessary conditions of a society. The main idea in the article, however, was to define the relation between economic and moral considerations. Although the division of labour was considered to be the primary, and necessary, condition of society, it nevertheless implied the presence of a moral personality under whose auspices the division was to take place. A moral personality, according to Walras, was a person furnished with (aesthetic) senses, intelligence and a free will. As such, the economic perspective combined both considerations of interest and of justice: the division of labour implied morality, and morality in turn was explained and justified by the division of labour. This mutual relation determined the nature of the theory of society.

As Figure 5.1 shows, the economic perspective implied that the questions concerning society were related, on the one hand, to social wealth and its production in terms of social interest; and on the other, to the distribution of social wealth in terms of justice. As such, the social question, which we have already characterized as being central to the understanding of Walras's theory, was for the time being delimited to the *economic* social question. The solution to this question was, in fact, the solution to the question of an adequate *economic* organization of society.

> The solution to what one names the economic social question, and which is not the entire social question, depends on two kinds of very different, though equally essential, preliminary considerations: purely economic considerations and purely moral considerations. Here is exactly what I wish to say in this respect. To resolve the question of the economic organization of society is, in summary, to lay down the conditions: 1. of the most abundant production, and 2. of the most just distribution of social wealth among men in society.
>
> (Walras 1896a)[8]

Walras's economics was therefore primarily interested in finding the conditions for two categories of relations. The first category concerned the relations between persons and things in the process of producing social wealth, or, in Walras's words, 'human actions in respect to natural forces'.[9] The *raison d'être* of production, in abstract terms, would be the subordination of the destiny of things to human destiny. The second category concerned the relations between persons and their fellows in the distribution of social wealth, or, 'the impact of the human will or of human actions on the will or actions of other men'.[10] The *raison d'être* of this second category was found in the mutual co-ordination of human destinies. Although the answers to the 'economic' social question which had hitherto been put forward by Walras are not very original, and are, moreover, verbatim extracts from his father's work, the new questions that arose in consideration of these answers are much more fundamental:

> before laying down, and in order to lay down, these conditions one must know two things: what is social wealth and what is man in society.
>
> (Walras 1996a)[11]

The questions thus posed in 1868 were to take Walras all the way back to the drawing board in his attempts to establish economics as a formal science. The economic perspective, therefore, inevitably entails the structuring of ideas, and out of these a philosophy of economics must emerge.

## 'CLASSIFIED' FACTS

> Say's disciples . . . classify the theory of value in exchange under the theory of production while others classify the theory of property under the theory of distribution. This is the sort of political economy which is being fashioned and taught today. Is that not reason enough to hold that the structure is cracked and the façade deceptive and that in such a case it is the right and the primary duty of the economist carefully to formulate a philosophy of his science?
>
> (Walras 1988)[12]

One of Walras's objections to the manner in which his contemporaries were proceeding concerned the continuing debate about the definition of economic science. In several articles Walras expressed his strong disagreement with the economists of his day, who would persist in muddling the different objects and methods in, and nature of, economic science. According to Walras, economic science would eventually obtain its proper characterization as a science. This, however, would require a classification of sciences in general, in order to provide a niche for each science.

The classification of sciences, in Walras's day, consisted of a division into natural and moral sciences. A natural science would in this respect deal with natural phenomena; likewise, a science dealing with human phenomena was a moral science. Walras also retained this distinction between natural and moral sciences, which he could relate to his ontological differentiation. But this was only one part of the classification. What this classification failed to do, according to Walras, was to state explicitly the differentiation in method. In terms of his methodological procedures, Walras stressed that one set of sciences 'identifies, describes and explains' general phenomena. In a sense, one could add that it also 'identifies, describes and explains' the causes of the general phenomena, that is, the 'forces'. This was affirmed by Walras, in particular for the 'forces of nature':

> Obviously all one can do about manifestations of the forces of nature is to identify, verify and explain them.
>
> (Walras 1988)[13]

By their very nature, the scientist can observe these 'blind and ineluctable forces of nature' and can do nothing more than that, since they are considered to be beyond the influence of man. This limitation does not apply to the 'forces of the human will', since according to Walras:

> In dealing with the workings of the human will, not only is it possible to identify, verify and explain them, but having done that, one can then direct[14] them.
>
> (Walras 1988)[15]

The consequence for Walras's methodology is that science is no longer restricted to observation and explanation but, in addition, also 'advises, prescribes and directs'. In this respect, Walras extended his positive concept of science, which he called 'pure' science, with a set of criteria with which to direct the forces of the human will. This latter set was called 'applied theory', although it remains within the domain of theoretical science.[16]

Clearly, Walras's methodology in his 'applied theory' is only applicable to a study of human beings, or rather the related phenomena, as opposed to non-human beings, for only the forces of the former can be directed. This is, indeed, an important point in Walras's theory. Since he introduces the possibility of exercising a certain amount of influence on the human will, in whatever manner, the human-induced processes in society are no longer necessarily fatalistic and determinist. In fact, the solution to the social question can be found in the process of guiding mankind. Hence, as stated by Walras, (economic) science

> may be considered as an *explanation of what is* and *as a programme of what ought to be.*
>
> (Walras 1988)[17]

In this respect, 'what is' and 'what ought to be' are connected by the methodology used, in which the 'truths' obtained in Walras's 'pure' science serve to formulate the rules of conduct in his 'applied' science.

In addition to the division of sciences into natural and moral sciences, therefore, Walras introduced the distinction between 'pure' and 'applied' sciences in order to include the difference in method: 'pure' science observes and explains phenomena, whereas 'applied' science prescribes rules of (human) conduct. Walras thus arrives at a double distinction as described in his article '*De la culture et de l'enseignement*':

> There is a *pure natural* science which establishes facts and relations stemming from the play of nature's fatal forces and there is a *pure moral* science which establishes facts and relations stemming from the exercise of man's free will . . . . There is an *applied natural* science furnishing rules of conduct of persons versus things, and there is an *applied moral* science furnishing rules of conduct of persons versus one another.
>
> (Walras 1987)[18]

These four possible combinations: pure natural sciences, pure moral sciences, applied natural sciences and applied moral sciences, can be summarized as in Figure 5.2.

The grid framework in Figure 5.2 can in principle be imposed on any science. In some sciences, however, one or more cells will remain vacant, implying absence or irrelevance of a certain fact or type of method. The type of 'pure sciences' we can expect in the two relevant cells is described by Walras as follows. Pure sciences proceed 'by parting from the most simple manifestations of it [the phenomenon] to arrive at the most complex manifestations'.[19] Examples of these are: mathematics, physics, chemistry and natural history. The types of 'applied sciences' are much more restricted. As we mentioned above, applied sciences relate to the prescription of rules of conduct, always designed to guide the forces of the human will. The question here is: rules of conduct

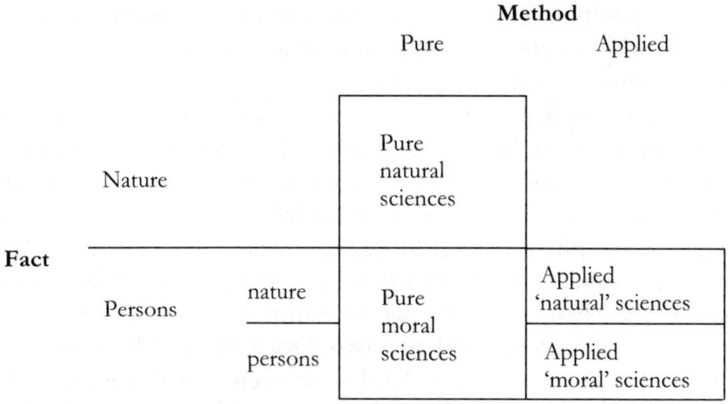


*Figure 5.2* The Walrasian classification of sciences

in relation to what? Again, following the distinction adopted by Auguste Walras,[20] the distinction is between natural phenomena and human phenomena. This implies that applied natural sciences deal with the rules of conduct in the relation 'man'–'thing', on the one hand. On the other, applied moral sciences deal with the rules of conduct in the relation 'man'–(fellow)'man'. Walras describes this as 'the history of human action in all its varieties'. Examples of such action are: languages and literature, religion, art, science, industry, habits, law, war and politics. Using these divisions, we are able to construct a classification for Walras's economic theory, as we will see shortly.

## TOWARDS A PHILOSOPHY OF ECONOMICS

In the shadow of an 'economic' social question, Walras's prime ambition seemed to be the formulation of a science that determined the conditions of production and distribution of social wealth. As we have noted above, the nature of a science, for Walras, was characterized by the point of view adopted. As such, economic science was the study of the universe from the economic point of view. In the '*Philosophie des Sciences Economiques*',[21] as well as in some unpublished manuscripts in the archives at Lausanne, Walras re-examined his ontological writings in order to set out the specific contours of an economic science. A science, then, defined as the study of phenomena related to a corporeal entity,[22] would in the case of an economic perspective have to indicate which economic phenomena are to be studied and to which corporeal entity they relate.

According to Walras, the economic perspective, which amounts to the division of labour, had resulted in the establishment of necessary economic relations between persons. A first general phenomenon that should be studied by an economic science is, therefore, the phenomenon of *exchange*. Walras asserted that, when envisaged from a certain point of view, social life presented itself as a series of exchanges and the world manifested itself as a market in which successive sales and purchases took place. The manifestation of the phenomenon of exchange occurs in those corporeal entities which are potentially exchangeable. In Walras's terminology this constitutes *social wealth*. Hence, an economic science studies phenomena of exchange in relation to all those things which can be exchanged, in other words, in relation to social wealth. Social wealth, in this respect, was considered to comprise *useful* things *limited in quantity*.[23]

In dealing with the exchange of useful things limited in quantity, i.e. exchanging scarce things, three other general phenomena arise, as explained by Walras in the *EPE*.[24] In the first place, the exchange of social wealth implies that the things exchanged are valued by the traders, for otherwise the things would not have been exchanged. As such, according to Walras, social wealth has a special 'property' which is 'that of being exchangeable against any other scarce thing in such and such a determinate ratio'.[25] The phenomenon that results from this 'property' subsumes the exchange relationships between elements of social wealth, and is called *value in exchange*. According to Walras, value in exchange can be considered as being a 'natural' phenomenon, in the sense that it is determined by the 'blind and ineluctable forces of nature'. This proposition is peculiar at first sight, because it seems to be the traders themselves who attach such 'value in exchange' to the things exchanged. What Walras appears to be getting at is the fact that the cause of the phenomenon should not be sought in the domain of human actions. Instead, it is the case that value in exchange is a result of 'natural' conditions such as the useful characteristics of the thing and its scarcity. Although one may alter the 'natural' conditions, and thus cause value in exchange to vary, (individual) human action will not be able to influence such variations directly. This seems to be in accordance with Auguste

Walras's observation that 'political economy is the science of value.'[26]

In the second place, Walras has it that the exchange of social wealth implies that it is worthwhile to produce useful things, 'limited in quantity', in order that they be exchanged. In that sense, the exchange of social wealth gives rise to the phenomenon of *industrial production.* Walras did not only think in terms of making social wealth less scarce, but also in terms of making production well proportioned, i.e. avoiding the shortfalls and surpluses in the production of specific scarce goods. Industrial production is, hence, regarded as the *economic* organization of industry rather than as the *technical* production of social wealth. As such, the phenomenon of industrial production is a human phenomenon because it is brought about by the 'forces of the human will', which are free to influence that production.

In the third place, the exchange of social wealth implies that useful things, 'limited in quantity', may be liable to appropriation. When Walras points out that there is no reason why useless things or things which are available in unlimited quantities to anyone interested in them should ever be appropriated, clearly Walras is speaking in scientific terms, and the vagaries of real life are being rendered into abstractions. The appropriation, which is based on the consideration of interest, may give rise to the phenomenon of *property.*[27] Property, in turn, is related for Walras to an equitable distribution of social wealth. As such, it springs from the 'forces of the human will', but in contradistinction to the appropriation itself, it is not motivated by considerations of interest but rather by considerations of justice. In this sense, property is 'appropriation in conformity with justice'.[28]

With the introduction of the phenomena of appropriation and property, Walras introduced a social dimension into industrial production. Whereas industrial production was concerned with the subordination of the destinies of things to human destinies, Walras was well aware of the fact that the appropriation of things implied the mutual co-ordination of human destinies.

> Once the conditions of appropriation are fulfilled in the nature of things, it is within our power to determine whether this appropriation shall be carried on in one way rather than in another. Obviously, this power does not reside in each of us individually but in all of us taken collectively. We are dealing

here with a human phenomenon that is shaped, not by the separate will of each individual, but by the collective activity of society as a whole.

(Walras 1988)[29]

Hence, the economic perspective gave way to a viewpoint based on the phenomena of *value in exchange*, *industrial production* and *property*. Walras's philosophy of economics, then, was concerned to define the questions which needed to be asked in studying the manifestations of the phenomena; this in order to establish the science of those phenomena. As explained by Walras in the *EES*,[30] economic science would be completed once the nature, causes, laws and consequences of social wealth were perfectly known, and, subsequently, once the conditions of optimal production and distribution had been established. In this sense, the completion of economic science implied an approximate solution to the 'economic' social question. What remained to be answered, in this respect, was the question of the nature of 'man in society'. The importance of this latter question will become even more obvious when we classify Walras's economics according to the taxonomic scheme[31] set out above.

## THE ECONOMIC SCIENCES

Walras's ideas on an economic science only took shape gradually. His initial ideas, as expressed in a letter to A. Guéroult in 1859,[32] vaguely distinguished natural facts from moral facts, although all of the constituent elements of a science in the making were present in embryonic form. It transpired that Walras chose to stay close to the results of his father's work which had been the inspiration of his initial ideas. During the early 1860s, plans for an extensive work on economics were laid in the course of which Walras proposed to the French mathematical economist Du Mesnil-Marigny[33] that he should co-author a four-volume standard work on economics. Although the plan was never actually carried out, Walras nevertheless retained the outlines of his classification, in which the distinction between 'pure' and 'applied' economics appeared for the first time. In his letter of application for the economics chair at the Academy of Lausanne, Walras emphasized what he had already mentioned at an earlier stage in his *Recherche de l'idéal sociale*:

> As far as I am concerned, I divide all of social and political economy into three parts, namely:
>
> 1. the study of the natural laws of *exchange value*, and *exchange*, or the *theory of social wealth*. This is also what I call *pure economics*;
>
> 2. the study of the most favourable conditions for *agriculture*, *industry*, *trade*, *credit*, or the *theory of the production of wealth*. This is also what I call *applied economics*;
>
> 3. the study of the best conditions for *property* and *taxation*, or the *theory of distribution of wealth*. This is also what I particularly call *social economics*.
>
> (Walras 1868)[34]

In the preface to the first edition of the *Eléments d'économie politique pure* (1874), Walras envisaged the final format of his research as a three-volume treatise, discussing the 'elements' of the various segments of an economic science.

## Structuring the order

The taxonomic scheme set out above captured Walras's conception of science by introducing the double distinction of, on the one hand, the type of phenomena studied, i.e. natural versus human, and on the other, the type of 'scientific' method employed, i.e. observation, description and explanation as against advice, prescription and directive. In the particular case of an economic science, a similar taxonomic scheme can be constructed as in our Figure 5.3.

In this scheme, the study of social wealth in itself, which is associated with the phenomenon of value in exchange, is classified under the heading of 'pure natural economics' because value in exchange was considered to be a natural phenomenon. By its very nature it can only be observed, described and explained.

Establishing the conditions which would cause an increase in the quantity of social wealth, a growth associated with the phenomenon of industrial production, is placed under the heading of 'applied "natural" economics'. The term 'natural' (judiciously placed between quotes) indicates the relation between persons and things in which the 'forces of nature' are subordinated to the 'forces of the human will'. Clearly, the art of determining such conditions is of a prescriptive nature. Determining the conditions which render the appropriation of social wealth legitimate is also of a prescriptive nature, though in this case the conditions

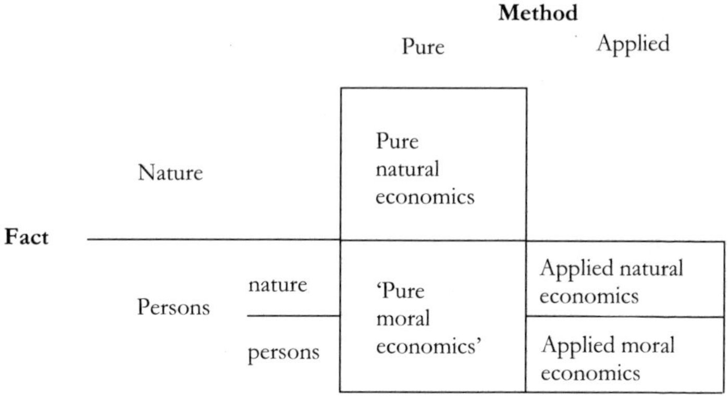


*Figure 5.3* Walras's economics 'classified'

relate to the mutual co-ordination of human destinies. Such activity was classified by Walras under the heading of 'applied moral economics'.

The segment in Figure 5.3 that deals with studying the nature, causes, laws and consequences of human or moral phenomena, does not, strictly speaking, fall under the domain of Walras's economics. The corporeal entity in an economic science, associated to economic phenomena, has been identified as social wealth, either studied in itself or in relation to persons. The corporeal entity in a pure moral science would, consequently, be a person in which the human phenomena are manifested. By definition, therefore, 'pure moral economics' does not exist in Walras's terminology, but is adopted here in order to maintain the symmetry of the taxonomic scheme. Walras, for that matter, referred to this specific segment as either 'moral philosophy' or as the 'pure science of man and of society'. This latter feat of nomenclature exactly expresses what is meant, i.e. the observation, description and explanation of man and his functioning in society. As such, it provides the definition of man and society which are used, together with the definition of social wealth, in both types of applied economics.[35]

The classification illustrated in Figure 5.3 also explains why Walras insisted on talking about different types of economic sciences, and how he was intending to incorporate them in the three books he had initially planned. Indeed, one may attempt to

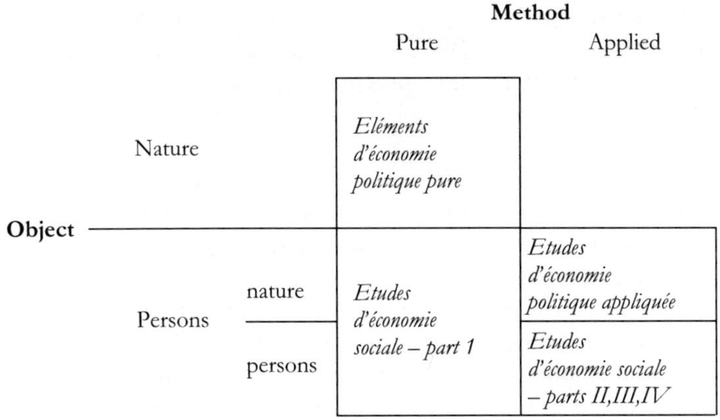


*Figure 5.4* Walras's economics 'filed'

'file' the main works in Walras's œuvre by adopting the taxonomic scheme, as has been attempted in Figure 5.4. Figure 5.4 makes apparent where, and to what extent, each segment in the classification was covered by Walras. It is striking, in that respect, that although the 'economic' social question required full coverage of his applied 'natural' economics and applied moral economics, Walras devoted most of his career to the segment dealing with his pure natural economics.[36] A possible explanation for this apparent over-emphasis can be found in the fixed sequence of the segments in the scheme.

## Ordering the structure

> In my opinion . . . the theory of the art, or applied science, should precede the practice of the art, and that pure science should precede applied science.
>
> (Jaffé 1965)[37]

The establishment of the fourfold typology of economic sciences was not an end in itself. Although by thinking in terms of modules, Walras was able to elaborate on each segment in turn, he always stressed their interdependencies. As already indicated by Walras, the determination of the optimal conditions of production for social wealth, and its distribution among persons, requires exact knowledge of what precisely 'social wealth' is and what 'persons' are. As Walras asserted on various occasions, pure economics should always precede applied economics. The assertion that 'observation', 'description' and 'explanation' should precede 'advice', 'prescription' and 'directive' is, in that respect, almost a tautology. In Figures 5.3 and 5.4, the ordering sequence moves from left to right.

With respect to the distinction between pure natural and pure moral economics, a comment should be made concerning methodology. The observation, description and explanation of phenomena in Walras's pure natural economics was mainly an inductive operation in which generalization of observations led to principles and laws.[38] The methodology of a 'pure moral economics', or 'moral philosophy', on the other hand, was regarded by Walras as being of an entirely different nature. This latter methodology was characterized by Walras as purely deductive reasoning in which basic axioms led to more complex conclusions.[39] In terms of the 'economic' social question, the distinction, and to a higher degree the sequence, of pure natural economics and pure moral economics seems to have lost most of its relevance, however:

> The distinction of pure science into pure natural science and pure moral science would be less necessary. If the distinction is made, one must always avoid believing that pure natural science would suffice to elaborate on applied [natural] science and pure moral science for [applied] moral science. That would be a mistake.
>
> (Walras 1896a)[40]

In this context, the pure economics, i.e. the entire left-hand column in Figure 5.3, serves as the 'hard core' of Walras's normative solution to the social question. The importance he attached to a solid scientific foundation to any reformist theory also applied to what Walras once believed to be a viable doctrine:

> I sincerely believe that Saint-Simon or any other reformer, with a less improvised philosophy and a less superficial science, could have been the Newton of social science.
>
> (Walras 1987)[41]

We will turn to Walras's pure economics next.

# 6

# THE ELEMENTS

## ELEMENTS OF EXCHANGE

Walras's pure natural economics studies value in exchange, as the phenomenon of social wealth (the corporeal entity), with respect to its nature, its causes, its laws and its consequences. By considering the phenomenon of value in exchange as a property of things, which accomplishes that things are neither obtained freely nor given away freely but are instead bought and sold in a certain relation, the relation of this phenomenon to social wealth is established. As such, value in exchange always implies the exchange of two things or *commodities*. The demand for a commodity is matched by the supply of another commodity, which, in turn, was matched by the demand for the former. The supply of, and demand for, a commodity gives rise to the phenomenon of value in exchange.

According to Walras, value in exchange would be the 'natural' outcome of the interplay of supply and demand in a process of competition in the market.[1]

> The phenomenon of value in exchange manifests itself in the market, and we must go to the market to study value in exchange.
>
> (Walras 1988)[2]

The manner in which the value in exchange was brought about, however, would be determined by the degree of competitiveness in the market.

> Value in exchange left by itself will appear naturally in the market in which competition prevails. . . . Value in exchange will appear more or less rigorously according as this competition is more or less able to function.
>
> (Walras 1874)[3]

Hence, the market would need to be perfectly organized, in order to enable free competition, if the phenomenon of value in exchange were to reveal itself in an undistorted form. According to Walras,[4] the best-organized markets are those in which there is transparency of the transactions. This transparency may be achieved by centralizing the transactions with the aid of intermediary agents.

> In the market, buyers and sellers are usually present; but their presence is not a necessity, however: they could give their orders to [intermediary] agents and the market will be operated by them.
>
> (Walras 1987)[5]

Walras first looked at the price mechanism in the Paris Stock Exchange in the anticipation that it would (to some extent) serve as a starting point for the type of market under consideration in his theory. As stated by Walras:

> The study of the Stock Exchange is a subject of interest to the entire political and social economy. The commodities that are sold there are well defined and very valuable; their prices fluctuate considerably, which is an important observation. These circumstances have already made the market of fixed capital stocks into a market close to perfection; but pure economics should nevertheless analyze it critically in view of the formulation of a typical market.
>
> (Walras 1898a)[6]

This market contained some features, considered as essential by Walras, that would characterize free competition. In this mechanism the transactions of purchases and sales were performed by stockbrokers or agents[7] who centralized the transactions in such a way that 'the terms of every exchange are openly announced and an opportunity is given to sellers to lower their prices and to buyers to raise their bids'.[8] The central features here are *full information for*, and *unrestricted participation by*, the buyers and sellers in the market.

Clearly, these features are unlikely to be found in the actual exchange process in the wider economy, in which a variety of cases can be observed. Sometimes the type of market adopted in theory is *practically* impossible, as observed by Walras:

> This substitution [of sellers and buyers by intermediate agents]

> is often impossible, for the reason that the buyer will need to see and touch the commodity, in other words, to be himself in the market.
>
> (Walras 1987)[9]

Walras's logic, however, required the study of the general, theoretical case of exchange before studying special practical cases. Free competition, by its very nature, was considered by Walras as the general case. In this representation, free competition was considered as the case in which no institutional obstructions could hamper the outcome of the exchange process. Free competition was only restricted by the constraints and distortions which institutional arrangements impose on information or participation. Walras's general theory of exchange would cover all special cases of exchange, such as monopolies for example, at a later stage. Hence, the study of the phenomenon of value in exchange would initially have to be carried out under an ideal and hypothetical situation of free competition:

> Thus in an ideal market we have ideal prices which stand in an exact relation to an ideal demand and supply.
>
> (Walras 1988)[10]

## An inquiry into the nature and causes of value in exchange

> I think that in the methodical study of a general phenomenon, such as value in exchange, the inquiry into its nature should precede the research for its origin.
>
> (Walras 1988)[11]

The earliest intimations of Walras's pure natural economics can be followed along the lines of three unpublished manuscripts entitled '*Application des mathématiques à l'économie politique*', the first of which is designated as '(1*ère tentative*, 1860)', the second as '(2*e tentative*, 1869–1870)' and the third as '(1871), 3*e tentative*'.[12] In these attempts to apply mathematics to economics, Walras was trying to grasp an idea of the mechanism of exchange.

The very first '*tentative*' attempted to elucidate the absolute value of a commodity, denoted by Walras as '*valorie*', in a function of demand and supply. Here, Walras explored the relation between the absolute value of a commodity and the totality of human desire to acquire it. As such, Walras concluded that the absolute value of a commodity is equal to the ratio of the total sum of all individual desires to the total supply.

In the second '*tentative*', Walras had not progressed to any great extent. As indicated by a note on the manuscript, this attempt was only meant to supplement his *Recherche de l'idéal social* with three '*leçons*'.[13] In this manuscript, Walras introduced a concept of utility to express those qualities of a good which enable it to satisfy the desires of man. The ratio of the utility of a good to the available quantity of a good was, subsequently, denoted as *rareté*, thereby echoing the expression used earlier by his father:[14]

> Indeed, let us call the *rareté* of a good the relation between the utility possessed by this good and the existing quantity of it . . . or the relation between demand and supply.
>
> (Walras 1870)[15]

By defining '*rareté*' as the ratio of demand and supply, Walras was in effect still pursuing an explanation of the absolute value of the commodity, rather than an explanation of the exchange process.

In the third *tentative*, Walras tried to establish alternative representations of the exchange ratios between commodities by means of geometrical figures. In these figures he compared the demand curves of two commodities in which values were represented by an area under the curve. By representing exchange as an exchange of values, Walras compared the area for each commodity that was exchanged. The conclusion that followed from this third *tentative*, indicates that at this time, Walras had already grasped the idea that the equality between the ratio of values in exchange and the inverse ratio of the quantities exchanged would determine the equilibrium situations in exchange. As such, he had found a crucial relation in the examination of the *nature* of exchange. During the early 1870s, Walras continued his study of the process of exchange by concentrating on the establishment of equilibrium prices on the one hand, and on the stability of these equilibria on the other.

In the *Eléments d'économie politique pure*, Walras turned to a price-adjustment mechanism that worked on the basis of an excess supply or excess demand, and argued that equilibrium prices could, indeed, be attained. Once effective demand was equal to the effective supply of each commodity, the market was said to be in equilibrium. The stability of these equilibria was studied graphically. Other mathematical expressions of the exchange process were mere representations of ideas which had been expressed by non-mathematical means in the work of earlier economists, though these mathematical expressions were, in their own right, considerable innovations for economic science.

Faithful to his own methodological procedures, Walras went on to examine the 'cause' of exchange and value in exchange. The 'cause' of these phenomena was found in the property of things which he had called 'utility'. The utility of a commodity, then, was considered to stand in a certain relation to the individual's desires for this commodity. Because each individual was considered to have his own desires, differing from other individuals' desires, the utility of a commodity would be different for each individual. As such, Walras focused on the relation between commodity and man at the individual level first.

Although Walras did not explain the origin of the concept of utility in his work, a rather speculative reconstruction can be attempted on the basis of both the *Elements* and his ontological work.[16] As such, one could distinguish *virtual* utility and *effective* utility, thereby stressing, on the one hand, the total (virtual) human wants, and, on the other, the (effective or) 'real' manifestation in terms of wants satisfied.[17]

Taking *virtual* utility, then, to relate to wants that can potentially be satisfied by commodities, Walras distinguished two dimensions: the magnitude of the wants in their totality and the urgency of the wants. The magnitude of the wants was related to *extensive* utility and could be expressed as the amount of commodities that would be desired if their price were not an obstacle, that is, at a price zero.[18] The urgency of the (virtual) wants was related to *intensive* utility. According to Walras, the urgency of the wants could not be expressed as a quantity. *Intensive* utility, then, is assumed to express the relation between the urgency of the successive wants and the capacity of the commodity to diminish this urgency.[19] In this context, both *extensive* and *intensive* utility can be considered to represent the same Space–Time concept as is found in Walras's ontological work, in which *extensive* utility represents the Space dimension and *intensive* utility represents the Time dimension. 'Time', in this sense, should be seen in terms of a sequential ordering rather than as actual time.

Both *extensive* and *intensive* utility were assumed by Walras to depend on the number of people who feel or who continue to feel the wants to a certain degree. This, in fact, implies that an individual's assessment of (virtual) wants is partly determined by introspection and partly by a subjective evaluation of influences from the surroundings, such as the *a priori* evaluation of scarcity in the market.[20] In addition, both *extensive* and *intensive* utility are assumed to be fixed:

> I am assuming that, during this interval [i.e. period], the utility, both extensive and intensive, remains *fixed* for each party, which makes it possible for me to include time implicitly in the expression of utility.
>
> (Walras 1988)[21]

This assumption is quite essential, as it appears, to Walras's static analysis. The fact that the *extensive* utility is assumed to be fixed not only implies that the individual preferences are fixed in extent, but also that the number of people in the population is fixed. Although this assumption is relaxed later, as we shall see in Chapter 8, for the determination of static exchange relations, the analysis cannot do without it. The assumption of fixed *intensive* utilities does not imply, however, that they all have the same magnitudes. In fact, Walras postulated that intensive utilities would decrease if an increasing quantity of commodities were being acquired, i.e. where the degree of urgency was being tempered.

> I postulate that intensive utilities always diminish from that of the first unit or fraction of a unit consumed to that of the last unit or fraction of a unit consumed.
>
> (Walras 1988)[22]

The *ordering*, however, of intensive utilities does remain fixed in a static situation.

The introduction of virtual utility, in either of its dimensions, primarily provided an explanation for the 'cause' of exchange: wants can potentially be satisfied through exchange. Although virtual utility remains undiscussed in the analysis that follows, it does seem to have some other consequences at this stage: virtual utility expresses the maximum that effective utility can achieve.

The term *effective* utility was used for the first time by Walras around 1871, as can be inferred from early manuscripts. Instead of relating utility to the virtual wants an individual could have, effective utility related to the wants of an individual that were satisfied by any given quantity consumed. In this sense, effective utility was related to a personal subjective reaction to a commodity or the evaluation by man based on the wants satisfied. Some of the virtual wants were thus transformed into effectively satisfied wants. As such, the intensive utility *ex ante* was translated into the intensity of the wants satisfied *ex post*. As the intensive utility decreased with an increasing quantity consumed, the intensity of the wants satisfied, analogously, also decreased with increasing quantities consumed. This latter connection, however, was considered by Walras to apply exclusively in the individual case.[23]

At this juncture, Walras reasoned in the *EPE* that in terms of wants satisfied, there is always a *last* want satisfied. The *intensity* of this last want was called *rareté* and was, according to Walras, highly subjective and quintessentially human. As long as this intensity proved to be positive, it could serve as a motive for supply and demand, assuming, as Walras did, that the object of trading 'is to gratify the greatest possible sum total of wants'.[24] The sum total of wants, in this context, comprises the wants per individual aggregated over all commodities.

Because *rareté* was considered to be a subjective experience, i.e. the experience of the satisfaction of a last want, it could only be attached to an individual and not to any specific commodity. As such, *rareté* could neither determine the phenomenon of exchange directly nor that of value in exchange, since these latter phenomena were assumed to express a relation between commodities. Instead, as noted by Walras, *rareté* determined individual demand and, indirectly, the individual supply of a commodity. In a note, written at the end of his career, Walras expressed this point in a nutshell:

> Distinction between *final utility* (the increment of effective utility) and *final degree of utility* (*rareté*). The *final utility* is the product of the increment of a supposedly infinitesimal small quantity (positive or negative, demand or supply) and the *final degree of utility* (*rareté*)
>
> $$\text{final utility} = dq \times r$$
>
> The maximum of effective utility of (*A*) and (*B*) for a trader will be reached when at a certain bid the final utilities are equal.
>
> $$dq_a \times r_a = dq_b \times r_b$$
>
> $$\frac{r_a}{r_b} = \frac{dq_b}{dq_a} = p_{a,b}$$
>
> This condition only determines *supply* and *demand* and not the exchange.
>
> (Note by Walras 1898)[25]

Since value in exchange had already been defined as the natural outcome of the interplay of demand and supply, Walras reasoned that *rareté* is the 'cause' of value in exchange, although an indirect one.[26]

## Social wealth and the mechanism

The first instalment of the *Eléments d'économie politique pure* appeared in 1874 and the second three years later, in 1877. Upon his arrival in Lausanne in 1870, Walras had occupied himself with the elaboration of the pure natural economics. As it turned out, he would require the rest of his life, virtually up to his death in 1910 for the refinement of the *Elements*, although hardly any aspect of his initial plans changed in the four consecutive editions.[27] The *Elements* was, and is, a theory of social wealth, a qualification which was added as a subtitle from the second edition onwards. Social wealth, as set out above, was to be the corporeal entity in which the phenomenon of value in exchange would be manifested.

The 'corporeal entity' social wealth comprised all of the material and immaterial things which were both useful and only available in limited quantities, in other words, all *scarce* things. This definition was, in fact, inherited from his father, who was particularly interested in the process of the appropriation of scarce things. By concentrating on scarce things, however, Léon Walras was able to connect his ontological framework with a scientific conception of exchange, in which all commodities were limited in extent. Among these commodities limited in extent, there were those which were also limited in duration.

Hence, his classification of social wealth distinguished durable goods, or 'capital', from non-durable goods, or 'income'. 'Capital', then, included land, personal faculties and capital goods proper, and could be used more than once in its purpose. 'Income', then, could only be used once, after which it ceased to exist. Each successive use of 'capital' was called by Walras a 'service', and, because of its 'non-durable' character, was included in the category 'income'. Analytically, Walras distinguished consumers' services from productive services, although the model itself does not incorporate this differentiation. Among the elements of this 'income' category, Walras also distinguished consumers' goods and raw materials. Money was added by separating it into two categories because of its mixed nature: as cash holdings it was considered as a (circulating) 'capital' and as savings it was considered as an 'income'.[28]

In the *Elements*, Walras distinguished thirteen elements in the categorization of social wealth, which, as we shall see, will serve to explain the development of the modelling of exchange. These elements are the following:

In the category 'capital':

| | |
|---|---|
| 1 landed capital,<br>2 personal capital,<br>3 capital goods proper, | yielding consumers' services |
| 4 landed capital,<br>5 personal capital,<br>6 capital goods proper, | yielding productive services |
| 7 new capital goods, | |
| 8 cash holdings of consumers and | |
| 9 cash holdings of producers. | |

In the category 'income':

10 consumers' goods (including consumers' services),
11 raw materials (including productive services),
12 new income goods and
13 money savings.

As it appears, Walras tried to model a mechanism that contained all thirteen elements, taking from reality the ideal-types deemed necessary. To this end, he constructed several theories presented as nested models, which, once fully elaborated, constituted the whole account.[29] Commenting on these sub-theories, Walras stated:

> All these theories are, admittedly, abstract; but when they are progressively enfolded [absorbed] in one another by a process of systematic synthesis, they take us right into the midst of reality.
>
> (Walras 1988)[30]

The theoretical exposition in the *Elements*, therefore, consisted of a gradually expanding world into which an increasing number of variables were introduced. Walras successively presented, what we have called, the *Exchange model*, the *Production model*, the *Capital formation model* and the *Money model*.[31]

The *Exchange model* formed the heart of the overall mechanism. In this model, Walras examined the workings of free competition in the exchange of two or more commodities in the commodity market. In this respect, only one element of social wealth was examined, i.e. the element of consumers' goods, item 10 in the categorization above. In the market, suppliers and demanders of consumers' goods meet, and exchange the commodities on the basis of their evaluations of the utility it will procure them. Each trader, for that matter, has his own judgement of the commodities, referred to by Walras as the 'individual trader's schedule'. Based on this 'trader's schedule', the traders will bid for the commodities in accordance with the prevailing price, in an effort to obtain the greatest possible satisfaction of wants. According to Walras, one would have to impose two conditions on the exchange model in order to guarantee the optimal situation. These conditions were, that:

I the rate of exchange of two commodities would apply to all traders, in other words, there is only one price for each commodity; and

II the rate of exchange of two commodities is proportional to the rate of exchange of these commodities separately to a third commodity,[32] in other words, arbitrage is excluded.

Once both conditions were fulfilled, Walras felt entitled to refer to a *general market equilibrium*.

The exchange model was extended by including the items 1–6, 10, 11 and 12, thereby still *ex*cluding the items 7, 8, 9 and 13, i.e. new capital goods and money, from all elements that eventually will form the social wealth. This new model, which we called the *Production model*, examined the mechanism of free competition in two markets. For the production of the commodities, which will be traded in the *Exchange model*, the producers-entrepreneurs required productive services and raw materials. These productive services were offered by the owners of the capital yielding these services in a second market: the services market. The raw materials in the model are assimilated in the productive services that entered into the production of these raw materials. Hence, 'landowners', 'workers' and 'capitalists' offered land-services, labour-services and capital-services respectively. In return, these capital-owners demand consumers' goods in the commodity market and consumers' services in the services market. This can be depicted as in Figure 6.1, in which a flow of services offered is directed towards the services market, and continues either directly to the consumers

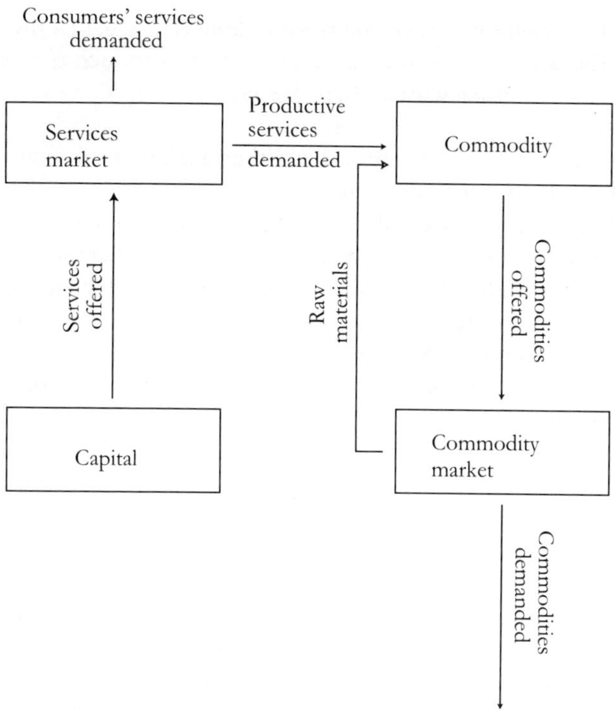


*Figure 6.1* Production and exchange

or to the fabrication of the commodities. The flow of commodities, in turn, is directed towards the commodity market and is thus offered to the consumers.

The *Production model*, then, amounted to a determination of the prices of consumers' goods and services and of raw materials and productive services[33] by means of a theory of exchange in which production takes place but is not explained. In this respect, the particular behaviour of the consumers, i.e. the traders in the *Exchange model*, remained the same. The producers-entrepreneurs, on the other hand, were mainly guided by their profit or loss position rather than by considerations based on utility. The conditions I and II of the *Exchange model* for the attainment of a general market equilibrium, in which the greatest possible satisfaction of wants is assured, applies equally to the *Production model*. In addition, the following condition should be fulfilled:

III the selling prices of the commodities are equal to the costs of the services and raw materials used to produce the commodities, in other words, there are no profits.

A general market equilibrium will then include both consumption and production of consumers' goods.

By adding new capital goods (item 7) and money savings (item 13), Walras extended the *Production model* into what we have called, the *Capital formation model.*[34] This latter model examined the mechanism of free competition in capital formation and credit, thereby extending the analysis to the explanation of the prices of capital goods proper. In the extended model the prices of the capital goods proper were related to the income they would yield, i.e. to their services. Having deducted for depreciation costs, Walras obtained the net income, the ratio of which to the price of the capital good proper, may be considered as the rate of return on the investment, or, in the phrase coined by Walras, the *rate of net income.*

In comparison with the *Production model*, Walras introduced two new features: first, producers could now produce either consumers' goods or new capital goods proper; second, the consumers could buy either consumers' goods and services or the new capital goods proper. The latter, however, were bought indirectly, through an intermediate credit operation, in the form of shares. These shares would procure the consumers the expectance of future income to which they attach a present utility. In addition, a third market was therefore introduced, in which capital proper is traded; this is depicted in Figure 6.2.

Figure 6.2 illustrates the flows of services and commodities. The capital-services offered on the services market are demanded either for final consumption or for the production of commodities or new capital goods. The produced commodities are subsequently offered on the commodity market either as intermediate goods, i.e. 'raw materials', or as final consumers' goods. The former will enter into the production of new capital goods whereas the latter will leave the system. The new capital goods proper are offered on the capital market in the form of shares.

The conditions of a general market equilibrium in terms of the *Production model* also applied for the *Capital formation model*, to which one condition was added:

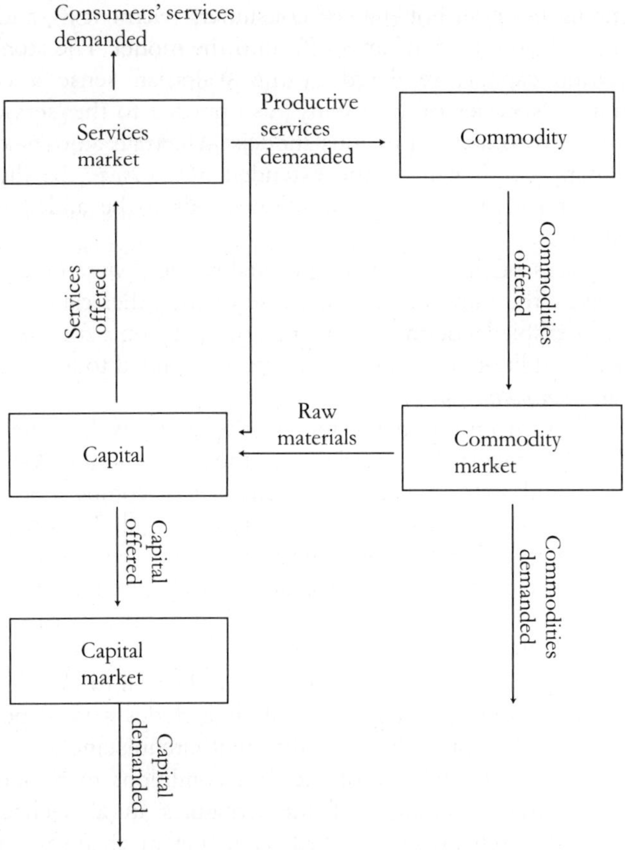


*Figure 6.2* Capital formation, production and exchange

IV the ratio of the net income of the capital service to the price of the capital good, is the same for *all* capital goods, in other words, there is one rate of net income.

The *Money model*, finally, included the remaining constituent items of social wealth, (i.e. items 8 and 9), thereby completing the entire mechanism of exchange. This definitive model also allowed for stocks, not yet taken account of in the previous models. Both consumers and producer-capitalists keep in stock any amount of consumers' goods or raw materials and final commodities respectively. These stocks can be kept *in kind* but also *in money*, thereby integrating the cash holdings of consumers (element 8), and cash holdings of producers (element 9), into the model. The stocks, or 'circulating capital', rendered in the Walrasian sense a certain amount of 'services of availability', as opposed to the 'services in use' referred to in the previous models. A certain amount of the consumers' goods can, in the extended *Money model*, be diverted from their role as final consumption goods to be added to the capital stock.

The prices of these circulating-capital services were determined in precisely the same manner as those of the other capital goods. This also enabled a definition of a rate of net income for circulating capital. In addition, condition IV above is extended to include both *fixed* and *circulating capital*.

As follows from the methodology adopted by Walras, the *Money model* in his theory is a static one: the four models 'observe', 'describe' and 'explain' the mechanism of free competition in the exchange of social wealth during a certain period. This, however, does not imply that the mechanism could not be considered as being dynamic. In fact, the mechanism itself operates in such a manner that the basic data, i.e. the initial quantities of capital and income and the preferences of the consumers, will change or will induce the 'technical' circumstances of production to change.[35] As observed by Walras,[36] once the analysis includes several periods, the market will continually meet different circumstances.

In this sense, knowledge of the four conditions mentioned, i.e I–IV, precedes knowledge of the dynamics in a science that describes the 'self-driven and self-regulating mechanism' of free competition. This knowledge of the conditions crystallizes in the formulation of 'laws' and in the examination of the consequences of the phenomenon of value in exchange.

## Laws and consequences

Walras divided his analysis of the mechanism towards equilibrium under free competition hypothetically into three phases. A first phase analysed the exchange process preceding an equilibrium situation in which preliminary groping ('*tâtonnement*') of prices tended towards an equilibrium. A second phase concentrated on the effective establishment of an equilibrium with constant data. Walras called this the 'static' phase. In the third phase, the data were allowed to change and the deviations from the equilibrium were analysed. In this, so-called 'dynamic' phase the new capital goods, for instance, as described in the *Capital formation model*, were put to use.

The 'laws' that followed from Walras's models could also be seen in the light of these phases. The concept of 'law', in this respect, was one which Walras owed to Montesquieu.[37] 'Laws', then, were interpreted as the necessary relations which followed from the nature of things. In this sense, the concept of 'law' was interpreted as a recurring regularity which could be observed in studying phenomena. Relating to the first phase, Walras formulated the 'law of the establishment of equilibrium prices'. This 'law' followed from the first three models in which he had examined the tendency of prices in circumstances of disequilibrium, that is, in situations in which conditions I–IV were not fulfilled. This, so-called '*tâtonnement*'-process has often been considered as a 'dynamic' mechanism, although in Walras's theory it remains within the realm of the static theory. This 'law of the establishment of equilibrium prices' was, therefore, merely an algorithm with which to determine a route towards an equilibrium situation. The 'law of the establishment of equilibrium prices' stated, in addition, that equilibrium is actually achieved when conditions I–IV are fulfilled, thereby referring to the second phase.

Moving on to the third phase, Walras formulated a 'law of the variation of prices' in a stationary economy. The 'law' in this case, resulted in an analysis of price changes due to changes in either the preferences with respect to a commodity or in the initial quantity of the commodities possessed. In qualitative terms, the 'law' summarized the increases or decreases in prices according to their cause. The 'law of variation of prices' in the stationary economy, together with the 'law of the establishment of equilibrium prices', constituted the more general 'Law of Supply and Demand'.

In Walras's conception of science, however, it was not only of importance to formulate the 'laws' governing a system of free competition, but also to prove them. The 'proof' of the 'Law of Supply and Demand' was based on, first, proving the establishment of prices at which the commodities were exchanged, i.e. equilibrium prices, and, second, proving the stability of these equilibria. Due to the self-imposed requirement of generality, Walras argued that the rationality of the 'proof', rather than the description of the system, would depend on the use of analytical mathematics. The mathematical method, as a means of abstract reasoning, would provide the theoretical solution to the problem of the determination of equilibrium prices, by proving the equality between the number of equations and variables. The actual 'proof' of the 'Law of Supply and Demand', however, was found by Walras in demonstrating the conformity with the practical state of affairs in a market of free competition.

> It should be recalled . . . that what we have in mind throughout this volume is not to pose and solve the problem in question as if it were a real problem in a given concrete situation, but solely to formulate scientifically the nature of the problem which actually arises in the market where it is solved empirically.
>
> (Walras 1988)[38]

The (Paris) Stock Exchange was, in this respect, considered by Walras as a close approximation.[39] Walras concluded that this conformity of the '*tâtonnement*'-process with an actual movement of prices at the Stock Exchange could indeed be found, thereby hinting at a 'proof' of the 'laws' in a stationary economy.

These general principles served, as it seemed, to analyse the consequences of changing data in a progressive economy, i.e. in an industrializing society. These consequences, summarized in the 'laws of the variation of prices in a progressive economy', were mainly caused by the fact that, of all capital goods, only landed capital could not be increased. Having assumed that in a progressive economy the population and capital stock would increase, Walras concluded that the price of land and the price of its service will rise, whereas the price of capital services, i.e. the interest rate, will fall. Assuming the prices of capital proper to remain constant, the rate of net income will fall in a progressive economy. As for labour, Walras assumed that wages would remain unchanged in a progressive economy.[40]

This 'law of variations of prices in a progressive economy' seemed to be one of the major tenets of Walras's pure natural economics, thereby supporting some of the conclusions of classical economics. By rephrasing the conclusions in the evolutionist context this 'law of variations of prices' suddenly obtains a different impact:

> Pure economics, as I have just formulated it . . . defines in this manner . . . that there are two natural types of social wealth: 1. the *land* and 2. the *personal faculties of man*; in addition, it defines that the value of the second does not necessarily change

> whereas the value of the first rises necessarily in a progressive society which goes through the transition of a regime of *hunting and fishing* to the *pastoral, agricultural, industrial* and *commercial* regimes.
>
> (Walras 1987)[41]

## THE ELEMENTS OF SOCIETY

Walras's pure moral economics appeared for the first time in the *Recherche de l'idéal social* (1868). In these studies, Walras criticized traditional opinions on man and society on both philosophical and economic grounds. In their place, he suggested a synthesis of contemporary thought, in which he believed it would be possible to harmonize conflicting points of view. Intending in the first instance to write down the principles of social economics, in a manner comparable to the *Elements*, Walras was eventually forced to temper his ambitions and finally published a collection of articles and lectures spanning a period of thirty years in the *Etudes d'économie sociale* ((*EES*) 1896).

During the preparation of the publication of the *EES*, Walras received Giddings's[42] *The Principles of Sociology* (1896), which Walras considered as the definitive vindication of his own 'pure moral economics'. By that time, however, Walras's 'pure moral economics' had already been outstripped by other theories. What remained was that, in order to be able to determine the optimal condition of an economic organization of society, one would have to explain the individual as such:

> Pure economics is only the theory of social wealth. To go from there to applied economics and social economics one has to introduce a physiological and psychological individual, both individually and morally.
>
> (Jaffé 1965)[43]

Our concern, here, relates to the 'observation', 'description' and 'explanation' of man in society and its consequences for Walras's economic theory.

### Man in society

Walras's discussion on the nature and consequences of man in society can be found in the *Théorie générale de la société*, and in particular in the section entitled 'De l'homme et de la société'.[44] This section seems to be organized on the same lines as his ontological essay *Philosophie de l'Art*. In this respect, Walras distinguished between corporeal entities and phenomena which were abstract terms obtained by 'observation' in reality. In the case of a theory of society, dealing with 'human phenomena', the corporeal entity was 'man':

> To establish the theory of society in general, either economic or moral, and to establish it *a priori* and rationally, a preliminary operation is required to release, by abstraction, the definition of man from experience.
>
> (Walras 1896a)[45]

As was observed by Walras, 'man' had been the object of study for centuries, which had resulted in a multitude of mostly conflicting theories. The orthodox classification of the theories relating to the destiny of man into those emphasizing the physiological faculties of man (the materialists) and those emphasizing the psychological faculties of man (the spiritualists), was, according to Walras, overrated and incorrect. In fact, man could be observed from both points of view, each defining a different characteristic. Considered from the physiological point of view, 'man' would appear as a human being occupying himself with the satisfaction of his own wants through the division of labour. Considered from the psychological point of view, 'man' would reveal himself as a human being endowed with senses, intelligence and a free will. Hence, both points of view were complementary, rather than conflicting, in the explanation of man's destiny. These destinies of men could be regarded as independent of each other, in which case he referred to man as an *individual*. On the other hand, the destinies of men could alternatively be regarded as interrelated, in which case Walras referred to men as the *State*. In this respect, man was considered capable of differentiating between individual wants and collective wants:

> The general theory of society demonstrates that man in society is *individual* and *State* at the same time, that he has individual wants in as far as he applies to acquire a *personal position* and collective wants in as far as he proceeds to establish *social conditions*.
>
> (Walras 1898a)[46]

Hence, the absolute individualistic standpoint of both the materialists and spiritualists was rejected by Walras who insisted on including social relations.[47]

The State, in this respect, became an entity in its own right, and was thus emancipated from the (individualistic) definition of a State as the sum of all individuals. Both individuals and State were considered as abstract entities which would act, and interact, in society. As such, matters involving property and taxation could only be analyzed by addressing both aspects simultaneously. Although the State in the Walrasian theory was assigned the traditional responsibilities, i.e. to maintain order and security, to administer justice and to guarantee national defence, it was above all the 'natural' and necessary agent in institutionalizing *social conditions.* These social conditions were, in fact, the rules of society, established and maintained collectively by men. The social conditions were, in addition, the setting for the individuals, who by their own actions could accomplish their *personal positions.*

The analysis in Walras's 'pure moral economics', both in terms of method as well as in terms of criteria, subsequently concentrated on the examination of the rights and duties of the individual and the State. By distinguishing the political organization from the economic organization, Walras examined the role of each agent, whether individual or State, in a different organizational climate. The questions raised concerned the influence of the free will of man in relation to fellow men. It transpires that the answers to these questions could not be found by observations in reality. Hence, deviating from the methodology he had followed in his economic theory, Walras relied on deductive reasoning instead, which he defined as 'the method of conciliation'.

## The best of both worlds

Walras's 'method of conciliation', or 'synthetism', was above all intended to be a *new* method of social science. As explained by him, most theories in social science contained elements of 'truth', though they were not necessarily 'true' in themselves. The 'method of conciliation', then, would analyse the existing theories to find 'true' and 'false' elements, and rearrange the 'true' elements into a new theory. In this sense, the 'true' theory could always be constructed out of existing ideas, opinions or theories:

> Amidst a certain quantity of shapeless blocks, it will be there as a well-cut stone which we will keep for the construction of our building.
>
> (Walras 1896a)[48]

The method, as such, inclined to the eclecticism of Jouffroy[49] to whom Walras had once adhered in his youth. The 'synthetism' claimed to examine *all* theories objectively before filtering out the 'true' elements. In practice, this resulted in confronting two opposing (mainstream) doctrines which were analysed first and synthesized next, thereby obtaining 'the best of both worlds'.[50]

Two types of questions with respect to the rights and duties of man were raised once the method was applied to the theories concerning the influence of the free will of man in relation to his fellow man, that is, concerning the mutual co-ordination of human destinies. First, a question concerning the *political* organization of society, related to the problem of government and family, as was indicated in Figure 5.1. In view of the achievement of destinies, one could ask when man should employ his efforts individually, i.e. freely, and when he should employ them collectively, i.e. 'authoritatively'. According to Walras, this was a question of political *order*. Second, in view of the distribution of social wealth among men, a question concerning the *economic* organization of society was addressed. In this context, one could ask when man should profit individually, i.e. unequally, and when he should profit collectively, i.e. equally, from the efforts employed. This was a question of *justice*. Both questions were, according to Walras, in the spirit of the French Revolution, since they deliberately confronted matters of liberty and equality. The French Revolution had achieved great advances in the civil and political field, though it had not resulted in any 'synthesizing' of both concepts. This operation, i.e. the reconciliation of liberty and equality, was, according to Walras, now made possible by his 'method of conciliation'.

The question of order was resolved by stating that it was the individual's 'natural' right to pursue his own personal position freely, just as it was the State's 'natural' right, or rather duty, to establish the general conditions authoritatively. Hence, from a principle of 'pure moral economics', Walras argued that man should employ his efforts individually with regard to his personal position and should employ his efforts collectively with regard to the general conditions. This may seem altogether tautological, but, in fact, this principle implied that the State should not interfere in the arrangement of personal positions, for instance by levying taxes, nor should the individual, as individual, intervene in the establishment or maintenance of general social conditions.

The question of justice was resolved by stating that the individual not only had the right to pursue his personal position freely, but also had the right to profit from his own efforts in accomplishing his destiny. This could very well imply that, due to a difference in efforts among individuals, a difference in personal positions could arise compared to other individuals. The State, on the other hand, would not only have the right to establish the social conditions, but it would establish them to apply to everyone. Hence, as a second principle of 'pure moral economics' Walras stated that man should profit unequally when it concerned his personal positions and should profit equally when it concerned the general social conditions.

The actual synthesis of liberty and equality followed directly from both questions of order and justice: the individual could be both free and unequal whereas the State would be authoritative and guarantee equality. Since the individual could only exist in society, organized by the conditions established by the State, Walras concluded:

> *Freedom for the individual; authority for the State. Equality of conditions; inequality of positions.* Hence, this is on balance the superior law on order and justice.
>
> (Walras 1896a)[51]

## 'The superior law of social organization'

During the last months of 1867 and the first months of 1868, Walras gave six public lectures in Paris which expounded his 'law of social organization'. This law, endowing individuals with liberty and the State with authority thereby arriving at equal 'conditions' and unequal 'positions', was not received with the enthusiasm which Walras must have hoped for. The main criticism concerned the vague and enigmatic chain of concepts, which were continually being used and abused by others. As expressed by one of his critics:

> You speak of liberty and authority, authority and liberty. . . . But don't we hear every day from writers and orators who tell us about *Liberty* and *authority*, *order* and *Justice*? You have spoken to us with talent, conviction and sincerity, but so have the others!
>
> (Jaffé 1965)[52]

The 'superior law of social organization', and with it Walras's 'pure moral economics', underwent very little change from the late 1860s onwards, however. Walras's daily routines at the 'Caisse d'Escompte des Associations Populaires', and later at the Academy of Lausanne, prevented him from finding time to restate his ideas. This neglect, eventually, resulted in a rather harsh judgement of Walras' 'questionable philosophies about social justice' which, according to Schumpeter, 'have cost him [Walras] the goodwill of many a competent critic'.[53]

In our opinion, this statement deserves some refinement. The judgement may apply to the *Recherche de l'idéal social*, where Walras's general theory of society appeared as an isolated theory, although the 'law' already had a history of its own by then. As appears from the correspondence with his father, the 'law' was suggested by Auguste Walras as an improvement on the Saint-Simonian slogan 'to each according to his ability, to each ability according to its works'.[54] The improvement, according to Auguste Walras, would lie in clarifying that equality and inequality should each have their own domain but at the same time they should go hand in hand.

> The Saint-Simonians have proclaimed the maxim: *to each according to his ability, to each ability according to its works*; but this maxim has always remained rather vague and not very precise. . . . I admit, it is true, that this maxim ratifies the distinction I make between communitative justice and distributive justice and it seems to reserve separate domains for equality and inequality. But all this is not very transparent, and I much more prefer my own formula: equality of conditions, inequality of positions.
>
> (A. Walras 1912)[55]

At the time of the *Etudes d'économie sociale*, then, Walras's principles of society were embedded in his economic theory as a whole, thereby giving it a different meaning altogether. In this new context, it presented the definitions and assumptions regarding man and society, which were to be used in his applied economics. As such, Walras's 'pure moral economics' at the time of the *EES* had a different pretention altogether than it had at the time of the *RIS.* The more so, since the question of political 'order' does not reappear in Walras's *economic* theory; only the conclusions involving equality of conditions and inequality of positions are reflected in his applied economics, as we shall see. The 'pure moral economics' only hooked the criterion of 'justice' onto Walras's economic theory, in so far as it related to the distribution of social wealth. The criterion of 'social justice' in matters of distribution, together with the criterion of 'social interest' in matters of production, consequently laid the foundations on which the conditions for an optimal economic organization can be built. Or, in Walras's own words,

> The *Recherche de l'idéal social* provides us with the philosophical basis of my conclusions, or the pure science of man in society; the *Eléments d'économie politique pure* establishes its basis, or the pure science of social wealth. . . . From pure economics, together with social philosophy, I deduce . . . *applied economics* and *social economics.*
>
> (Jaffé 1965)[56]

# 7

# THE APPLIED

> To state it as simply and as cursorily as possible, we have two problems to solve with respect to social wealth: firstly, to indicate the mode of production for an abundant social wealth, and, secondly, to indicate a convenient manner for its division among men in society. This is what we could call in more elevated terms, the theory of production and the theory of distribution of wealth; the theory of agricultural, industrial, commercial and financial production of wealth, and the theory of distribution of wealth by means of property and taxes among individuals and the State. Scientifically the social question will cease to exist once these two problems have been solved and these two theories have been developed.
>
> (Walras 1987)[1]

## ORGANIZING FREE COMPETITION

The discussion on 'is' and 'ought' in economics came to Walras's attention through the work of J.-B. Say and his students.[2] Whereas Say, according to Walras, had defined political economy as a natural science, his students proposed to modify this definition by introducing elements of both a natural science and a moral science into economics. It was proposed that the combination of a natural and a moral science should form a distinction between, and a synthesis of, the *science* and the *art* of political economy. Thus, the science of political economy would concern itself with the observation and description of real phenomena from which rules would be deduced to form the basis of the art.[3] The term '*art*' also appeared in Walras's work, though carrying a different meaning. In Walras's work, *art* related to that body of knowledge prescribing rules of human conduct in the organization of production.

The scientific theory with regard to these rules of human conduct in the organization of production, i.e. the theory of the art, was called the applied natural economics. The study of production, in this sense, was mainly directed towards the economic organization of industry rather than the technical operations. The main stimulus inspiring a theory of production following these lines was the scenario that foresaw an abundance of production[4] made possible by the industrialization of society. To this proposition, Léon Walras added an argument involving efficient production in which the supply of commodities would be 'proportional' in the sense that supply would be attuned to the demand. Both arguments were to be developed in the light of, and validated by, the indications of history:

> The object of the guild system was, clearly, to assure proper apportionment in production. It is claimed for the system of freedom of trade and freedom of enterprise – for what is called the system of *laissez-faire, laissez-passer* – that it harmonizes apportionment with abundance.
>
> (Walras 1988)[5]

According to Walras, *laissez-faire*, as such, was often misinterpreted by the liberal economists of his day as 'doing nothing'. Instead, Walras claimed, *laissez-faire* should imply the act of allowing free competition to exist and thus guaranteeing the optimal conditions for abundant and proportional production. This emphasis on an active concept of *laissez-faire*, was supported by the observation that specific instances of competition could possibly deviate from the ideal situation developed in Walras's pure economics. Applied natural economics, then, would relate the general foundations of pure economics on which free competition was developed to the specific situations of agricultural, industrial and commercial production. This would, first, enable recognition of those situations to which the principle of free competition does not apply and, second, facilitate the framing of a possible rule of conduct that would be optimal, from a theoretical point of view, in those cases.

The principle of free competition rested, in fact, on three cornerstones. The first implied the individual consumer's ability to estimate the utility of commodities and services manifested in the individual demand. The application of the principle of free competition was, therefore, restricted to individual wants and their satisfaction through goods and services of private interest. This, as can be concluded, excludes the goods and services of public interest:

> The principle of free competition, which is applicable to the production of things for private demand, is not applicable to the production of things where public interest is involved.
>
> (Walras 1988)[6]

The second cornerstone assumed that producers could enter or withdraw from any productive branch, thus inducing profits to move to zero. Hence,

> the principle of free competition is not generally applicable to the production of things which are within the province of natural and necessary monopolies.
>
> (Walras 1988)[7]

The third cornerstone implied an 'authoritative' State: in terms of the conditions of the functioning of *laissez-faire*, Walras claimed that the State should not only organize and maintain the proper conditions, but, in fact, should also remedy the consequences of the deviations from free competition.

Walras's applied natural economics examined these cases in greater detail by studying the role of the economic agents in matters of production. As it appears, it concentrated, above all, on an argument in favour of a 'regulated market economy'.

## Individual vs. public interests

Walras's pure natural economics was based on the assumption that each individual would pursue his own destiny and that optimal exchange conditions could thus prevail. The 'pure moral economics', on the other hand, explained social relations in terms of individual and collective needs. The applied natural economics, then, was in a position to marry pure natural economics with 'pure moral economics' by virtue of the fact that it prescribed rules of *human conduct* for the production of *social wealth*. The criterion of *interest* was based on the relation between 'man' and 'thing' in which the idea of material well-being was the only relevant factor.[8] The concept of *interest*, therefore, merits closer examination.

The concept of interest was introduced by Walras to distinguish political and social economy from the social sciences.[9] 'Interest', in this respect, was primarily interpreted as 'social interest' referring to the society as a whole. In the *Etudes d'économie politique appliquée*, Walras elaborated the concept of 'interest' by distinguishing private and public interest which were manifested in a corresponding distinction between goods and services. Thus, Walras distinguished on the one hand goods and services associated with *private* interest, which satisfy the wants of man individually and are, consequently, different for everyone.

> These services and products [of private interest] are those that will interest men as individuals, freely pursuing their personal positions, that is, pursuing the satisfaction of their diverse and unequal need.
>
> (Walras 1898a)[10]

On the other hand, goods and services of *public* interest, are those which satisfy the collective wants of all men and which satisfy them all to the same extent. Hence,

> services and products of public interest are theoretically those that will interest men as members of the community or the State, emanating from the authority to establish social conditions, that is, from the satisfaction of needs that are the same and equal to all.
>
> (Walras 1898a)[11]

Thus, the main difference which separates goods and services of private interest from those of public interest is the fact that the need for the former is only felt by individuals whereas the need for the latter is exclusively felt by the community or State.[12]

By distinguishing these types of 'interest', Walras in fact created the means by which a rule of (human) conduct for the production of different types of products and their respective satisfaction of needs could be formulated. In Walrasian theory, the possible alternatives for the organization of production were restricted to private enterprise or State enterprise. Walras's applied natural economics, then, was mainly concerned with the allocation of the production activities to these two alternatives:

> the principle objective of applied economics is, hence, to indicate those cases, on the basis of social interest, where entrepreneurial activity can be left to individual initiatives

> and where it must be set aside for the State's initiatives or to be organized by the State.
>
> (Walras 1898a)[13]

The distinction between private and public interest led Walras to separate three distinct and alternative cases of organization of production. The first case dealt with services and products of private interest. In his pure natural economics Walras had argued that free competition would theoretically be conducive to an optimal situation, assuming that individuals pursue their own private interests. In his applied natural economics Walras therefore concluded that it would be in the interest of society to allow the individual as a producer-capitalist to produce those services and products of *private* interest which were amenable to free competition.

The second case dealt with the services and products of *private* interest which are produced under conditions in which free competition is restricted. Free competition, according to Walras, assumed the free movement of entrepreneurs to profitable branches of production. There are several reasons, however, why such free movement might be restricted. According to Walras, these types of restrictions tend to cause monopolies which are not in the interest of society. Walras therefore concluded that the State, in this case, should either regulate the organization of the production of these kinds of products, in the absence of free competition, or else participate itself in the production. In both instances the State would have to ensure that a situation exists the results of which correspond to those of an equilibrium situation of free competition: i.e where the price of the service or product equals the cost of producing it.

The third case concerned the services and products of *public* interest. The need for this class of products was, by definition, only felt by the community as a whole and not by the individual. Consequently, the individual would not produce these products at all and, unless the State performed this task, the society would remain deprived of this class of services and products entirely. Hence, it would be in the interest of society to induce, if not compel, the State to produce services and products of public interest. Walras defined this type of productive organization as a 'moral monopoly'.

In each of these three cases of organization of production, the task of the State is a different one. At one extreme, the State does not intervene at all in the case concerned with services and products of private interest in which free competition was not restricted, whereas at the other extreme, i.e. in the case concerned with services and products of public interest, society would not be able to obtain such services and goods but through State intervention. In this sense, the case concerned with services and goods of private interest, but in which free competition was restricted, represented an intermediate situation with regard to the task of the State. In the next section we will review some of these 'restrictions on *laissez-faire*'.

## Restrictions on laissez-faire

Starting with free competition as the general case, a restriction on free competition would result in exceptions from this case.[14] The generality of free competition in the Walrasian theory resulted from the pure natural theory in which 'the blind and ineluctable forces of nature' acted unhampered by human influences in their manifestation of the phenomena of exchange and production. Only after the introduction of the 'forces of the human will', would restrictions on the 'natural' case of free competition become possible.

The restrictions on *laissez-faire* envisaged by Walras related exclusively to the production and exchange of services and products of private interest.[15] As we have seen above, restrictions on free competition induced Walras to opt for some degree of State intervention. But, as pointed out by him:

> [W]e have . . . to draw a clear distinction between restrictions on *laissez-faire, laissez-passer* in matters pertaining to the production or circulation of wealth, and State intervention in the distribution of wealth. Maximum and minimum prices, prohibitive or protective tariffs, monopolies and the issuance of paper money are comprised in the first category.
>
> (Walras 1988)[16]

With this in mind, Walras seemed to imply that in matters of the organization of production, State intervention was merely contingent upon restrictions compromising the 'natural' situation, whereas in matters of distribution of wealth State intervention was much less conditional. The contingency of the role of the State in the organization of production can also be inferred from the subjects Walras classed under the heading of restrictions on *laissez-faire*. These subjects, in fact, related to an increasing degree of market asymmetry, which was arrived at by successively dropping the conditions of:

I the equality between the selling price of products and their cost of production, and
II a uniform price on the market for each product or service.

In cases in which conditions I and II were both being fulfilled, the State would not intervene in the production of services and commodities of private interest, as we saw above.

The idea of price fixing in a competitive market was dealt with by Walras in a discussion on maximum and minimum prices. Present-day theory shows that ideas about price fixing in Walras's analysis have survived the test of time remarkably well, albeit that Walras imagined it 'very difficult to enforce such restrictions'.[17] Both a maximum and a minimum price[18] endanger condition I above, since the equality of selling price and cost of production is not necessarily attained. Walras's conclusion is that where a maximum selling price has been set (a price lower than the general cost of production), no production whatsoever will take place.[19] In the situation of a minimum price, which is set higher than the general cost of production, the producers will always sell at a profit.[20] Walras therefore concludes that no justification can be found for price fixing, since either outcome is less than optimal.

Similar arguments were applied to prohibitive and protective tariffs in Walras's discussion of a theory of international trade.[21] His main conclusion in matters of international trade is simply that free trade is the optimal situation. This conclusion seems to be dictated by a mere extension of the principle of free competition:

> Free trade is simply the extension of the regime of free competition to the economic matters of the world at large.
> (Walras 1898a)[22]

The two conditions above, i.e. selling price equals cost of production and individual product prices are uniform, are in Walras's theory of international trade consistently extended. The selling price of internationally exchanged commodities will be equalized to the costs of production when the productive services are free to move between the importing industries and the exporting industries. The condition of a uniform price will be fulfilled when price-adjusting arbitrage is allowed. Prohibitive and protective measures, whether tariffs or quotas, are considered as restrictions on free competition. As in the case of price fixing, prohibitive and protective measures will lead, according to Walras, to a less than optimal situation.

Both price fixing and prohibitive and protective tariffs are restrictions on free competition which, potentially, can be removed by either the State or any other private institution responsible for the restriction. Hence, when condition I is not fulfilled, Walras allows for State intervention, although exclusively to remove the restriction, after which a situation of free competition may be expected.

Quite a different matter arises when the circumstances of production themselves create restrictions on free competition. In Walras's market of free competition it is assumed that the cost of production is the same for all entrepreneurs, from which Walras concluded that all entrepreneurs manufacture equal quantities of products.[23] When the (fixed) cost of production is very high, or when entrepreneurs do not manufacture equal quantities of products, Walras claimed that there is a tendency towards a monopoly.

In the case of high fixed costs, the initial investment will create an entry barrier, thereby obstructing a free flow of entrepreneurs to and from the production sector. The large enterprises will, according to Walras, take over the smaller enterprises or will merge, in order to monopolize the market. In this respect, Walras speaks of a 'natural monopoly'. In those cases in which the circumstances of production demand that there be only one supplier, Walras speaks of a 'necessary monopoly'.

When entrepreneurs do not manufacture equal quantities of products, this implies in Walras's analysis that some entrepreneurs will make losses and some will make profits. In the end, only those entrepreneurs who make profits will enlarge their production, thereby striving for a monopoly situation.

> Thus, in consequence of certain characteristic properties of fixed and variable costs, an industry, which starts out under free competition with a large number of small enterprises, tends to be divided among a smaller number of enterprises of medium size, and then among a still smaller number of

> large-scale enterprises – to end, finally, in a *monopoly first selling at cost of production and then selling at a price yielding a maximum profit.*
> (Walras 1988)[24]

In addition to being able to determine the selling price at his convenience, a monopolist will be able to apply price discrimination to his product. This implies that the entrepreneurs will be able to charge each consumer a different price in order to maximize their profits. The possibility itself will clearly impair the condition of the uniformity of price for each product, as observed by Walras. The monopoly situation, therefore, involves a twofold restriction on free competition: neither condition I nor II is fulfilled.

Whether a monopoly is *a priori* in the interests of society or not, is difficult to determine in Walras's analysis. In fact, it depends on the type of product and the interests involved. Any monopoly production of services and products of *private* interest, or 'economic monopoly', depends on the balance between individual and social interests. When this balance turns out to be unfavourable for society, Walras argues that the State should intervene to remedy the restriction on free competition. State intervention was considered by Walras, in this particular case, to be much more radical than in other cases. The State should either organize the market such that condition I is fulfilled and *a fortiori* condition II, for instance through concessions; or engage in the production itself by selling the commodities at cost price. As indicated by Walras, not all monopolies can be dealt with similarly,[25] and as such each case of monopoly should be evaluated carefully.

An evaluation of this kind takes place in Walras's applied natural theory with respect to the issuance of paper money. Engaging in the discussion on the degree of (practical) regulation of the issuance of banknotes, Walras analysed the various alternatives in the article '*Théorie mathématique du billet de banque*' (1879b). The different alternatives range from issuance by the State (a moral monopoly), issuance by a single bank (an economic monopoly), issuance by an indefinite number of banks (free competition), to, indeed, a prohibition on the issuance of all paper money.

On the basis of the framework above, Walras concluded that the issuance of paper money, as a means of short-run credit, is above all a product of *private* interest. This precludes a 'moral monopoly' by definition. Whether the issuance of paper money should take place in the context of an economic monopoly or free competition is, according to Walras not immediately clear: in either case the risk for society of a monetary or financial crisis due to private interests in banking practices outweighs, according to Walras, the benefits of the (private) issuance of banknotes. He concluded that, even under the guarantee of State regulations, the disadvantage of a monetary crisis is more pronounced than the advantages of a paper currency. The outcome of the evaluation is then, for Walras, in favour of a prohibition on the issuance of all paper money.[26]

Summarizing, then, Walras's applied natural economics

> concludes, for theoretical reasons of economic interest, in favour of State intervention in matters of money and monopolies, but in favour of freedom for individual initiatives in matters of agriculture, industry, commerce, credit and speculation.
>
> (Jaffé 1965)[27]

## THE PROPERTY OF TAXATION

In discussing Walras's pure economics and his applied natural economics, we have abstracted from two issues. In the first place, we only briefly hinted at the matter of the *appropriation* of social wealth, which served as a (pre)condition to the pure models of exchange, although it remained undiscussed in the analysis itself. In terms of the attainment of the 'personal positions' and the establishment of the 'social conditions', Walras developed his '*Théorie de la Propriété*'[28] to fill this gap. In the second place, we hinted at the possibility of the individual attaining his 'personal position' by means of conditional freedoms, though we left undiscussed the manner in which the State could establish the 'social conditions'.

Both of the issues we have abstracted from were treated in Parts II, III and IV of the *Etudes d'économie sociale* (1896). These parts consisted of a collection of separate studies which were to form, what we have called, the applied moral economics. The *EES* was mainly concerned with the relations among people, in other words, the mutual co-ordination of human destinies. Just as Walras's applied natural economics had established the conditions for the abundant and proportionate *production* of social wealth, his applied moral economics set out to establish the conditions of a just *distribution* of social wealth.

The issues of appropriation and ownership of social wealth, as well as the manner in which the State could establish the 'social conditions', were parts of this theory of distribution of social wealth, and as such, would have to be solved simultaneously. The demarcation between a theory of property and a theory of taxation was based on the fact that man could be considered either individually or collectively:

> The theory of property and the theory of taxation are simply two aspects of one and the same theory of the distribution of wealth in human society, the first representing this society as composed of separate individuals and the second representing it as a collectivity in the shape of the State.
>
> (Walras 1988)[29]

These theories of property and taxation will be discussed in turn in the following sections. It should be noted that Walras confined himself to the evaluation of the system of property as it existed in his day, one which had to some extent generated the social problems of his time. As in the case of the organization of production, which had evolved in time (to the better), Walras likewise believed that evolution in time of the system of property was one of gradual progress, which he referred to as 'my system of historical evolution of property' (*'mon système d'évolution historique de la propriété'*)[30]:

> [t]he earlier systems of slavery and serfdom had the obvious disadvantage of forcing some classes of the community to work for the benefit of other classes. Our present system of private property and taxation is reputed to have put a complete end to this exploitation of man by man.
>
> (Walras 1988)[31]

This, of course, was due to the influence of the free will of man, and therefore the subject of Walras's (applied) moral economics.

## On property

It was not until 1896 that Walras formulated his '*Théorie de la Propriété*'. The theory of property formulated 'what ought to be' based on the principles he had arrived at, concerning the relations among individuals and between individuals and State.

With an allusion to the work of his father, Léon Walras denoted the origin of his theory of property as follows: 'my theory of property comes from the Ecole Normale' (Jaffé 1965).[32]

Hinting at the common background of his father's work and of his own work, Léon Walras tried to justify his reliance on the use of a natural law-based applied moral economics. In his *Réfutation de la doctrine de Hobbes sur le droit naturel de l'individu* (1835), Auguste Walras had developed his arguments concerning human rights *vis-à-vis* things in general, and the relations among men in society pursuing these rights, on the basis of a conception of natural law for the individual.

Following the lines set out by his father's work, Léon Walras adopted 'the good old natural law' in his own work. Natural law, in this respect, was considered by Walras as a set of rules derived from the 'nature' of man and was, as such, regarded as an applied science rather than as a pure science. This, in fact, characterized Walras's natural law conception as an 'ought'-statement imposed by the free will of man. It implied an idealistic point of view which diverged from, what Walras called, the 'naturalistic', i.e. fatalistic and determinist, points of view of the Physiocrats and J.-B. Say.[33] In terms of Walras's economics, however, natural law only appeared to serve to underpin his theory of property, thereby giving the phenomenon of appropriation a standard of justice.

Walras's theory of property, then, was based on the concept of property rights, which was defined as:

> A person's property right to a thing is the right of this person to use the thing to satisfy a need, even by consuming it.
> (Walras 1896a)[34]

The property rights of a person, as such, simultaneously implied the other person's duty to respect that property. In this sense, property rights created moral relationships among persons.[35]

Walras simplified the matter of how property rights related to social wealth by defining the elements of income as derivatives of capital. The definition of property rights was therefore supplemented by a pair of lemmas. The first was stated as follows:

> An owner of a thing is the owner of the service of that thing.
> (Walras 1896a)[36]

This lemma logically resulted from the relation between capital and services. If one was entitled to consume a thing immediately one would also be entitled to consume the thing during a longer period, that is, by consuming its services. The consequence of this lemma was that the ownership of services would result from the property rights of capital. Hence, in natural law, one would only have to formulate the rules that apply to capital.

The second lemma introduced the idea of exchange:

> An owner of a thing is the owner of the [money] price of that thing.
>
> (Walras 1896a)[37]

This lemma, in fact, logically resulted from the concept of exchange in which one was entitled to consume all of one's possessions or exchange all or part of them. Hence, the obtained (money) price in exchange for the thing offered would necessarily become one's property. The consequence of this second lemma, was that the ownership of commodities would result, through the services offered in exchange, from the property rights of services, and thus from the property rights of capital. Hence, the domain of natural law could, once again, be reduced to land, personal faculties and capital goods proper only.

The latter point, of course, presumed that 'fair' trade prevailed, that is, that exchange does not wrong any of its participants. This implied for Walras that free competition would have to be 'just':

> One has to demonstrate here that free competition does not benefit buyers at the expense of sellers, or the reverse . . . . This is, I believe, the *key* to the scientific theory of property.[38]

According to Walras, a necessary stipulation to demonstrate the 'justice' of free competition would be the liberty of the individual. A sufficient stipulation was then that the 'justice' of the conditions enabling free competition should be in evidence, i.e. uniformity of price, and price of the products equalling cost of production. In the case of the involvement of money, a final stipulation would be the stability of the value of money. These two (plus one) sufficient stipulations were, according to Walras, entirely in conformity with the justice he had in mind.

Finally, among the elements of capital, capital goods proper were considered in Walras's theory as 'artificial' capital, that is, mere products of labour and land. As such, capital goods proper would be owned by those who had manufactured them or who had obtained them through exchange. The property rights to capital goods proper could, therefore, be derived from the property rights to labour and land. Hence, the application of natural law was definitively reduced to the question of ownership of personal faculties and land, and its distribution among the economic agents, i.e. individuals and the State.

The theory of property, as part of Walras's applied moral economics, was, in fact, a theory concerning a 'just' rule of conduct for interpersonal relations. As such it was based on the principle arrived at in Walras's pure moral economics: inequality of positions, equality of conditions. Each individual has the right and duty to pursue his own destiny and is responsible for the accomplishment of it. To this end, the individual will have to be free to act and will consequently have to be able to employ his personal faculties freely. The personal faculties are therefore, by natural law, the property of the individual. The individual as owner of his personal faculties will, according to the first lemma, be the owner of his own labour. Consequently, the individual will, according to the second lemma, also be the owner of his salary or of the commodities or capital goods proper bought with his salary. In this way, natural law, according to Walras, determines what belongs to individuals.

Land, on the other hand, was according to Walras, given to all past, present and future generations. Since all men have the same right to pursue their own destiny, they should all profit equally from the available natural resources in accomplishing their destinies. This, in fact, relates to the principle of equality of conditions. Land will therefore belong, by natural law, to the community, that is, to the State. The State as owner of the land will therefore be the owner of the services of the land according to the first lemma. According to the second lemma, the State will also be the owner of the rent or of the commodities or capital goods proper obtained by this rent.

Natural law, thus, provided Walras's solution to the question of property of social wealth. As we shall see in the next section, the distribution of property has its consequences for the State's operations.

## On taxation

The theme of taxation runs throughout Léon Walras's work. Since his 'conversion' to political economy in 1858, Walras had occupied himself with denouncing the injustices of the tax system in the nineteenth-century France which he inhabited. In 1860, Walras attended an international conference on taxation at Lausanne, at which he presented the received Walrasian wisdom concerning the proposals for a tax reform.[39] Following his move to Lausanne in 1870, Walras continued to contemplate the concept of taxation, though only in the theoretical domain. The main idea was to formulate a theory of taxation in accordance with his conception of natural law, and based on the principles of his pure moral economics. This theory of taxation, together with the theory of property, would subsequently constitute Walras's applied moral economics.

A theory of taxation posed the question of how to provide for the needs of the State in the most 'just' manner in order to enable the State to carry out its duties. The liberal '*économistes*' of Walras's day tended to transpose this into the question of how individuals could, and should, contribute to the State's needs, on the basis of justice. The possible alternatives for the State to tax the individuals had at all times triggered the creativity of the policy makers. Taking Walras's classification of social wealth as a starting point, one can, in principle, distinguish the taxation of capital from the taxation of income, whether in terms of services or of commodities.

In the case of taxation of capital, the State levies a tax on the capital in some relation to its value. Hence, the value of land, personal faculties or capital goods proper determines the level of the tax. The tax itself is not deducted from the capital since this would destroy the source of wealth, but rather from the income derived from it. The taxation of services would imply a tax levied on the services of capital, i.e. services of land, of the labour and of the services of the capital goods proper. The State will in this case collect the tax by taking away part of the rent, wages or interest from the landowners, the workers and the capitalists respectively. In fact, the State can tax the economic agents *directly*, after they have obtained their income through exchange. The taxation of commodities is an *indirect* taxation. In this case the tax is added to the price of the commodities which are bought by the landowners, workers and capitalists. By buying these commodities, rent, wages and interests are reduced indirectly, by means of the taxes.

Walras's objection to these types of taxation mainly concerned the categories of income implicitly exempted from taxation:

> We must not fail to include among the consumers' services, i.e. among the items of income subject to taxation, the income from the personal faculties of the members of the leisure class who do not work, as well as the income from the land of those landowners who do not rent their land to others and the income from the capital goods of those capitalists who do not lend their capital goods to others.
>
> (Walras 1988)[40]

The objection was, in fact, a reproach directed towards the injustice of these types of taxation and therefore a reproach laid at the liberal economists' door. But even if all categories of income could be subjected to taxation, the question of whether such taxation should be proportional or progressive still remained, that is, whether the individual should contribute to the expenses of the public services in proportion or in progression to the advantages obtained by them. But clearly this was all in the individualistic tradition.

Any taxation of either capital or income, was in Walras's theory considered as unjust, since it represented a restriction imposed by the State on the personal positions. For Walras, the very idea of a contribution by individuals to the State was in contradiction to the results of his pure moral economics and to natural law. The State, in this sense, was considered to have its own needs and its own means of fulfilling them, namely land. The theory of taxation, concerning the question of how to provide the State with an income, consequently shifted from the idea of an income made up of individual contributions towards the idea of income being generated by the State itself. As such, the State in Walras's theory would have its own property, an entitlement based on arguments referring to justice:

> If the State were in possession of the land, and it would live from the rents received from the entrepreneurs or lessees, it would have a certain income to spend.
>
> (Walras 1896a)[41]

The idea of justice would, then, be represented in allowing each economic agent what is rightfully his: '*Ius est suum cuique tribuere*'. Thus we also see that Walras's theory of property and his theory of taxation are inseparably linked. The mutual co-ordination of human destinies, guided by rules of justice, will render the personal faculties to the individuals and the land to the State. This also implies, according to Walras, that wealth is the consequence of, and the reward for, labour and thrift; whereas poverty is the consequence of, and penalty for, idleness and prodigality. In an oblique reference to the implementation of his ideas, Walras observed that rendering the personal faculties to the individuals would meet few obstacles, although rendering the land to the State would be quite a different matter. The actual situation in Walras's day was one in which land was privately owned. Walras was convinced that this situation had arisen despite the fact that the French Revolution could have prevented it. Mere confiscation of the land by the State, however, was considered by Walras to be as great an injustice as maintaining the status quo. The question then remained as to how the State could obtain the privately owned land.[42]

It is interesting to note that the solution to this question was provided, incidentally, by H.-H. Gossen in his *Entwickelung der Gesetze des Menschlichen Verkehrs* (1854). Arguing on similar grounds to those chosen by Gossen, Walras advocated a gradual nationalization of the land by the State in the long run. The State would in that case buy the land from the landowners and obtain the rent in return from the lessees. Gossen's idea was that it would be profitable for the State to purchase the land since the price of the land would be increasing continually. This same idea of continually increasing land prices was one of the major tenets of Walras's pure economics, but was now linked to his social economics through the idea of an evolution of society:

> In a society, in which the land falls in the domain of individual property, and which is also a progressive society, as for instance a society passing from the agricultural stage to the industrial and commercial stage, 'the State will conduct a paper transaction by repurchasing the land at current prices due to the surplus-value' [of land].
>
> (Walras 1987)[43]

The theoretical process of transferring the land to the State was described by Walras in his '*Théorie mathématique du prix des terres et de leur rachat par l'Etat*' (1880) and in '*Un économiste inconnu. Hermann-Henri* Gossen' (1885). The idea of increasing rents and the possibility of the State repurchasing the land had already been examined by Gossen. Following Gossen's work, Walras's exposition was entirely based on the new system in which the State would buy the land and lease it to the farmer-entrepreneurs. By obtaining a steadily increasing rent, the State would be able to repay the loan which had been obtained to buy the land.

The main question converged on the matter of a 'just' price for the land. According to Walras, the State should indemnify the landowner fully by paying the price that includes all future rents as far as they were foreseen by the landowner. This, however, also includes future increases in the rents as far as they were foreseen. Hence, the State would have to pay a price that already contains the future growth of the rents, and, therefore, the State would seem to be unable to repay the loan.

As pointed out by Walras, the analysis assumed a constant rise in the rents. Due to an unpredictable future this growth rate need not be constant but could increase more than proportionally. By buying the land, the State would be able to repay its debt using these additional benefits:

> At each increase of the growth-rate of this surplus-value the price of land will rise, on top of the increase relative to the existing surplus-value, due to the occurrence of a new surplus-value. It is this profit on which the landowners have no right because they have neither foreseen nor calculated it.[44] Since they have not paid for it [the additional increase] when they bought the land, it should be reserved for the State, who will thus be able to repay the instalments for the price of the land by means of the rent.
>
> (Walras 1896a)[45]

Hence, the conditions for the most equitable distribution of social wealth, together with the conditions for optimal production, served as guidelines for the reform of the economic organization of society. The whole theoretical construction, based on 'pure' premises and subsequently 'applied' in the light of considerations of interest and justice, was to resolve the economic social question.

# 8

# ECONOMICS OF TRANSITION

## SAVINGS AND CAPITAL FORMATION

Aware of the gap that separated the reality of nineteenth-century France from the ideal, Walras was at pains to emphasize the transitional nature of the phase society was going through. As a result of exogenous changes of circumstances the old conditions which suited the agricultural stage led to social tensions in an industrializing society which were summarized under the rubric of 'the social question'. As the transition from one stage to the other, i.e. from the agricultural stage to the industrial and commercial stage, required time for the conditions to be adapted, the threat of social upheaval during the transitional period loomed large in the background.

Wary of social violence, Walras went on to indicate, on the one hand, that the social tensions were in fact the result of an exogenous historical evolution, and on the other hand, where and to what extent the transition, in theory, could be guided. This evolutionist approach in Walras's work has led us to speak of Walras's *evolutionist economics.*

> As testified by history, I say that our so called social organization is simply a transitional state between an old, dissolving, society and a new, recomposing, society.
>
> (Walras 1873a)[1]

Several indications in his pure and applied economics, illustrate that an elaboration upon Walras's static framework could introduce an idea of progress of society. In the evolution of 'economic regimes', each successive economic regime involved an increase in the capital stock which was mainly due to new or different methods of production at each stage. The only means to obtain this increase of capital stock would be through the creation of a surplus of production which outstripped consumption, that is, by means of savings.[2] Implicitly, this presupposes an effective mechanism that transforms savings into capital. This led Walras to emphasize the institutionalization of credit, in which the mechanism that transforms savings into capital was given a central role in short-term developments.

As was observed in Chapter 6, this question was allowed for in Walras's *Capital formation model*, in which savings were spent on unspecified shares and were consequently destined to reappear as (new) capital goods. The actual and more detailed process of capital formation, however, was examined by Walras in the *EPA*. In the '*Théorie du crédit*',[3] as well as in '*La bourse, la spéculation et l'agiotage*',[4] Walras described the nature of the transformation of savings into capital:

> The transformation of savings into capital will take place either in circulating capital, i.e. in raw materials and goods in stock, or in fixed capital, i.e. in buildings, machines, instruments or tools of any kind.
>
> (Walras 1898a)[5]

As far as fixed capital was concerned, private initiatives could either be large-scale or small-scale in nature.[6] Circulating capital was considered as a separate type of investment. Hence, all savings would be classifiable under one or more of these three types of investment. These types of capital formation could subsequently be characterized as having everything to do with exchange, either *in kind* or *in money*, giving rise to different types of 'interest rates'. Hence, total savings, whether transformed into fixed capital or into circulating capital could be divided as follows:

> One part is used to purchase newly produced capital to be rented out at a certain *rate of return*; another part is lent out in money as fixed capital at a certain *rate of interest*; yet another part is lent out in money as circulating capital at a certain *discount rate.*
>
> (Walras 1898a)[7]

In Walras's Capital formation model, however, those who offer savings and those who demand savings did not exchange directly but only through specialized intermediaries. These latter agents received the savings from the capitalists and bought the 'shares' from the entrepreneurs. Stockbrokers and bankers, therefore, play an essential role in the transformation of money-savings into fixed and circulating capital, in which, as expressed by Walras, 'capital formation is the goal but speculation is the means' (Walras 1898a).[8]

The stock exchange, as such, occupies a central position in Walras's work in more than one respect: it not only served as a metaphor for the price mechanism of free competition, but is also the key institution in the transformation of savings into capital goods.

The transformation of savings into capital is primarily an operation in money terms. Money itself was introduced by Walras in the *Money model.* In this respect, one particular commodity was singled out, which could perform both the functions of a commodity as well as the essential functions of money. Gold, for instance, could then be observed in either its commodity form as bullion, or in a minted money form. The total quantity of gold, $Q_a$, could then be divided among the alternative uses, i.e. as a commodity or as money, by melting it down or minting it. Hence,

$$Q_a = Q'_a + \frac{H_a}{i} \tag{1}$$

in which $Q'_a$ represents an amount of commodity (A), $H_a$ is the amount to be paid to the suppliers of money services in order that those services should be available and $i$ represents the rate of net income.[9] When discussing the categorization of social wealth in Chapter 7, we briefly hinted at the various functions of money: money for transaction purposes, being subdivided into cash in the hands of the consumers and cash in the hands of the producers, and money savings.[10]

The amount of money services $D_a$, rendered by the cash in the hands of the consumers, and the amount of money services $\Delta_a$, rendered by the cash in the hands of the producers, were both expressed as a 'service of availability', that is, the availability of cash itself is valued. The amount of money services $E_a$, rendered by the money savings, were, on the other hand, used to acquire capital, as described in the Capital formation model. Hence, equation (1) can be elaborated by including the distinction in the functions of money:

$$Q_a = Q'_a + \frac{D_a + \Delta_a + E_a}{i} \tag{2}$$

The money savings, then, are used to acquire either newly produced fixed capital or circulating capital. Allowing for this distinction between fixed and circulating capital, $E_a$ can be subdivided into the money services involved in the acquisition of fixed capital, $E'_a$, and the money services involved in the acquisition of circulating capital, $E''_a$. Hence, equation (2) is amended into

$$Q_a = Q'_a + \frac{D_a + \Delta_a}{i} + \frac{E'_a}{j'} + \frac{E''_a}{j''} \tag{3}$$

in which $j'$ can be interpreted as the rate of interest in the market for fixed capital or the long-term rate of interest on money loans; $j''$ can be interpreted as the discount rate in the market for circulating capital or the short-term rate of interest on money loans.[11]

The process by which the capitalist lends, directly or indirectly, savings to the entrepreneur, in order for the latter to buy fixed and circulating capital with those funds, transforms money savings into money for transaction purposes. Hence, $E'_a$ and $E''_a$ are 'transformed' into $D_a$ and $\Delta_a$.[12] Alternatively, when an entrepreneur repays the loan to the capitalists or when the capitalists convert new incomes into new savings, money for transaction purposes is 'transformed' into money savings. This circular flow of money is the mechanism that underlies the capital formation theory, succinctly described by Walras as follows:

> One could exactly compare this *circular flow*, by which money goes from circulation to savings and from savings to circulation, with the one in which rain goes from the sea to the clouds and from the clouds to the sea.
>
> (Walras 1898a)[13]

## Commercial tides

> The role of money is as important in the economics of the social body as the role of blood is in the human body; perhaps the study of the microbes of monetary circulation is as difficult and urgent as the study of the microbes of blood circulation.
>
> (Walras 1898a)[14]

In a non-static circumstance, however, this circular flow of money is not a regular, continuous process, a fact which is mainly due to the distinction between long-term and short-term credits. In the '*Théorie du crédit*',[15] Walras insisted that the length of the credit term determines the formation of either fixed or circulating capital. In this context, the main difference between fixed and circulating capital is the terms on which the capital can be liquidated. According to Walras, circulating capital can be liquidated on a short-term basis by using up the intermediate products and by selling the final products in stock. On the other hand, fixed capital can only be liquidated after a longer period of time.

The irregularity of the circular flow of money, then, causes an irregular capital formation process. The distinction between the formation of fixed and circulating capital influences the amount of money for transaction purposes which, in turn, influences all prices. These prices, among which are included the rate of interest and the discount rate, determine the transformation of money savings into capital. Hence, the production of new capital takes place in differing intensities and, as observed by Walras, induces business cycles[16] to appear:

> This production of new capital goods, which is what capital formation is, does not operate in a regular fashion. Its movement is analogous to the movement of the sea: it is composed of a flux, a high tide, and a reflux, a low tide.
>
> (Walras 1898a)[17]

The main idea of these cyclical movements, or 'commercial tides', in Walras's work seems to have been inspired by Jevons's *A Serious Fall in the Value of Gold ascertained and its Social Effects set forth* (1863). In this essay, Jevons observed cyclical movements of prices, in which each cycle spanned a ten-year period.

Following Jevons, Walras took price movements as a starting point but only to combine them with the idea of irregular capital formation. Within such a notion of 'commercial tides', high tides corresponded to a high rate of capital formation. Such a period was further characterized by high discount rates and high prices for primary commodities. At the same time, the prices of the consumers' goods and services would rise due to an increased demand for productive services in the capital goods sector. Low tides corresponded to a period of a low rate of capital formation with low discount rates, low prices for primary commodities and falling prices of consumers' goods and services.[18]

It should also be observed that 'commercial tides' did not at all times oscillate around the same (horizontal) level. As Jevons had suggested, one could, in fact, distinguish two separate movements only differing in frequency: first, the short-term cycles caused by the irregular process of capital formation, and second, what Jevons called, the 'permanent fluctuations' or long-term waves.[19] These latter 'fluctuations' could be regarded as positively or negatively sloped trends around which the short-term cycles oscillated. These long-term trends were determined by the relative scarcity of capital, as we shall see in the next section.

The cyclical movements of prices were, in general, associated with periods of prosperity and periods of depression. In Walras's work similar ideas can be found with respect to the explanation of depression. Walras observed that the upswing of a cycle displayed a slower pace than the downswing.[20] This implied that the decrease in prices took place at a more rapid pace than the increase of prices. These sharply decreasing prices, then, coincided according to Walras with a crisis. In the discussion on crises, Walras distinguished several types of crisis depending on the initial cause and on the type of market. As such, he distinguished monetary crises on the one hand, and industrial, commercial and financial crises on the other. All types of crisis, however, were in one way or another associated with the expansion or contraction of credit operations during the transformation of savings into capital.

Monetary crises, then, would come about as the result of a process of a diminishing quantity of money. Walras employed a quantity theory of money to explain the relation between the quantity of money and prices.[21] In this respect, a reduction in the quantity of (metallic) money, for instance due to the extraction of money from circulation through the formation of capital, induces the prices of the goods and services to fall. Hence, the increased *scarcity* of (metallic) money is the *cause* of the monetary crisis.

According to Walras, the same phenomenon of decreasing quantities of money would appear during the industrial, commercial or financial crises. In contradistinction to the monetary crises, however, the relative scarcity of money in the other types of crises would appear as an *effect* rather than as a cause. The actual cause of industrial, commercial or financial crises, was to be found in the speculation in goods and services of either industrial, commercial or financial origin. This was explained by Walras as follows.

Speculators in the industrial, commercial or financial markets anticipate certain increases in prices by increasing their demand for the specific commodity. The increase in the demand for the commodity will induce the price to rise. The operations of the speculators, as such, will serve as a signal for the other economic agents, who will consequently increase their demand thereby inducing the price to rise still further.

> When a certain number of speculators have reasons to believe that the price of certain products will rise, it is usually based on good information. They buy and induce the price to rise. But the rising price is a public fact indicating the speculation involved. Hence, many others will be attracted who will also buy and will thus induce the price to rise still further.
>
> (Walras ca. 1880)[22]

The outcome of the speculation would, therefore, be an entirely unintentional 'overshooting' of the prices that would otherwise indicate the relative scarcity of commodities and money. Due to rising prices the supply of the commodities would increase considerably. The actual crisis, according to Walras, will manifest itself when excess supply induces prices to take a downward plunge. The suppliers who would find themselves confronted with losses would default on their payments and thus induce a chain of bankruptcies. The eventual effect of such a crisis is, in Walras's theory, the contraction of credit operations. Transactions based on fiduciary money are no longer accepted and payments in metallic money will be required. Assuming a constant quantity and velocity of the circulation of money, the relative scarcity of money will increase. Hence, in the case of industrial, commercial or financial crises, an increase in the relative scarcity of money is an effect rather than a cause.

The differences between causes of industrial, commercial or financial crises on the one hand, and of monetary crises on the other, led Walras to approach these two categories differently when discussing ways and means of dealing with their effects. As explained by Walras in '*Des Crises*', the industrial, commercial or financial crises displayed a tendency to resolve themselves. This tendency was attributed to both the speculators as well as to the credit institutions. In the upswing prior to the crisis, prices were assumed to rise due to an increased demand by both the speculators as well as by the other economic agents. According to

Walras there will always be a group of speculators, however, who at a certain moment decide to sell at a profitable price and, thus, put a brake on the rising prices. In addition, the speculators were considered able to observe differences in prices between sectors, and hence divert capital from one sector to another. The effect of their operations would also, in this case, imply a stop to the rising prices in certain markets. With respect to the credit institutions, Walras argued that with increasing prices the price of short-term credit, i.e. the discount rate, would also rise. The demand for short-term credits would, therefore, diminish if not cease to exist. In times of crisis, then, the discount rate of the circulating capital ('*taux de l'escompte*') is expected to be higher than the interest rate of fixed capital ('*taux de l'intérêt*'). Hence, the price mechanism will adjust to the circumstances of industrial, commercial or financial crises.

In the case of a monetary crisis the solution, according to Walras, would lie in the adjustment of the quantity of money. As we remarked in passing in Chapter 7, Walras rejected the idea of private money creation and assigned this task to the State. The main argument, in fact, was the inability of private credit institutions to appreciate the social consequences of their money creation activities. The State would, therefore, be the appropriate agent to remedy monetary crises. In the normal case of fluctuations of prices due to irregular capital formation, however, this type of crisis did not seem to require a special remedy through State intervention.

It is noteworthy, in this respect, that the entire analysis is conducted in terms which fall outside the strict assumptions of Walras's pure static mechanism of exchange. In his pure economics, consumers were assumed to demand less of a commodity whose price was increasing rather than demanding more of it. In addition, the consumers were supposed to base their decisions on the present situation rather than on the expected future prices. Furthermore, Walras's 'crisis theory' seems to allow for the existence of more than one price for the same good, i.e. a 'speculators' price' and a 'consumers' price'. These deviations from the static pure model can be put into perspective by envisaging the process in a sequence of time periods. As society evolved through stages, which were associated with the gradual accumulation of capital, it passed through transition periods of disequilibrium.

> For, just as a lake is, at times, stirred to its very depths by a storm, so also the market is sometimes thrown into violent confusion by *crises*, which are sudden and general disturbances of equilibrium.
>
> (Walras 1988)[23]

In an industrializing society, therefore, fluctuating prices in the short-term were, according to Walras, the rule rather than the exception. In the longer run, the relative scarcity of capital and the variations of prices in a progressive economy determined the evolution of society.

## ECONOMIC PROGRESS AND MONETARY REFORM

> In an economy which has just passed either from a hunting and fishing stage or from a pastoral stage to an agricultural stage, each individual finds all the land and land-services he wants, not only for tilling but also for his house and garden. . . . But in an economy which has reached an industrial and commercial stage, people live in very tall buildings and gardens tend to disappear.
>
> (Walras 1988)[24]

The evolution of the economic processes in the longer run was analysed by Walras in Part VII of the *Elements*, which dealt with the conditions and consequences of economic progress. This analysis was based on the considerations of the static pure models,[25] though allowing for the quantity of capital goods to change. In the static models of Chapter 6 we distinguished two different types of data involved. The first were the exogenously determined preferences of the consumers, the initial quantities of commodities and services possessed by the parties engaged in the exchange, and the production technique expressed by fixed coefficients of production. The second type of data consisted of the endogenously determined quantities of capital goods.

Economic progress, then, was regarded as an increase in production activity without changing the production technique comprised in the first type of data. This increase in production activity implied a proportional increase in the use of the services of land, labour and capital proper. The increase in the services of labour, through an exogenous expansion of the population, and an increase in the services of capital goods proper through savings, were not assumed to be the restrictive factors. The central problem, then, in an industrializing society as envisaged by Walras, was the fixed quantity of land, which, once fully cultivated, would induce progress to come to a standstill. Hence, the *condition* for economic progress was the substitution of capital services for the unavailable additional land-services in order to expand output.[26] In this respect, economic progress resulted from the transformation of savings into capital and, consequently, from changes in the second type of data, above.

Economic progress was given a definite form in the *Elements* after the inclusion of considerations on marginal productivity, set out along the same lines as in Walras's approach to marginal utility. In this respect, he left the realm of *fixed* coefficients of production. In fact, these considerations on marginal productivity were to explain the underlying motive of the demand for services and the supply of commodities by the producer in a more satisfying way. The boundary for entrepreneurial behaviour, in which the cost of production was made equal to the selling price in equilibrium, was supplemented by the condition of proportionality between the prices of the productive services and their marginal productivities.

The *consequences* of economic progress were analysed in Walras's theory in a very rigid configuration and were restricted to the variations in prices. The object of the analysis seemed to be to demonstrate that economic progress would affect the prices of productive services but would not necessarily affect the prices of final products. When economic progress is considered as an expansion of production activity, the relative scarcity of land would increase whereas the relative scarcity of capital may decrease, assuming considerable savings to have been set aside: thus, the price of land services, i.e. rents, will rise and the price of capital services, i.e. interests, will fall. As a consequence, the producers will each buy less land services at a higher price and more capital services at a lower price. Walras assumed that the cost of production would remain unchanged, despite the change in its composition. On the other hand, the suppliers of productive services will sell less land services, though at a higher price, and more capital services at a lower price. The suppliers were also assumed to receive the same income as before. Due to a proportional increase in population the price of labour was assumed to remain unchanged. In view of the unchanged cost of production of capital goods proper and the fall in the prices of capital services, Walras concluded that the rate of net income would also fall.

Consequently, the price of the personal faculties and the price of land would rise in proportion to the fall of the rate of net income. Hence, economic progress would affect the prices of both capital and its services, but would it also leave the prices of the final products unaffected?[27]

The question of variations in the prices of final products in a progressive economy had been a matter of discussion for some time. J.-B. Say, for instance, had argued that one of the consequences of economic progress was a decrease in the value of all final products, described as '*la vie à bon marché*'.[28] This statement, as it seemed, lacked any sort of proof and was, in fact, contradicted by empirical evidence at the time. According to Walras, the variations in the prices of the final products in a progressive economy would be reflected in the variations in the ratio of the *raretés* of the final products to the *rareté* of money denoting these prices. Since economic progress would increase the supply of final products, the *raretés* of these products were expected to decrease gradually:

> The progress of economic production tries to induce, and effectively induces, more and more the reduction of the intensities of the last wants satisfied, or of the *raretés*, for products; it will have reached its final limits when we will have everything at our discretion.
>
> (Walras 1898a)[29]

Whether the prices of the final products would change due to economic progress would also depend on the variations in the *rareté* of money. Hence, the quantity of money also seems to be the determining factor for the prices of final products in the long run.

In this respect, a negatively sloped trend of the prices of the final products could be explained by two alternative causes. First, the quantity of commodities may have increased through economic progress which, with a constant quantity of money, will cause the prices to fall. Second, the quantity of money may have decreased which, when the quantity of commodities remains unchanged, will cause the prices to fall. Although the *causes* of the negatively sloped trend will be different, the *effect* will be the same for both cases: the quantity of money will fall short of the quantity of commodities.

As was argued by Walras, the fluctuations in the value of money may well prove to be detrimental. Although in the short run the fluctuations in the value of money may cancel out, in the long run the fluctuations will affect the prices of the final products and will, consequently, affect the valuation of property. In the exchange of social wealth in particular, the value of money was assumed to remain constant. Any violation of this state of affairs, according to Walras, would create an undesired injustice. To remedy this problem a solution was formulated as follows:

> The final solution of the circulation problems consists of, on the one hand, the correction of the slow and persistent fluctuations of the value of money, which will affect property while disturbing the general economic equilibrium; and, on the other hand, it consists of letting the more or less swift and ephemeral fluctuations persist, which are the means to restore diverse and particular equilibria as parts of the general equilibrium.
>
> (Walras 1898a)[30]

Therefore, the short-term cycles were tolerated whereas 'permanent' fluctuations had to be regulated to assure stable prices of final goods in the long run. Price movements, then, were to be reduced to cycles around a horizontal axis.

The means of achieving the regulation of permanent fluctuations was explained most explicitly in Walras's '*Théorie de la Monnaie*'.[31] The undesirable effects of the long-term trends of prices, then, could in Walras's scheme be controlled by the State based on the introduction of a regulation mechanism through silver bullion. Although this regulation was debated in the late nineteenth-century monetary controversy on the currency principle versus the banking theory, the regulation through silver bullion in Walras's theory was primarily intended to adjust the prices to a desirable level on social grounds rather than to supply a sufficient amount of money for transaction purposes. In the end, however, the result would appear to be the same.

The actual process of suppressing the long-term trend would, in the case of a downward sloping trend, become operational by introducing silver bullion during the downswing of the *temporary* fluctuation, that is, in the stage of the crisis during which prices are falling and money is most in demand. In the case of an upward sloping trend, silver bullion should be withdrawn during the upswing of the temporary fluctuation. The amount of bullion that is introduced or withdrawn from the economy was based on a (chain-)index of price movements of all, or the main, commodities.

In this way the cycles remained at more or less the same level in time.

The introduction of a regulating silver bullion, together with a gold standard, would clearly imply a complete reform of the monetary system of Walras's day. The monetary scene at the time was, according to Walras, intellectually divided between adherents of a monometallistic system on the one hand, and advocates of a bimetallistic system on the other. The only agent, therefore, that would be capable of the introduction of such monetary reform was considered to be the State. The State would introduce or withdraw the silver bullion, but only do so to prevent (monetary) crises, just as it would intervene to establish other social conditions. The actual monetary reform, however, was not the introduction of a regulating silver bullion itself, but rather its place in between monometallism and bimetallism. As such, the monetary system suggested by Walras embraced hybrid forms of both systems which could succeed each other in a fixed sequence. This can be explained as follows.

Starting from gold as the monetary unit, the regulation of prices might require the introduction of silver bullion. The monetary system thus becomes a gold standard with a regulating silver bullion. A continuous introduction of silver could drive out the monetary gold, following Gresham's law, since some of the gold would be melted down for use as a commodity. The proportion of gold to silver will, therefore, change and inaugurate a period of a bimetallic standard. A prolonged addition of silver to the quantity of money will eventually drive out all monetary gold and the system will then have a silver monetary unit. Hence, by adopting a long-run approach, the monetary system could gradually be allowed to change into one of the four alternatives: either gold monometallism, gold standard with regulating silver bullion, bimetallism or silver monometallism. An actual choice of a monetary system was, therefore, governed by the specific circumstances of the composition of the quantity of money and the necessity to regulate the prices in the long run.

## Land reform and evolution

In Walras's theory economic progress was considered to be the cause of increasing prices of land in the longer run. Landowners, therefore, would benefit considerably from the consequences of economic progress without any additional efforts. This subject was discussed throughout the eighteenth and nineteenth centuries and had led to several arguments against the private ownership of land and in favour of nationalization.[32]

Auguste Walras, in '*La Vérité Sociale*' (1848), had advocated the nationalization of the land. Unlike thinkers such as Proudhon, for instance, Walras père strongly opposed the nationalization of the other types of capital, in particular capital proper. This difference in approach to land and to capital proper was explained by the degree of uncertainty and risk attached to the productive activity of either landowner or capitalist and the income it would yield. Although both activities could be regarded, as Auguste Walras did, as idle activities, the incomes through capital proper would always be affected by the risk of wear and tear of the capital, whereas the land did not seem to be subject to uncertainty with regard to deterioration. In addition, due to increasing prices of land in time, the rents would increase constantly without any additional effort on the part of the landowner that would justify this increase. Hence, Auguste Walras's argument was entirely based on standards of justice.

> Well, this increase [of the rent] will inevitably and constantly enrich the landowner, who has had no need whatsoever to bear the costs of insurance, no necessity to save on his income, and without having to impose on himself any deprivation.
> (A. Walras 1848)[33]

Presumably upon his father's instigation, this classical theme of a single class of men who 'reap where they never sowed',[34] was adopted virtually in its entirety by Léon Walras. In the early writings of Léon Walras the idea of landowners as an idle class was dominant. Placed in a historical background, the landowners in Walras's account were associated with the aristocracy in eighteenth- and nineteenth-century France. Although the aristocracy had been made to give up their public functions after the French Revolution, they had been able to retain large parts of their land which were formerly associated to these functions. As such, they formed, according to Walras, a parasitical class in society ('*une classe absolument parasite*').[35]

Auguste Walras's argument of continually increasing rents was later supported by Léon Walras by means of his pure model in a progressive context. Although the model, as such, 'demonstrated' an increase in the rents due to economic progress, the actual enrichment of the class of landowners remained unproven. Nevertheless, Walras argued that 'justice' would demand that the free benefits of economic progress should accrue to the society as a whole. In other words, the land should be transferred to the State:

> To leave the land in the hands of the landowners is to continue in the midst of society the indefinite enrichment of a parasitical class; to retrocede the land to the State is to make the community benefit from the effects of social progress.
>
> (Walras 1896a)[36]

The repurchase of the land by the State in a progressive economy was also based on the distribution of the benefits of economic progress from the point of view of justice.

During the 1870s a new dimension was added to the issue of private ownership of land by referring to the interests of society. With this second point of view, Walras argued that it was not only in contradiction with standards of justice, but neither was it in the interests of society to allow the private ownership of land. As the economy evolved from the agricultural stage to the industrial and commercial stage, the extensive division of labour would diversify the working population. This implied, according to Walras, that less labour would be engaged in the agricultural sector, although the sector would have to nourish an expanding population. Hence, the agricultural sector would have to adapt its production techniques to meet the needs of the nation:

> Agriculture should transform itself completely, i.e. to become intensive rather than extensive, large-scale and capital-intensive, on a double condition: technically and economically.
>
> (Walras 1896a)[37]

This transformation of the agricultural sector would imply an entirely different use of the land which would not occur under private ownership. Neither large estates nor small farms, as forms of private ownership, could guarantee an optimal use of the land. Hence, it would be in the interest of society to find another type of system in which the land could be used in the most advantageous manner from society's point of view. As such, the initial charge against the aristocracy in Walras's early writing gradually gave way to considerations of a more efficient use of the land.

This new system was described by Walras in the '*Théorie de la*

*Propriété*', in which the State would lease the land to the highest bidder. The farmer-entrepreneur, then, would only lease the land when he expected its produce to prove profitable to him. In this way, Walras assumed, the land will be used optimally in its role of satisfying the demands of an industrializing society. The evolution from an agricultural stage to the industrial and commercial stage, therefore, formed the incentive for land reform. Due to the crisis in the agricultural sector in Walras's day, the evolution was, however, not at all clearly visible to everyone. Nevertheless, this crisis would, according to Walras, only be of a temporary nature. The State should, therefore, buy the land while the landowners would still be unaware of what was in store for them and would not be discounting any (additional) future increases of the rents in assessing the price of the land.

> I believe . . . that humanity accomplishes presently a considerable economic evolution. . . . I believe that this evolution, which has resulted in a new surplus-value of the rent . . . has not yet been discounted by the landowners. Hence, I believe that if the State would repurchase the land before the evolution . . . it would find the abundant means to repay the price in the new surplus-value.
>
> (Walras 1896a)[38]

In this sense, the land reform should precede, according to Walras, the evolution of the economy. The evolution to the industrial and commercial stage, then, would induce the rents to rise, providing the State with the means with which to repay its debt. In the meantime, the negative influences of the evolution of the economy, in particular the inflationary effects in the long run, should be restricted through monetary vigilance by the State.

> Thus, we will peacefully effectuate the social evolution required by our economic evolution, by establishing rationally and experientially a system of property which will suit at the same time an agricultural regime and an industrial and commercial regime.
>
> (Walras 1987)[39]

# 9

# FROM ROMANTICISM TO LOGICAL POSITIVISM

> Man is a planet who, in the moral world, has its own orbit propelled by means of a double effort and a double progress: the effort of human reason who seeks the social ideal and the effort of human will who realizes this ideal.
>
> (Walras 1896a)[1]

## ENLIGHTENMENT AND ROMANTICISM

In cultural history the late eighteenth century and early nineteenth century stand for a period of transition, a transition departing from the ideas of the Enlightenment, or classical period, and moving in the direction of Romanticism. As in all transitional periods the ideas developed and expressed were somehow of a hybrid nature although, as time went by, the descending influence of classicism was intermittently superseded by the increasing influence of Romanticism. The heyday of Romanticism would differ by country, though could be placed somewhere in the 1770s in Germany, around the turn of the century in England, and in the 1820s in France.

The Romantic generation was very conscious of breaking away from the attitudes of rationalism of the eighteenth-century Enlightenment; simultaneously, it continued to display characteristics which seem to stress the continuity of Enlightenment and Romanticism: both Enlightenment and Romanticism shared a belief in process, change and progress and both believed that this change could be achieved by human effort. As set out by others,[2] these shared beliefs were undermined by fundamentally very different conceptions of the terms.

For the eighteenth-century Enlightenment the individual was

conceived as primary and the relations with other individuals, for instance in an organized society, as secondary. The whole was just the sum of the parts and to understand the whole one had to know the parts. In the mind of the Romantic the order was reversed: the individual was considered as a member of the whole and the existence of the individual was an outcome of the realization of the whole. The idealization of these social relations was an important characteristic in the developments in the area of social, political or economic thought. The concepts of process, change and progress would in the first case be defined in atomistic terms whereas in the second it would be in 'organistic' terms.

Second, the Romantics assumed the primacy of process as opposed to ends, of becoming as opposed to being, and struggle as opposed to passivity. The moral rebellion, which was displayed by most Romantics, was directed against tradition and customs and favoured the reform through an appeal to the ideals of liberty, equality and fraternity. The process towards the unity of civilization was the process towards the fulfilment of the individual's destiny. In the mind of the Romantic process and progress could be seen as an end in itself.

Third, for the minds of the Enlightenment uniformity was valued, which could be inferred from the nature of truth: to any problem there is only one true answer. Similarly, there is only one correct way for any task and diversity in opinion is a departure from the norm. For the Romantics this presupposition was reversed: diversity of men, of institutions, of times and ages, is 'natural' and perhaps even desirable. This implied that idiosyncrasies were preferred over universal standards. It also allowed for a bias towards historicism to illustrate diversity and, to some extent, necessity of change.

Although the Romantic philosophy of history was predominantly optimistic, Romanticism also contained elements of melancholy. As expressed by Baumer:[3]

> There was another side to the movement [of Romanticism], already hinted at, which was the reverse of optimistic . . . . It dominated the thought of French romantics like Alfred de Vigny and Alfred de Musset, the latter an admirer of Byron, and was reflected in the painting of Eugène Delacroix (*Dante and Virgil in Hell*, 1822). Musset called it *la maladie du siècle* and ascribed its vogue to the times in which young Frenchmen

> lived following the Revolution and Empire, between two worlds, between a past forever destroyed and a future but dimly guessed (*La confession d'un enfant du siècle*, 1836). No wonder they were melancholy. 'Je suis venu trop tard' . . . too late to believe, as in a past age of innocence and illusion.
> (Baumer 1973)

Léon Walras was born much too late to be considered as a Romantic, and ditto for the Enlightenment. Yet, as we have seen in Chapter 3, some of the traits in Walras's literary work of the late 1850s and early 1860s display close resemblance to the characteristics of Romanticism we described above. In addition, Walras's adherence to the historical processes, though not based on a Romantic philosophy of history, seems to be in the same tradition. Likewise, the idea of social reform held on to its place of prominence in Walras's work. These features seem to have in common that they deal with the process of individuals in society, or, in the terminology of Chapter 5, they deal with Walras's moral sciences. Simultaneously, one could argue that Walras's theory clearly exhibits features which fall in the classicist and rationalist tradition. This mainly applies to his pure natural economics, which addresses the manifestations of the forces of nature.

I would like to argue that Walras's evolutionist economics is rooted in this double tradition of Enlightenment and Romanticism. In pure natural economics[4] the model of general economic equilibrium seems to be expanded on the basis of the primacy of the individual and on a universal standard: the concept of equilibrium. This emphasis on 'being' rather than 'becoming', on uniformity and individuality gives Walras's pure natural economics its classical traits. At the other end, the applied economics[5] seems to emphasize the individual as a member of the whole, the necessity of change and reform and the possibility of diversity ('inequality of positions'). These traits seem to fall in the domain of Romanticism. The combination, then, of the idea of reform, the harmonious reconciliation of opposing doctrines, and the description and prescription of the organization of production and distribution were cast in a scientific, unifying mould. Looking back upon this accomplishment, while quoting the French Romantic Alfred de Vigny, Walras wrote:

> If it is true, as Alfred de Vigny says, that a good life is 'a reminiscence of childhood realized at an advanced age', no life

> has been better than mine. At the age of 24 I took off along my own track (at 30 I perceived it) seeing it distinctly traced out in front of me; during 40 years, I proceeded along it without hesitation, though not without difficulties, until the end.
>
> (Jaffé 1965)[6]

## THE EVOLUTION OF SOCIETY AND EVOLUTIONIST ECONOMICS

The belief in change and progress, in theory and in practice, runs throughout Walras's work. In '*Exposition et Conciliation des Doctrines Sociales*', Walras reviewed the evolution of social ideas by studying the process through which various social doctrines passed: from the ancient Greeks and Romans, through the Middle Ages, and up to the nineteenth century. With this exposition Walras was trying to draw attention to the changing nature of ideas concerning social wealth and the role of man in society. Simultaneously, he argued that a study and description of history would reveal that the progressive processes were induced by the underlying interaction of ideas and facts. In this respect, a historical overview of the social doctrines would emphasize the sequence of doctrines by referring to the practical reaction at each stage.

In Walras's work, the progress of society was explained by making a distinction between social ideas and social facts:

> In the progress of societies I distinguish two things: the progress of social ideals and the progress of social facts.
>
> (Walras 1896a)[7]

The progress of social ideas consisted, according to Walras, of a rewriting of the theory of society by defining a new foundation for society, hence formulating 'the ideal'. This would imply, as for Walras's case, that the nineteenth-century socio-economic environment in France be taken as the starting point. As we have seen in the previous chapters, this is what we have argued Walras actually did with respect to the social question. As we have argued, the establishment and institution of general social conditions was precisely Walras's solution to the social question. The theory of production, in this sense, established the conditions of the optimal transformation of productive services into products. The theory of distribution, on the other hand, established the conditions for a legitimate appropriation of productive services and a just attribution of the produce. The progress of social ideas, then, consisted of a sequential replacement of doctrines in time.

The progress of social facts consisted, according to Walras, in the actual reform of society effected by using the results of science in the real situation. The progress of social facts resulted from the replacement of the application of a doctrine by (another) application of another doctrine in time, as Walras had argued in the '*Exposition et Conciliation des Doctrines Sociales*'.

Given his abhorrence of violent revolutions, Walras assumed that a gradual implementation of these scientific results would imply a tendency of reality to conform to the ideal situation.

> Given a social reality, it is fitting that this reality transforms itself spontaneously and resembles the ideal as much as possible.
>
> (Walras 1896a)[8]

The implementation of the scientific results, therefore, only applied to the institution of general social conditions, which served as the given margins for individual actions.

This tendency in reality towards the ideal was in Walras's work entirely attributed to the spontaneous activity of the individual, who was considered to be able to act freely. The reason to leave progress in reality to the individual was based on a natural selection argument,[9] in which each individual would act in his own interest:

> From the perspective of interest, it is of importance that the personal faculties . . . belong to the individual . . . [thus] letting the force of selection manifest itself . . . by which humanity in reality tends to resemble its current ideal and can perhaps conceive another, ulterior ideal.
>
> (Walras 1896a)[10]

Progress of societies, then, assumed a process of interaction between changing social ideas and changing social facts. Changing insights in science induce changes in policy which in turn induce, through changing the facts, the insights to change.

> The ideas following from science induce new facts, which constitutes the practical progress; but these facts induce, in turn, new ideas, which constitutes the progress of theory.
>
> (Walras 1987)[11]

In terms of Walras's evolutionist economics, the theory, as we have seen above, was induced by the changing facts: the transition from the agricultural stage to an industrial and commercial stage. In this light we examined the 'laws of nature' and the desired institutional adjustments to influence the real facts. Conditioned by 'natural' tendencies of prices in an evolving society and an active reform of the economic organization by the State, real social improvement could only take place in due time. Walras's evolutionist economics, hence, embraced an idea of continual change leading to a new social organization. The direction of this change was led by the ideal formulated in science and supported by a history of stages. The change in reality was thus considered to be a process of improvement and, as we have seen, of natural selection.

In the terms of the mapping of evolutionist theories of Chapter 1, above, the question remains whether societal progress follows its natural course or whether progress necessarily leads to social perfection. For Walras, the concept of perfection was included in his distinction between reality and ideal.[12] The assumption underlying this distinction was that, by definition, an ideal is always perfect and perfection is always considered as an ideal situation. As progress was the road towards the realization of the ideal, this implied that progress and perfectibility in Walras's work were conflated. This viewpoint, i.e. equating social progress and social perfectibility, was supported by the viewpoint that progress was directed by the progress of ideas, hence giving its direction towards an ideal.

On the face of it, however, perfection as such would never be achieved. Although the sequential replacement of scientific insights may imply a process of improvement or perfection of science, and consequently leads to perfection of social facts, it does not imply that there is an end to progress. With the realization of an ideal it will cease to be an ideal. In the interim, however, new ideals can be formulated. This was also affirmed by Walras: 'my social ideal is not a fixed ideal' (Jaffé 1965).[13]

In fact, Walras allowed for differing social ideals with respect to either place or time. As such, humanity could approach its social ideal and already perceive an ulterior social ideal. The consistency in Walras's account was retained by assuming all ulterior social ideals to include all preceding ones. The achievement of any stage in this evolution, then, was subject to the conditions of time and place as were formulated in Walras's stages theory.

In the same terms, it is obvious that Walras's evolutionist

economics combines elements of 'liberty-orientated' evolutionist theories and 'justice-orientated' evolutionist theories.[14] In Chapter 1, the distinction between these two types of evolutionist theories was based on the distinction between theories in which perfection is achieved by changing ideas ('liberty-orientated') and those in which perfection is achieved by changing the social arrangements ('justice-orientated'). Simultaneously, it is obvious that social perfectibility in Walras's works only applies to theory and science and not to reality, which is imperfect by definition:

> As far as social perfectibility is concerned, it would seem logically necessary:
>
> [t]hat the idea of social perfectibility, implying the idea of a theoretical and scientific social ideal, extracted by reason from the social reality supplied by experience, regards the idea of perfection.
>
> (Walras 1896a)[15]

As we have observed above, perfectibility in Walras's science mainly relates to adapting the social arrangements to a new order. This would place Walras's theory, in the terms of Figure 1.1, in the domain of justice-orientated evolutionist theories.

## IN THE ARMS OF POSITIVISM

> Thus, first elaborate a pure economics in view of an applied economics and subsequently elaborate an applied economics in view of economic reforms . . .
>
> (Walras 1898a)[16]

Towards the 1830s, some Romantic writers turned to what may be called a humanitarian socialism. The general metaphor for society became the 'social organism', which would grow and develop according to its own laws. In this social organism the State was considered as a separate agent living in harmony with its citizens. This clearly meant a break with the conception of social relations held by the thinkers of the Enlightenment.

Walras was initially attracted to the emerging socialist studies of his day because of the predominance which they attached to the problems of society. The observations of the suffering of the poor and the oppression of certain groups had led to a wide variety of solutions and suggestions for reform. Walras's objection to the socialist theories, however, was related to their 'empirical' methodology, if they had any methodology at all. According to Walras, any study of society advocating a reformist programme would have to be based on scientific principles. The 'vulgar' empiricism of the socialists clearly deprived their social pontificals of a scientific status, so Walras claimed.

The liberal economists, in Walras's view, were to be taken much more seriously. Since Adam Smith and J.-B. Say, the studies of the economists had contributed to the edification of an economic science. Their main contribution, however, was to bolster the *laissez-faire* principle. Walras's objection to these '*économistes*' was their firm belief in a labour theory of value and in their theory of property which were mainly based on considerations of interest rather than on considerations of justice.

Walras's conviction that particular elements of socialist theories and *laissez-faire* economics could be reconciled had already appeared in his first book on economics, *L'économie politique et la justice*. Explaining the intention of this book, Walras wrote in a letter to Louis Jourdan:

> The main idea of my introduction holds that socialism should be a methodical work of reason and not of sentiment, or, that the theory of society should be founded as a rigorous science. I attempt to establish this thesis *a priori*; I also try to demonstrate *a posteriori* that on the one hand the empirical method has deluded contemporary socialism, and on the other, that despite a good political economy and a healthy ethics, the economists have refrained from a scientific elaboration of the social problem, or the question of the distribution of wealth.
>
> (Jaffé 1965)[17]

By this time Walras had completely left the Romantic attitude in which emotions played an instrumental role:

> In the presence of the pleas of society, the economist must remain calm and restrain his emotions to the benefit of his observations; finally, he must leave the . . . impressive field of reality to rise to the scientific domain of cold abstractions.
>
> (Walras 1860a)[18]

In the following decades, in which Walras developed his evolutionary economics this bend towards methodological rigour was present from the start, but always to combine it with a self-styled socialism. Surprisingly enough, and without any reference to Marx, he coined it *scientific socialism*. Walras's socialism, in this respect, was the doctrine which supplied a solution to the social question in terms of nationalization of the land and suppression of taxes. The methodological rigour was meant to supply his socialism a scientific aura. As such, Walras's scientific socialism followed naturally from his evolutionary economics and, consequently, could serve as panacea for all the worldly problems. In what seemed to be slightly exaggerated but certainly disappointed terms Walras wrote in 1897:

> Many of my generation had hoped to see this evolution in Europe, from an agricultural regime to an industrial and commercial regime, take a more definite shape through a scientific socialism.
>
> (Walras 1898a)[19]

The disillusion for Walras, however, would only partly lie in his socialism and all the more in his science.

Walras's scientific socialism relied heavily on three elements which were derived from his evolutionary economics: a specific interpretation of the State, a historical process of progression and the 'superior law of social organization' (equality of condition; inequality of positions). The State was represented as a separate agent in an organic whole. As such, the State was in Walras's theory inspired by, if not rooted on, a Romanticist personification of the State: 'the State should be the personification of the people' (Jaffé 1965).[20]

As we have seen above, the State was attributed its own resources (land) and income (rent), and given its own function.[21] The State would be able to buy the land in the long run on the basis of an assumption of rising prices. The underlying historical process of progression, which would support this assumption, can be viewed in the Romanticist attention to history and process. Walras's theory of stages serves in this line an instrumental role. In this social scheme of State and individual in an organic whole, Walras believed that diversity of the individual positions would not only be the natural outcome but also the required outcome for a humanitarian society. As expressed by Walras in 1909 in '*Ruchonnet et le socialisme scientifique*'[22]

> This is the socialism I have arrived at. It is a scientific, liberal and humanitarian socialism.
>
> (Walras 1987)[23]

By this time, however, the conception of science had already gone through a process of revision under the influence of Ernst Mach, Heinrich Hertz, Henri Poincaré and Pierre Duhem.[24] The revision of the conception mainly focused on the method and aims of science, which laid the foundations of, for instance, the work of the Vienna Circle. The concern here was mainly with the logical structure of science and theorizing rather than the consequences of science for a general world-view. In terms of Walras's scientific socialism this would imply that the attention would be drawn away from the policy implications and that it would concentrate on the methods applied in his science.

The methodological procedures articulated by Walras in the 1860s were in that respect in line with the standard view in the middle of the nineteenth century. By the end of the nineteenth century conceptions of observation, hypotheses and laws had drastically changed. For Walras, observations would lead to abstractions or ideal-types, which could be placed in a causal relation through hypotheses. As the hypothetico-deductive model of scientific explanation gradually developed after the turn of the century, hypotheses were given the status of premise. For Poincaré, for instance, an hypothesis was a convention containing empirical information, neither true nor false in itself but supported by a consensus. In one of the few, but telling, encounters between Walras and Poincaré the question of hypotheses was raised. In a correspondence on the validity of Walras's work Poincaré wrote in 1901:

> I would have thought that before any mathematical inquiry there are hypotheses, and for this inquiry to be fruitful, one should (as for the application in physics for that matter) analyse these hypotheses. It is when one forgets about this condition that one exceeds the limits.
>
> For example, in mechanics, one often neglects the friction and bodies are regarded to be infinitely smooth. As for you, you regard men to be infinitely selfish and infinitely shrewd. The first hypothesis may be admissible as a first approximation but the second may require some reservations.
>
> (Jaffé 1965)[25]

The laws in Walras's method were not logically deduced from its premises, as would become the new standard, but were either formulated as a possible or desirable tendency or simply stated; as for Walras's 'superior law of social organization' it was not a law by any standard but simply a rephrased Saint-Simonian slogan. As for the consequences of Walras's laws, they were neither verified nor falsified but simply applied in a normative context. Hence, the laws could neither explain nor predict but only prescribe. As the hypothetico-deductive model gradually emerged in economic science it placed Walras's scientific method in a rather pale light.

In retrospect, Walras's scheme of land nationalization and the suppression of taxes, as outcomes of his scientific socialism, already went down with the setting of the Romanticist influence but certainly never stood a chance in a twentieth-century science. On the other hand, Walras's evolutionist economics bridged the period from the mid-nineteenth century to the end of the nineteenth century. As such, Walras's evolutionist economics served as a transitional thread in economics, from Romanticism to logical positivism.

# NOTES

## 1 EVOLUTION AND PROGRESS

1 'Natural order is the physical constitution which God himself has given to the universe', Dupont de Nemours in the *Introduction aux oeuvres de Quesnay*.

2 '*L'Histoire universelle* embrasse la considération des progès successifs du genre humain et le détail des causes qui y contribue. Les premiers commencements des hommes; la formation, le mélange des nations; l'origine, les révolutions des gouvernements; les progrès des langues, de la physique, de la morale, des moeurs, des sciences et des arts; les révolutions qui ont fait succéder les empires aux empires, les nations aux nations, les religions aux religions; le genre humain toujours le même dans ses bouleversements, comme l'eau de la mer dans les tempêtes et marchant toujours à sa perfection. Dévoiler l'influence des causes générales et nécessaires, celles des causes particulières et des actions libres des grands hommes; montrer les ressorts et la mécanique des causes morales par leurs effets: voilà ce qu'est l'histoire aux yeux d'un philosophe.' (A.R.J. Turgot, *Plan de deux discours sur l'histoire universelle*, ca. 1751, in Turgot 1844).

## 2 THE WORLD ACCORDING TO WALRAS

1 'J'avais à peu près votre âge [22] lorsque mon père m'ayant complètement initié à sa théorie de la valeur d'échange et à sa théorie de la propriété . . . j'aperçus, par une intuition aussi nette que rapide, la vérité de son système, et résolus de consacrer ma vie à établir rigoureusement la série des déductions qui devaient rattacher *ses principes* d'économie politique pure à *ses conclusions* d'économie sociale' (*CLW*, Letter 493, to Pasquale del Pezzo, 26 February 1881; emphasis added).

2 I refer to pleasant discussions I had with some members of the Centre Walras in Lyon.

3 Although never expressed explicitly, it seems there was a strong tendency towards Saint-Simonism in Auguste Walras's work.

4 'Je demande une Revue, un Journal où développer des vérités scientifiques; je ne trouve que des organes de parti ou des spéculations d'industrie; et je ne puis me résoudre à renoncer à mon but sans avoir tout essayé pour me mettre en rapport avec vous qui seul peut-être voyez encore dans le journalisme un instrument de progrès, et un refuge pour les idées plus que pour les annonces. (*CLW*, Letter 16, to Adolphe Guéroult, undated).

5 This becomes evident from a manuscript in Auguste Walras's handwriting which is part of the collection at the Fonds Walras (Lausanne). In the manuscript, Auguste Walras fulminates against Proudhon in words which can be found verbatim in Léon Walras's *L'économie politique et la justice.*

6 '*Mon père et moi avons consacré toute notre vie à l'élaboration d'une économie politique et sociale assez différente de celle qui règne, quant aux bases et quant aux conclusions, soit économiques, soit morales*' (*CLW*, Letter 250, to Edouard Pfeiffer, 12 March 1874; emphasis in original).

7 Louis Bonaparte (1808-73), nephew of Napoleon I.

8 See for an excellent description of the socio-political setting, Boson (1951), Chapter IV.

9 'J'étais alors un de ces jeunes gens dont la Révolution de [1848] février avait uni les têtes et les cœurs en un mouvement sur lequel s'était abattu brutalement le coup d'Etat de décembre 1851' (*CLW*, Letter 1280, to Juliette Edmond Adam, 9 December 1896).

10 A.-A. Cournot (1877), *Revue sommaire des doctrines economiques*, Section VI, 'La Question Sociale'.

11 Preface to *Francis Sauveur*; translation by Jaffé in 'The antecedents and early life of Léon Walras', *History of Political Economy*, 16, 1, 1984.

12 'Et croyant, comme j'y crois, à l'humanité, au progrès éternel, c'est dans le développement même du progrès humanitaire que j'en irai chercher les causes' (*Francis Sauveur*, Walras, 1858a, pp. xv–xvi).

13 'L'amélioration et le perfectionnement pratiques de notre état social actuel: l'extinction du paupérisme, l'assiette de l'impôt, l'organisation définitive du travail et de la propriété impliquent la connaissance théorique des conditions normales économiques d'une société idéale, et, plus généralement, l'étude rationnelle de toutes les conditions sociales: civiles, politiques, etc.' (*EPJ*, p. lix).

14 In the next chapter we will give a more rigorous exposition of this distinction of reality.

15 Etienne Vacherot (1809–97), French philosopher.

16 Note that 'perfection' in Walras's words related to the final result rather than to the process of perfectibility.

17 The question of 'how' must be deferred until Chapters 7 and 8.

18 'Nous préférons croire que le temps est venu de préparer scientifiquement, de discuter librement, avec calme et sans colère, d'exécuter avec prudence et fermeté les réformes économiques les plus désirables et les plus fécondes' ('*Des réformes économiques*', in: *Le Travail*, July 1866, 1, 1, p. 4).

19 See Chapter 8.

20 Edmond Scherer (1815–89), editor of *Le Temps.*

21 *EES*, p. 20. This text dates from 1863. About the origin of his socialist ideas Walras wrote in a letter to Laure de Saint-Beuve:

> My father had 'progressive' opinions, as they say, which he has transmitted to me. He and I, we have been two *socialists* ('Mon père avait des opinions 'avancées', comme on dit, qu'il m'a transmises. Nous avons été lui et moi deux *socialistes*') (*CLW*, Letter 1262, to L. de Sainte Beuve, 23 October 1896; emphasis in original).

22 *EES*, p. 20.
23 The point, here, is not to promote either liberalism or socialism but to illustrate that there are several ways of solving the 'social question'. Whether Walras has given a correct interpretation of liberalism or of socialism is therefore not the main issue; it is the characteristic approach, which is attributed to a doctrine, that is evaluated. In that respect, pigeonholing Walras as a 'socialist', a 'semi-socialist', a 'liberal socialist' or, for that matter, a 'social liberal', should be seen in this light.
24 'J'ai . . . gardé toute ma vie cette double conclusion: 1. qu'il faut faire des *réformes* et non des *révolutions*; 2. que toute réforme, avant d'être effectuée *politiquement*, doit avoir été préparée et mûrie *scientifiquement*' (*CLW*, Letter 1602, to Louise Renard, 25 October 1905; emphasis in original).
25 'Cette organisation [sociale] n'est donc point à détruire, ni même à refaire en entier: elle n'est simplement qu'à perfectionner d'après les indications de l'histoire, de l'économie politique, de la philosophie, de toutes les sciences' (*EPJ*, p. v).

## 3 INDICATIONS OF PHILOSOPHY

1 'Nôtre rôle est moins d'affirmer la science dont il s'agit que de la mettre à part en précisant son objet, son caractère et sa méthode' (*MEPS*, p. 261).
2 'Nous désirons bien vivement, ta mère et moi, que tu termines, cette année, tes cours à l'École des Mines, et notre vœu le plus cher, c'est que tu les termines convenablement, en recueillant, à la fin de l'enseignement que tu y as reçu et que tu y reçoies encore, les titres, certificats, attestations qui peuvent te recommander à ceux qui auront besoin de toi, et qui se trouveront conduits à faire appel à tes connaissances. Tu tromperais cruellement nos espérances, si tu sortais de là comme une sorte de fruit sec, et, si perdant de vue le but que tu avais en y entrant, tu rêvais un autre genre d'existence que l'une ou l'autre des carrières auxquelles tu te prépares depuis quatre ans' (A.-A. Walras 1912, 'Lettres inédites de et à Léon Walras', 19 February 1858).
3 See *CLW*, Letter 13(4), from Francisque Sarcey, 4 November 1858.
4 'Pendant le second hiver que je passai à Paris, le monde m'ayant fait ces avances qu'il prodigue indistinctement à tous les jeunes gens, j'y

cédais sans toutefois renoncer à mes habitudes de travail et à ma vie réglée. Pour employer le terme dont on est convenu d'appeler cette occupation, *j'allai dans le monde*' (*FS*, p. 40).

5 'Peu à peu, l'ardeur de connaître envahit cet esprit candide. Les imaginations vives se peignent en rose les accidents d'une vie un peu bohême' (*FS*, p. 38).

6 'les faits du monde intérieur', (*FS*, p. xxvi).

7 'La morale n'est autre chose que l'équilibre et l'accord de l'intérêt individuel et l'intérêt général. . . . nous avions distingué le but vers lequel nous devions nous diriger, et la route qu'il nous fallait aller prendre, l'égalité sociale' (*FS*, p. xxix).

8 As we will demonstrate in the next section, the arts in general played a role in his endeavour.

9 These manuscripts are part of the collection of the Fonds Walras Lausanne; the manuscripts are undated but were presumably written towards the end of 1858. Although the pages appear without numbering we will refer to the manuscript as *PA*, [p . . . ] . A first manuscript, entitled 'Philosophie de l'Art; première partie: Ontologie – Chapitre 1. Synthèse du fait ontologique', consists of forty foolscap pages. A second manuscript, entitled 'Philosophie de l'Art; Première partie: Ontologie – Deuxième Chapitre. Phénomènes physiques et moraux', consists of seven foolscap pages. This second manuscript also includes a text in Walras's handwriting regarding the 'Prix Bordin', reporting the possibility of submitting essays on the principles of the 'Science du Beau'. Several drafts of both the first and the second chapter show the gradual changes in the texts. Together with these manuscripts, a three-page table of contents gives an overview of the initial plan for the book.

10 'S'il n'y a pas au sujet de l'art de question plus grande et plus belle que celle du Réel et de l'Idéal, il n'y en a pas qui soit aussi plus complexe et plus épineuse. Elle prend son origine au sein de la Métaphysique; et je l'irai chercher jusque là. Je passerai par l'*ontologie* pour arriver à l'*Esthétique*' (*PA*, chapter 1, [p. 2]).

11 It is not very likely that Walras had read the original philosophical works of the authors he mentioned, such as Plato, Aristotle, Kant, Descartes, Malebranche, Berkeley, Gassendi, Cabanis or Condillac, albeit without any reference to their writings. Walras had presumably only read the secondary literature, such as the writings of his father and of the French philosopher Théodore Jouffroy (1796-1842), French philosopher and professor at the Ecole Normale and Collège de France and author of *Mélanges philosophiques* (1833), whom Walras quoted extensively. In his personal library, presently at the Centre Walras et Pareto at the University of Lausanne I found only one book by Kant.

12 'Je suis éclectique avec Jouffroy dont l'autorité me décide' (*PA*, Chapter 1, [p. 13]).

13 'Il suffit que je vous aie sincèrement nommé le maître [Vacherot] de qui . . . je suis un disciple' (*EES*, p. 12. Text dates from 1863).

14 See, in particular, the *EPA*, p. 459: 'The work of Vacherot, *La*

*métaphysique et la science*, appeared in 1858, at a point in time in which I tried to fill this gap and complete my philosophical studies. I read it without any difficulty, with meticulous attention and with a vivid interest; it has remained my favourite book. If I haven't found my system there completed I have taken it from there bit by bit.' ('L'ouvrage de Vacherot, *La métaphysique et la science*, parut en 1858, au moment même où j'entreprenais de combler cette lacune et de compléter mes études philosophiques. Je le lus sans la moindre difficulté, avec une attention scrupuleuse et le plus vif intérêt; il est resté pour moi un livre de chevet; et si je n'y ai pas trouvé mon système tout fait, je l'en ai tiré peu à peu.)

15 Adolphe Guéroult, (1810–72).

16 'Pour procéder en bonne logique, il y aurait d'abord à rechercher en dehors des préjugés religieux qui entravent le progrès des idées sociales, dans le domaine de la Métaphysique du XIXe siècle, une Théorie de la Réalité qui pût servir de base à une Théorie de la Science en général' (*CLW*, Letter 16, to Adolph Guéroult, not dated).

17 'Materialism is to know nature through the experiences of the senses, and to deduce from them the knowledge about man and God.' ('Connaître la nature par le témoignage des sens, et en déduire la connaissance de l'homme et la connaissance de Dieu, c'est le *matérialisme*') (*EES*, p. 75).

18 'Spiritualism is to know man through the testimony of the conscience, and to deduce from it the knowledge about God and nature.' ('Connaître l'homme par le témoignage de la conscience, et en déduire la connaissance de Dieu et la connaissance de la nature, c'est le *spiritualisme*') (*EES*, p. 75).

19 'Indépendamment de l'élément purement affectif introduit dans nos perceptions externes par l'exercise des sens, il y a, dans ces perceptions, un autre élément subjectif, savoir l'unité qui leur est donnée par notre esprit . . . nos perceptions intimes, si elles ne comprennent pas d'élément affectif dû à l'exercise de la conscience, comprennent néanmoins, elle aussi, comme un élément subjectif, l'unité que leur donne l'imagination ou la faculté qu'a notre esprit de synthétiser les intuitions de l'expérience' (*EPA*, pp. 413–14).

20 'Prior to any other consideration, that which purely and simply exists, is *substance*, by virtue of the affirmation of being.' ('Ce qui existe purement et simplement, antérieurement à toute autre considération, en vertu seulement de l'être affirmé, c'est la *substance*') *(PA*, chapter 1, [p. 14]).

21 See, in particular, A.-A. Walras (1833), *De la nature de la loi, Recueil de la Société Libre d'Agriculture, Sciences, Arts et Belles-Lettres du département de l'Eure*, 4 (April).

22 'To the phenomenon of pure and simple substantial existence I add the phenomenon of the universal and necessary modality. Hence, I obtain the double phenomenon of material existence and virtual existence.' ('J'ajoute au phénomène de l'existence substantielle pure et simple le phénomène de la modalité universelle et nécessaire; et

j'obtiens le double phénomène de l'existence matérielle et de l'existence virtuelle') (*PA*, chapter 1, [p. 20]).

23 'By uniting force and matter, substance becomes Reality.' ('Par l'association de la force avec la matière, la substance devient Réalité' (*PA*, chapter 1, [p. 23]).

24 '*Il existe, dans l'Espace et le Temps, en étendue et durée – par l'association de la force avec la matière – une réalité, ou ensemble d'individus – comme des corps soumis à des phénomènes, ou comme des phénomènes tenant à des corps*' (*PA*, chapter 1, [p. 31]; Walras's emphasis).

25 'Les véritables conséquences de la réalité, et les seules aussi dont l'étude soit possible et féconde. ce sont donc les fait généraux' (*PA*, p. 40).

26 This article consists of forty-eight pages divided into four sections. It is part of the collection of the Fonds Walras, Lausanne.

27 See, for instance, J. N. Keynes (1904: 35), in which 'art' was defined as 'a system of rules for the attainment of a given end'.

28 'Je vois que tu as mis un peu de côté ta *Philosophie de l'Art*, et je ne puis pas désapprouver le sage parti que tu as pris, à ce sujet. Un ouvrage de cette nature est un travail de longue haleine. Il faut s'y préparer par de nombreuses recherches, par de vastes lectures, par de sérieuses réflexions. Il faut mûrir son plan, et en distribuer tous les détails. Cela vient petit à petit, et, plus on attend, plus on se ménage la chance de faire un livre solide et durable. Je pense que tu as entrevu toutes ces idées, et que je n'ai aucun besoin d'insister là-dessus' ('Lettres inédites de et à Léon Walras', 5 December 1858, in A.-A. Walras (1912)).

29 'L'homme ne doit pas seulement connaître les individus; il doit savoir aussi les rapports d'ordre et de causalité des phénomènes' (*Paradoxes Economiques II*, p. 9).

30 *Journal des Economistes*, December 1860, pp. 373–91. Reprinted in *MEPS*, pp. 42–62.

31 The list of subjects addressed can be found in *MEPS*, p. 42, n. 1.

32 See *MEPS*, p. 42, n. 1.

33 See *CLW*, Letter 72, to Urbain Gilbert Guillaumin, February, 1862.

34 'Il est aisé de comprendre qu'une théorie de la science en général est indispensable pour constituer la théorie de la science sociale, la théorie de l'économie politique, ou la théorie de toute outre science particulière. En l'absence d'une *philosophie de la science* à la fois expérimentale et rationelle qui n'existe point encore à vrai dire, il est sans doute permis d'en esquisser quelques traits dans un cas donné' ('Philosophie des sciences économiques', *Journal des Economistes* (1860), p. 197. The article 'Philosophie des sciences économiques' was extracted from the *EPJ*. This quote can also be found in the *EPJ*, p. 5, n. 1; emphasis in original).

35 Or, as Walras put it in the *Elements of Pure Economics* (*EPE*) (§16), the corporeal entities are the 'theatre' of the phenomena.

36 *EPE*, §16. The French word '*faits*', translated by Jaffé as 'universals', could better be translated, in our opinion, as 'phenomena' or 'facts', in accordance with Walras's own terminology.

37 'The general fact is *universal* and *permanent*: it can manifest itself individually in reality at all places and at all times.' ('Le fait général est *universel* et *permanent*: il peut se manifester individuellement dans la réalité dans tous les lieux, en tous temps') (*Journal des Economistes* (1860), p. 196).

38 *EPE*, §17.

39 *EPE*, §18.

40 *EPE*, §18.

41 'S'il nous était utile et possible de percer la terre de part en part, de dessécher l'océan, de rapprocher du soleil notre planète, cela nous serait permis sinon commandé, par cela seul que c'est tout à la fois un droit et un devoir pour nous que de subordonner la fin des choses à notre fin' (*EPJ*, p. xi).

42 At a later stage Walras admitted that he was aware of the Kantian doctrine only through the work of Charles de Villers of 1801 and Victor Cousin's lectures published in 1842. (See *EPA*, p. 459.) In Walras's personal library at Lausanne one can find Charles-F.-D. de Villers, *Philosophie de Kant ou Principes fondamentaux de la philosophie transcendentale*, Metz: Collignon, 1801; and Victor Cousin, *Leçons sur la philosophie de Kant*, Paris: Librairie philosophique de Ladgrange, 1842.

43 'J'ai dit que les socialistes affirmaient, avec raison, la question sociale, mais qu'ils prétendaient, à tort, la résoudre en dehors des données de la science et avec la seule ressource de leur expérience personnelle, c'est-à-dire par la méthode empirique' (*CLW*, Letter 123, to Jean Macé, published in *Le Travail*, 31 December 1867).

44 '*L'observation*, *l'expérience*, *l'induction*, *l'hypothèse* . . . , tels sont les principaux procédés qui conduisent à la solution des questions posées . . .' (*Journal des Economistes* (1860), p. 197).

45 The manuscript is undated but appears to have been written in the early 1860s. Since the manuscript is untitled we will refer to it as 'Methodological procedures'.

46 The manuscript itself does not contain the relevant expression.

47 'L'Observation et l'Expérience travaillent, et de jour en jour une masse croissante de manifestations individuelles de faits généraux toujours plus consciencieusement étudiées, et mieux connues, pénètrent dans la science. Mieux connus dans leur nature, les faits généraux réclament des explications plus précises. Les hypothèses succèdent aux hypothèses' (Léon Walras, 'Methodological procedures').

48 D. Pokorný, (1978).

49 In the '*Esquisse d'une doctrine économique et sociale*' (*EPA*, pp. 449–95), Walras reported how this subject had led to a disagreement with the editor of the *Journal des Economistes*, Henri Baudrillart. Baudrillart had previously published a study entitled *Des rapports de la morale et de l'économie politique* (1860), in which economics was primarily seen as a moral science. A review by Walras of Baudrillart's book, now in the archive at Lausanne, discusses this liberal, i.e. 'spiritualist', approach to economics. In ironic turns of phrase, Walras ridiculed the naive moral philosophy, which he accused of twenty-five centuries of

misery and crime. Clearly, more than enough material for a lively discussion.

50 'Toutes les destinées individuelles se trouvent directement en rapport les unes avec les autres. Ils forment donc l'objet propre de l'activité sociale, et ils sont les éléments du fait général de la *Société*' (*EES*, p. 120; emphasis in original. This text dates from 1867).

51 *EPE*, §7.

52 It is interesting, in this respect, that Walras was said to be credited with having introduced the concept of adaptation in psychology; see *EPA*, p. 461.

53 *EPE*, §7.

54 'Pour critiquer l'organisation sociale actuelle, et pour établir la théorie de la société rationelle et idéale, le publiciste doit constamment se tenir au double point de vue du bien et de l'utile, de la philosophie morale et de l'économie politique' ('*Paradoxe Economique* II', p. 18).

## 4 INDICATIONS OF HISTORY

1 See S. Charléty, *Histoire du Saint-Simonisme (1825-1864)*, Gonthier, Paris, 1965 and C. Crossley, *French Historians and Romanticism*, Routledge, London, 1993.

2 See *EPA*, pp. 504-505.

3 A few years earlier, in 1857, Walras had met Maxime Du Camp, one of Lambert's recruits, who had commented on Walras's *Francis Sauveur*.

4 'Mon livre [*EPJ*] une fois publié, j'en adressai un exemplaire à Lambert-Bey avec lequel j'étais en relations et qui voyait en moi un disciple à recruter. Quelque temps après, j'allai faire une visite à Lambert-Bey, rue de Tournon, dans la maison de l'éditeur Douniol. . . . il avait lu mon ouvrage avec soin et m'en fit une critique vigoureuse' (*EPA*, p. 466).

5 'Je ne sais s'il vous souvient que, vers 1860, nous nous rencontrâmes un soir chez Georges Le Roy, rue de la Ferme des Mathurins. Nous étions six: Le Roy, Habenack, et vous d'un côté; mon ami Gustave Maugin, le Dr. Thulié et moi de l'autre. Il s'agissait pour vous de nous convertir au saint-simonisme. La discussion dura jusqu'à 1h du matin. Nous sortîmes, mes deux camarades et moi, sans avoir été entamés. Il faut vous dire que, pour ma part, j'étais inconvertible, ayant déjà reçu en dépôt le germe d'une doctrine sociale à laquelle je suis resté attaché et au développement de laquelle j'ai consacré ma vie' (*CLW*, Letter 553, to H. Fouquier, 9 June 1883).

6 See *CLW*, Letter 34, to U.G. Guillaumin, 3 June 1860.

7 'Je vois que tu es circonvenu par les Saint-Simoniens. J'espère que tu ne te laisseras pas à leurs belles paroles. C'est une des sectes que je connais le mieux, puisque j'en ai longtemps étudié les doctrines, et sur laquelle je puis te donner quelques renseignements. Je ne sais pas si tu as remarqué que, dans mon travail sur le livre de M. Thiers sur la propriété, j'ai fait ma profession de foi sur l'école saint-simonienne. En tous cas, je crois pouvoir te rappeler les points qui m'ont toujours

empêché d'abonder dans le sens de l'école saint-simonienne' (A.-A. Walras to L. Walras, 1 April 1860).

8 'Le mort de Henri Fouquier me rappelait ces jours-ci un souvenir de la nôtre assez différent: celui d'une soirée passée chez Georges Le Roy, le neveu de Mme Du Camps, rue des Mathurins, où Roy, Ch. Habenack et Fouquier devaient nous convertir, Thulié, toi et moi, au St. Simonisme et d'où nous sortîmes sains et saufs, mais sans prétendre pourtant que je n'ai rien emprunté, pour ma part, aux Saint-Simoniens' (*CLW*, Letter 1513, to Gustave Maugin, 31 December 1901).

9 See e.g. *CLW*, Letter 553, to H. Fouquier, 9 June 1883.

10 See C. Crossley (1993, p. 126).

11 See e.g. 'L'industrie moderne et l'économie politique' of 1861, in *MEPS*, Ch. 3.

12 See pages 60–65 below.

13 'Je fais un très grand cas de l'histoire; mais je crois qu'elle ne peut seule et sans le secours de l'économie politique pure suffire à l'application et à la pratique' (*CLW*, Letter 827, to W. Wundt, 1 March 1888).

14 See 'Notice autobiographique', *CLW*, vol. 1, p. 2.

15 The 'Comité du salut public' was the dictatorial body founded by Robespierre in 1793.

16 See Chapter 5.

17 Public lectures delivered before the Société libre d'Agriculture, Sciences, Arts et Belles-Lettres du département de l'Eure.

18 'J'aurais pu te proposer un autre sujet qui me préoccupe moi-même depuis longtemps, mais qui est encore plus vaste que le précédent, et qui demande bien des travaux, bien des recherches. Je veux parler d'une histoire du *régime économique* des sociétés. C'est un travail dont j'avais conçu et rédigé une sorte d'esquisse, lorsque je faisais mon cours d'économie politique à Evreux, en 1832. De même qu'il y a pour les corps, en physique, trois états d'agrégation, l'état *solide*, l'état *liquide*, l'état *gazeux*, je concevais pour les sociétés humaines 5 manières de vivre, ou 5 régimes économiques, qui sont: l'Etat *chasseur*, l'Etat *pasteur*, l'Etat *agricole*, l'Etat *industriel*, l'Etat *commercial*. Je définissais chacun de ces états, j'en donnais des exemples. Je les étudiais ensuite dans leurs causes et dans leur effets. Je signalais les conditions qui président à leurs établissement. Et enfin, chose la plus grave et la plus importante, mais aussi la plus instructive et la plus curieuse, je voulais rechercher quels étaient les effets de ces différents régimes sur la population, sur son bien-être, sur ses lumières, sur ses moeurs, sur la paix, sur la guerre, sur la législation, sur les formes du gouvernement, etc, etc.' (A.-A. Walras to L. Walras, 16 December 1860, in A.-A. Walras 1912).

19 See Chapter 1.

20 These lectures are part of the collection of the Fonds Walras (Lyon). The *Cours d'économie politique* is partitioned in lessons. The '*Esquisse d'une histoire économique*' is part of lesson 3.

21 'La nécessité, la liberté, le progrès, voilà les trois faces diverses qui

présente ce fait unique qui constitue dans sa simplicité primitive, l'ensemble de cet univers que nous appelons la vérité. La science naturelle, la morale, l'histoire seront alors les trois principaux démembrements de la science universelle' (A.-A. Walras, 'Cours d'économie politique', in A.-A. Walras 1990).

22 'Je conviens que la richesse considérée sur son véritable point de vue, la véritable richesse si vous voulez, est un fait progressif, que l'opulence des nations est un des élements nécessaires de leur civilisation générale, et que cette opulence grandit ou diminue, comme une foule d'autres faits qui font partie de cette civilisation. Mais je nie que la richesse considérée sous ce point de vue soit l'objet de l'Économie politique. Et voilà comment j'échappe à la contradiction dans laquelle je paraissais être tombé. L'Économie politique est la science de la valeur; entre la richesse et la valeur il y a une intervalle immense, il y a un abîme. La valeur n'est point un fait progressif et l'économie politique reste indépendante de l'histoire' (A.-A. Walras, 'Cours d'économie politique', in A.-A. Walras 1990).

23 'Les cinq états que nous avons décrit forment sans doute une série ascendante de progrès et de perfection. Ils peuvent servir à tracer la marche de la civilisation' (A.-A. Walras, 'Cours d'économie politique', in A.-A. Walras 1990).

24 Running ahead of the description of the different stages one may give one example to illustrate the comparison between the texts:

| Auguste | Léon |
|---|---|
| 'Dans l'état agricole l'homme s'addresse directement à la terre, et la force à produire les végétaux qui sont le plus à sa convenance, tels que le riz, le blé, le maïs, le manioc, la pomme de terre, et les autres substances alimentaires qui se composent de fruits, tels que le raisin, la pomme, l'olive' | 'Dans l'état agricole l'homme commence à s'addresser directement à la terre pour forcer à produire des végétaux [qui sont le plus à sa convenance] comestibles tels que riz, blé, maïs, manioc, et des fruits: raisin, olives, etc.' |

25 See L. Walras (forthcoming).

26 This same idea appears in Auguste Walras's 1832 lectures with reference to the physics analogy: 'Although three aggregation states for bodies are distinguished, this does not imply that all bodies in nature are susceptible to each aggregation state.' ('C'est ainsi que quoiqu'on reconnaisse trois états d'agrégation pour les corps, on ne prétend pourtant pas dire par là que tous les corps de la nature soient susceptibles de ces trois états d'agrégation') (A.-A. Walras, 'Cours d'économie politique', in A.-A. Walras 1990).

27 *EES*, pp. 205–39.

28 The manuscript is part of the Fonds Walras collection (Lausanne). It consists of 12 foolscap, numbered, pages in Walras's handwriting. A small note attached to the manuscript reads:

I read this article to my father in Hôtel de Saxe in September, October 1861. 'Ah!, he said, these type of articles will not be accepted.' (Je lisais cet article à mon père à l'Hôtel de Saxe, en 7bre 8bre 1861. 'Ah!, disait-il, on te refuse des articles comme ceux-là!)

29 See J.-P. Lévy (1972), J.Droz (1983).
30 An elaboration of the concept of economic equality will be given in the subsequent chapters.
31 Although *L'Economie politique et la justice* was presented as a refutation of the 'socialism' of Proudhon, to a certain extent it also represented a reaction to the ideas of reformists in general. The socialists, in the eyes of Walras, were a heterogeneous group of socially concerned intellectuals disseminating a whole variety of options for social (re)organization with matching policies. The contending orthodox '*laissez-faire*' policy of the liberal economists, on the other hand, had been claimed by these '*économistes*' to be by far superior to any other policy. According to Walras, however, also '*laissez-faire*' as a doctrine lacked a strong scientific basis and, as such, had been unsuccessful in silencing the socialist opinions of its opponents.
32 W. Jaffé, 'Walras's economics as others see it' (*Journal of Economic Literature*, vol. 18, June, 1980).
33 See, for instance, Walras (1987: Ch. 2).
34 *Gazette de Lausanne*, 22 July 1880, reprinted in the *EES*, pp. 240–6.
35 L'économie politique nouvelle a complètement éclairci l'ancien problème dit 'de la population et des subsistances' . . . et qui se pose ainsi: 'Comment faire subsister de plus en plus confortablement sur un territoire *limité* une population *croissante* déjà parvenue au régime industrielle et commercial?' (*MEPS*, p. 513, 'Ruchonnet et le socialisme scientifique' (1909); emphasis in original).
36 'Nous savions qu'à l'époque actuelle, grâce aux chemins de fer, nous sortons de l'état agricole pur pour entrer dans l'état industriel et commercial qui est aussi *financier*' (*EPA*, p. 468).
37 H.-E. Barrault (1923).
38 'Les conditions de la société changent lentement dans le cours des siècles, en vertu de causes intimes et générales, dont on démêle l'action à travers tous les incidents de l'histoire et en même temps de brusques secousses, auxquelles on donne le nom de révolutions, déterminées par des causes locales et accidentelles, exercent çà et là des actions dont la sphère varie d'étendue' (A.-A. Cournot (1872), vol. I, p. 5).
39 'Si défectueux que puisse parfois nous paraître notre état social, il faut l'accepter sans révolte parce qu'il est nécessaire, sans regrets parce qu'il renferme en lui le principe indestructible de son amélioration normale' (*EPJ*, p. v).
40 'L'installation même du régime industriel et commercial réclame la solution de la question sociale' (*EES*, p. 453. This text dates from 1896).
41 'Pour résoudre la question sociale, nous avons à effectuer de grands

progrès dans les conditions de la production et de la distribution de la richesse' (*EES*, p. 245).

42 These doctrines are discussed by Walras in the unpublished '*Théorie de la répartition de la richesse social*'. This manuscript consists of 239 foolscap pages and was presumably intended as a more systematic work on social economics. The '*Théorie de la répartition de la richesse social*' is part of the archive of the Fonds Walras (Lausanne).

43 *EPE*, §7.

44 'Il faut dire toutefois qu'on n'a guère fait jusqu'ici l'histoire au point de vue économique. On a fait surtout l'histoire des guerres et des conquêtes, on a fait aussi l'histoire des gouvernements et des révolutions politique; mais on a négligé l'histoire du travail et de la production agricole, industrielle et commerciale. Cette sorte d'histoire se trouve surtout dans les ouvrages qu'écrivent les Allemands sous le nom d'ouvrages d'économie politique' (Walras (forthcoming)).

45 'Comme l'ont très bien remarqué les maîtres de l'école historique eux-mêmes, nos types économiques de *marchés*, de *produits*, de *services*, d'*entrepreneurs*, de *propriétaires fonciers*, de *travailleurs*, de *capitalistes*, de *prix courants*, de *fermages*, de *salaires*, d'*intérêts*, se rapportent à l'état industriel et commercial et non à l'état agricole, à l'avenir et non au passé' (*EPA*, p. 468).

46 See Chapter 5 et seq.

## 5 INDICATIONS OF SCIENCE

1 See pages 42–3.

2 See *CLW*, Letter 72, to Urbain Gilbert Guillaumin, February, 1862.

3 To be found in the archives at the Fonds Walras (Lausanne).

4 See page 43.

5 See pages 48–51.

6 Second article in the series '*Paradoxes Economiques*', (ca. 1860) [unpublished].

7 'Qu'a été jusqu'ici l'économie politique? – Rien. Que doit-elle être désormais? — Tout' ('*Paradoxe Economique II*', p. 1).

8 'La solution de ce qu'on appelle la question sociale économique, et qui n'est pas la question sociale tout entière, dépend de deux ordres de considérations préliminaires très différentes mais également essentielles: des considérations purement économiques et des considérations purement morale. Voici exactement ce que j'entends dire à cet égard. Résoudre la question de l'organisation économique de la société, ce serait, en somme, déterminer les conditions: 1. de la production la plus abondante possible et 2. de la répartition la plus équitable possible de la richesse sociale entre les hommes en société' (*EES*, p. 175).

9 *EPE*, §19.

10 *EPE*, §19.

11 'Avant de faire et afin de faire cette détermination [of the conditions],

il y a deux choses qu'il faut savoir: ce que c'est la richesse sociale, et ce que c'est que l'homme en société' (*EES*, p. 175).

12 *EPE*, §8.

13 *EPE*, §17.

14 Jaffé translated the French '*gouverner*' as 'to control'; in our interpretation 'to direct' is a better translation in this context.

15 *EPE*, §17.

16 This position is similar to J. N. Keynes's (1904) definition in *The Scope and Method of Political Economy* of 'positive science' and 'normative or regulative science', respectively.

17 *EPE*, §15; emphasis in original.

18 'Il y a une science *pure naturelle* qui constate des faits et des rapports ayant leur origine dans le jeu des forces fatales de la nature, et une science *pure morale* qui constate des faits et des rapports prenant leur source dans l'exercise de la volonté libre de l'homme. . . . Il y a une science *appliquée naturelle* fournissant des règles pour la conduite des personnes vis-à-vis des choses impersonnelles, et une science *appliquée morale* fournissant des règles pour la conduite des personnes vis-à-vis les unes des autres' ('De la culture et de l'enseignement', in *MEPS*, p. 414; emphasis in original. Text dates from 1878).

19 *MEPS*, p. 414.

20 See page 57.

21 *Journal des Economistes*, vol. 25, February 1860, pp. 196–210.

22 See page 41.

23 Note that this is fully consistent with Walras's ontological definition of a corporeal entity, being an 'individual limited in extent', i.e. limited in quantity. In Chapter 6 we will go into the matter of social wealth in greater detail.

24 *EPE*, lessons three and four.

25 *EPE*, §24.

26 See page 58.

27 Note that property as a phenomenon, implying ownership of 'things', should not be confused with the 'property' we saw earlier, defined as the 'quality' of a 'corporeal entity'.

28 *EPE*, §23.

29 *EPE*, §35.

30 *EES*, p. 31.

31 See Figure 5.2.

32 *CLW*, Letter 16, to Adolphe Guéroult, undated.

33 Jules Du Mesnil-Marigny (1810-85).

34 'Je partage, quant à moi, toute l'économie politique et sociale en trois parties, savoir:

1. L'étude des lois naturelles de la *valeur d'échange* et de *l'échange*, ou *théorie de la richesse sociale.* C'est aussi ce que j'appelle *économie politique pure*;
2. L'étude des conditions les plus favorables de *l'agriculture*, de *l'industrie*, du *commerce*, du *crédit*, ou *théorie de la production de la richesse.* C'est aussi ce que j'appelle *économie politique appliquée*;

3. L'étude des meilleurs conditions de la *propriété* et de *l'impôt*, ou *théorie de la répartition de la richesse*. C'est aussi ce que j'appelle particulièrement *économie sociale*' (*RIS*, p. 10).

35 See pages 97–103.
36 We will come back to this point in Chapter 6.
37 'Je suis d'avis que . . . la théorie de l'art, ou science appliquée, doit précéder la pratique de l'art, et que la science pure doit précéder la science appliquée' (*CLW*, letter (1025), to Vilfredo Pareto, 14 September 1891).
38 See page 47.
39 '*Paradoxe Economique II*', pp. 18-19.
40 'La distinction de la science pure en science pure naturelle et science pure morale serait moins nécessaire. Si on la fait, il faut, en tout cas, se garder de croire que la science pure naturelle suffit pour l'élaboration de la science appliquée [naturelle] et la science pure morale pour celle de la science [appliquée] morale. Ce serait une erreur' (*EPA*, pp. 453–4).
41 'Je crois sincèrement que Saint-Simon ou tel autre réformateur, avec une philosophie moins improvisée et une science moins superficielle, eût pu être le Newton de la science sociale.' Note by Walras, dated February 1862, in *MEPS*, p. 134.

## 6 THE ELEMENTS

1 See page 74.
2 *EPE*, §40.
3 'La valeur d'échange laissée à elle-même se produit naturellement sur le marché sous l'empire de la *concurrence*. . . . Selon que cette concurrence fonctionne plus ou moins bien, la valeur d'échange se produit d'une manière plus ou moins rigoureuse' (*Eléments*, §41).
4 *EPE*, §41.
5 'Sur le marché, les acheteurs et les vendeurs sont ordinairement en présence les uns des autres; mais la présence de ces échangeurs n'est pourtant pas nécessaire: qu'ils donnent leurs ordres à des agents, le marché se tiendra entre ces derniers' (*MEPS*, p. 315).
6 'L'étude de la bourse est un sujet où toute l'économie politique et sociale est intéressée. Les marchandises qui s'y vendent sont très bien définies et très précieuses; leurs prix sont très variables; la constatation de ces variations est très importante. Ces circonstances ont déjà fait du marché des titres de capital fixe un marché très perfectionné; mais l'économique pure aurait cependent à y exercer sa critique en vue d'en faire le marché type' (*EPA*, p. 482).
7 In the *MEPS* Walras indicated that neither the presence of the stockbrokers nor the agents would be necessary:

> Mais, théoriquement, la présence des agents est-elle plus nécessaire que celle des échangeurs eux-mêmes? Pas le moins du monde. Ces agents sont les exécuteurs purs et

> simples d'ordres inscrits sur des carnets; qu'au lieu de faire la criée, ils donnent ces carnets à un calculateur, ce calculateur déterminera les prix d'équilibre non pas certes aussi rapidement, mais à coup sûr plus rigoureusement que cela ce pourrait se faire par le mécanisme de la hausse et de la baisse.
>
> (*MEPS*, p. 316)

8 *EPE*, §41; in the *EPA*, p. 432. Elsewhere Walras wrote: ' The typical market . . . is the one where sales and purchases are made through intermediary agents who receive the orders from sellers and buyers and who will only transact after having assessed the price, as current price, for which effective supply equals effective demand. . . . a typical market demands a stock exchange list in which current prices would be registered officially.' ('Le marché type . . . est celui où les ventes et achats se font par l'intermédiaire d'agents qui reçoivent les ordres des vendeurs et des acheteurs et n'opèrent qu'après avoir déterminé, comme prix courant, le prix pour lequel l'offre effective et la demande effective sont égales. . . . un marché type exige une mercuriale où les prix courants soient officiellement inscrits.')

9 'Cette substitution soit le plus souvent impossible, en raison de la nécessité pour l'acheteur de voir et de toucher la marchandise, d'être lui-même sur le marché' (*MEPS*, p. 316).

10 *EPE*, §30.

11 'Je pense que, dans l'étude méthodique d'un fait général comme celui de la valeur d'échange, l'examen de sa nature doit précéder la recherche de son origine' (*Eléments*, §40).

12 All of these '*tentatives*' are part of the Fonds Walras (Lausanne). The full title of the latter manuscript is: '*Application des mathématiques à l'économie politique* (1871), *3e tentative*'. In the first two '*tentatives*', the rudimentary exchange equations were expressed in simple algebra. In the third '*tentative*', the exchange was depicted analytically in a rather primitive, but, in fact, more abstract geometry. Jaffé (1965) mentions only the first two '*tentatives*'.

13 There is no evidence to indicate that this addition actually took place.

14 See A.-A. Walras (1831, 1849).

15 'Appelons en effet rareté d'une marchandise le rapport de l'*utilité* que possède cette marchandise à la *quantité* qui en existe, . . . ou le rapport de la *demande* à l'*offre*' ('*Application des mathématiques à l'économie politique, 2e tentative*', p. 14; Walras's emphasis).

16 See Chapter 3.

17 On the question of real utility, the following note can be found in the Fonds Walras (Lausanne):

'Two principle objections have been made regarding our fundamental formulae.

The first can be derived from the impossibility to "measure satisfaction" and, consequently, to enter this magnitude in the calculations.

This objection was raised by Mr Laurent at the *Institut des Actuaires français* (see the *Bulletin* of the institute of July 1900, p. 85) of which I am a corresponding member and of which Mr. H. Poincaré is an honorary member. I have trusted to be able to appeal to the judgement of the latter, who has answered that "the proof that of two satisfactions one may find one larger than the other *follows from the preference of one.*" I find this an excellent answer. It is in this manner that traders supply the measure of their own satisfactions: with respect *to their preferences.* Naturally, this is more or less judicious; but that is not the question. The establishment and variation of prices studied by pure economics are determined by proven wants and not by reasonable wants. Demand results from real needs and not from normal needs. It has been suggested to keep the name of *utility* for the latter and to name all other needs *desirability, ophelimity.* It seemed to me simplest to declare once and for all that economics takes the word *utility* in the well-defined sense of *real* utility and not *ideal.*'

('On a fait à nos formules fontamentales deux objections principales.

La première se tirerait de l'impossibilité de "mesurer une satisfaction" et, par suite, de faire figurer une telle grandeur dans un calcul.

Cette objection ayant été produite par M. Laurent à l'*Institut des Actuaires français* (Voir le *Bulletin* de l'Institut de Juillet 1900, p. 85) dont je suis membre correspondant et dont M. H. Poincaré est membre d'honneur. J'ai cru pouvoir en appeler du jugement de celui-ci, lequel m'a répondu que "la preuve que de deux satisfactions il pouvait trouver l'une plus grande que l'autre, *c'était qu'il la préférait.*" Cette réponse me parait excellent. C'est ainsi que tous les échangeurs fournissent la mesure de leurs satisfactions: respectives *par leurs préférences.* Plus ou moins intelligemment, bien entendu; mais là n'est pas la question. Les établissement et variations de prix qu'étudie l'économique politique pure sont ceux qui sont déterminés non par les désirs raisonnables, mais par les désirs éprouvés. Les demandes résultent non des besoins normaux mais des besoins réels. On a proposé de réserver le nom d'*utilité* aux premiers et de donner celui de *désirabilité*, d'*ophélimité* . . . aux autres. Il m'a paru plus simple de déclarer une fois pour toutes que l'économique prenait le mot d'*utilité* dans le sens bien défini d'utilité *réelle* et non *idéale* . . . ') (emphasis in original).

18 In the Walrasian ontology of Chapter 3 this could be rephrased as 'virtual utility limited in duration'.

19 i.e. 'virtual utility limited in extent'.

20 Jaffé's criticism in the *EPE* (translator's note 8[2]), that the reference to the 'number of people' is unfortunate due to the individual, psychological character of the reaction to goods, seems to miss the point. The 'number of people' can only be found in Walras's virtual concept of utility, in which no actual reaction to goods has yet been deemed to have taken place.

21 *EPE*, §74; emphasis in original.

22 *EPE*, §74.

23 In this respect, it is possible that extensive utility becomes devoid of meaning since it expresses the quantity of commodities where the intensive utility is zero, hence, where the intensity of the wants satisfied is zero. Since the analysis is restricted to those quantities

of commodities that have a positive intensity of wants satisfied, extensive utility falls outside its scope.

24 *EPE*, §76.

25 'Distinction de l'*utilité finale* (incrément d'utilité effective) et du *degré final d'utilité* (rareté).

L'*utilité finale* est le produit de l'incrément de quantité supposé infiniment petite (positif ou négatif, demande ou offre) par le *degré final d'utilité* (rareté)

$$\text{utilité finale} = dq \times r$$

Le maximum d'utilité effective de ($A$) et ($B$) pour un échangeur a lieu par l'égalité des utilités finales au *prix crié.*

$$dq_a \times r_a = dq_b \times r_b$$

$$\frac{r_a}{r_b} = \frac{dq_b}{dq_a} = p_{a,\ b}$$

Cette condition ne détermine pas l'échange, mais seulement la *demande* et l'*offre*' (Note entitled 'Observation à M. Gide (Juin 98)' in the archives at the Fonds Walras (Lausanne). This translation of the issue into mathematical terms was worked out for the first time by the mathematician P. Piccard in 1871, on request of, and in close cooperation with, Walras).

26 Walras's conclusion, that *rareté* is the 'cause' of value in exchange, was rejected by Jaffé in the *EPE* (translator's note 10[3]). Jaffé argued that one could not speak of a causal relation in a static environment. In our opinion Jaffé's objection is slightly beside the point: Walras's methodological procedure of finding a 'cause' of the phenomenon of value in exchange does not take place in the 'real' world. The conclusion that *rareté* is the indirect cause of value in exchange, however, does require a connection between the 'world of ideas' and the 'real world'.

27 This does not imply that the character of the consecutive editions remained the same.

28 In the *Elements*, Walras also gave an entirely different explanation for the mixed nature of money: money was considered as 'capital' from a social point of view, whereas from an individual point of view money was considered as 'income'. In the extensions of the model, however, this explanation loses all significance.

29 For an extension on this see van Daal and Jolink (1993: Part II).

30 *EPE*, §164.

31 See van Daal and Jolink (1993).

32 This third commodity, in terms of which the prices of the other two could be expressed, was often referred to by Walras as the *numéraire.*

33 In the mathematical model it appears impossible to separate the prices of the consumers' services and the prices of the productive services.

34 Although the *Capital formation model* includes money savings, 'money'

itself will remain undefined until the *Money model*. 'Money' in the present model is considered as a circulating medium which can be used without costs. This role changes in the *Money model*. In the *Capital formation model*, however, 'money savings' is expressed in terms of barter exchange.

35 In modern terminology this change in the 'technical' circumstances is better known as 'factor substitution'.

36 *EPE*, §322.

37 See *MEPS*, pp. 248–9.

38 *EPE*, §110.

39 See *EPE*, §116.

40 We will elaborate on this point in Chapter 8.

41 'L'économie politique pure, telle que je viens de la définir . . . établit ainsi que . . . il y a deux espèces naturelles de richesse sociale: 1. la *terre* et 2. les *facultés personnelles de l'homme* et qu'en outre, la valeur des secondes ne variant pas nécessairement, celle de la prémière va nécessairement en croissant dans une société progressive qui passe successivement du régime de *chasse et de pêche* aux régimes *pastoral, agricole, industriel et commercial*' (*MEPS*, p. 508).

42 Franklin Henry Giddings (1855–1931), American sociologist; professor at Columbia University from 1894 to 1928.

43 'L'économie pure n'est que la théorie de la richesse sociale. Pour passer de là à l'économie politique appliquée et à l'économie sociale, il faut introduire en scène l'homme physiologique et psychologique, individuel et moral' (*CLW*, Letter 253, to Antoine Auguste Cournot, 20 March 1874).

44 *EES*, pp. 99 ff.

45 'Pour faire la théorie de la société en général, économique ou morale, et pour la faire *a priori* et rationnellement, une opération préalable est nécessaire: dégager par abstraction de l'experience la définition de l'homme' (*EES*, p. 189; emphasis in original).

46 'La *théorie générale de la société*, nous apprend que l'homme en société est à la fois *individu* et *Etat*, qu'il a des besoins individuels en tant qu'il vaque à l'obtention d'une *position personnelle* et des besoins collectifs en tant qu'il procède à l'établissement de *conditions sociales*' (*EPA*, pp. 265–6; emphasis in original).

47 See also pages 48–51 and 68–9.

48 'Il y aura là comme une pierre bien taillé, au milieu d'une certaine quantité de blocs informes, que nous retiendrons pour la construction de notre édifice' (*EES*, p. 177).

49 See page 38.

50 In matters of metaphysics, Walras considered the two opposing doctrines to be, on the one hand, 'empiricism' and, on the other, 'idealism' (*EES*, p. 75). 'Empiricism' itself could be divided into 'materialism' and 'spiritualism'. Turning to moral philosophy, then, the same doctrines would be addressed though 'empiricism' would be called 'liberalism' and 'idealism' would be called 'socialism'. The distinction into 'materialism' and 'spiritualism' was subsequently translated into moral philosophy as 'utilitarianism' and 'moralism'

respectively. Finally, in matters of social science, 'liberalism' on the one hand, was called 'individualism', and 'socialism', on the other, was called 'communism' (see outline below).

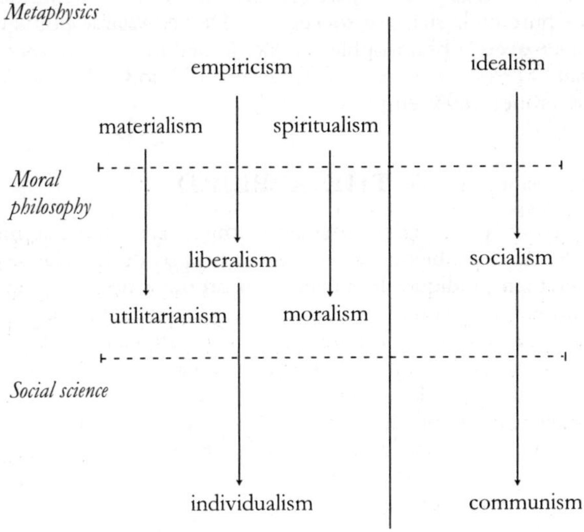


The terms themselves should be seen in their nineteenth-century context and may well lack the precision required in twentieth-century definitions. Our concern here is restricted to social science.

51 '*Liberté de l'individu; autorité de l'Etat. Egalité des conditions; inégalité des positions.* Telle est donc bien, en dernière analyse, la loi supérieure d'organisation de la société sur la base de l'ordre et de la justice', (*EES*, p. 162; emphasis in original).

52 'Vous parlez de liberté et d'autorité, d'autorité et de liberté. . . . Mais n'entendons-nous pas tous les jours écrivains et orateurs nous parler de *Liberté* et d'*autorité*, d'*ordre* et de *Justice*? Vous nous en avez parlé avec talent, conviction et sincérité, mais les autres aussi!' (*CLW*, Letter 126, from an unknown correspondent, 23 March 1868).

53 See Schumpeter (1954, p. 828).

54 'A chaque suivant sa capacité, à chaque capacité suivant ses œuvres'. See also Crossley (1993).

55 'Les Saint-Simoniens ont proclamé la maxime: *à chacun suivant sa capacité, à chaque capacité suivant ses œuvres;* mais cette maxime est toujours restée assez vague et assez peu précise. . . . Je conviens, il est vrai, que cette maxime consacre la distinction que je fais entre la justice communitative et la justice distributive, et qu'elle semble réserver la domaine de l'égalité et celui de l'inégalité. Mais tout cela n'est pas très clair, et je préfère de beaucoup ma formule: égalité des

conditions, inégalité des positions' (A.-A. Walras to L. Walras, 1 April 1860, in A.-A. Walras 1912; emphasis in original).

56 'La *Recherche de l'idéal social* fournit la base philosophique de mes conclusions ou la science pure de l'homme dans la société; les *Eléments d'économie politique pure* en forment la base scientifique ou la science pure de la richesse sociale. . . . De l'économie politique pure, combinée avec la philosophie sociale, je déduis . . . l'*économie politique appliquée* et l'*économie sociale*' (*CLW*, Letter 1172, to Guillaume de Greef, 27 November 1893; emphasis in original).

## 7 THE APPLIED

1 'Nous avons, pour parler aussi simplement, aussi familièrement que possible, deux problèmes à résoudre à propos de la richesse sociale: premièrement, indiquer le moyen d'en produire beaucoup, et, secondement, indiquer la manière de la partager convenablement entre les hommes en société. C'est ce qu'on peut appeler, en termes plus relevés, théorie de la production et théorie de la répartition de la richesse, théorie de la production agricole, industrielle, commerciale et financière de la richesse, et théorie de la répartition de la richesse par la propriété et par l'impôt entre les individus et l'Etat. Ces deux problèmes résolus, ces deux théories élaborées, il n'y aura plus, scientifiquement, de question sociale' ('Discours d'installation', *MEPS*, pp. 365–6).

2 See *EPE*, lesson 2.

3 This distinction between 'science' and 'art' can also be found in an 'English version' in the work of Senior and Mill. At a later period, John Neville Keynes, in *The Scope and Method of Political Economy* (1891), added a second distinction, by differentiating between a 'positive' science and a 'normative' science, and an 'art'.

4 In fact, Auguste Walras had already advanced the idea that abundant production would induce a general price decrease, thereby ameliorating the position of the labourers. See, for instance, A. Walras (1848), 'La Vérité Sociale par un travailleur', unpublished manuscript dated April 1848 preserved at the Fonds Walras (Lausanne); extracts of the manuscript were published in Leroy (1923).

5 *EPE*, §33; emphasis in original.

6 *EPE*, §223.

7 *EPE*, §223.

8 One should bear in mind that in Walrasian philosophy, the relation man–thing is dominated by the idea of the subordination of things to man.

9 See Figure 5.1, in which economics was not considered to be included in the social sciences entirely.

10 'Ces services et produits [d'intérêt privé] sont ceux qui intéressent les hommes en tant qu'individus vaquant librement à l'obtention de leurs positions personnelles, c'est-à-dire à la satisfaction de besoins divers et inégaux pour chacun d'eux' (*EPA*, p. 197).

11 'Services et produits d'intérêt public . . . sont théoriquement ceux qui intéressent les hommes comme membres de la communauté ou de l'Etat procédant d'autorité à l'établissement des conditions sociales, c'est-à-dire à la satisfaction de besoins qui sont les mêmes pour tous et qui sont égaux pour tous' (*EPA*, p. 198).

12 It is interesting to note at this stage, that Walras attributed a 'utility curve' to the State which is comparable to a utility curve for the individual. This clearly resulted from the holistic view of the State:

> 'It is certain that the utility-curves for products or services of public interest will be indispensable to complete the mathematical theory of economic equilibrium.' ('Il est certain que la conception des courbes de besoin ou d'utilité des produits ou services d'intérêt public serait indispensable pour compléter la théorie mathématique de l'équilibre économique.'), (*EES*, p. 433, n. 1)

This idea, however, never reached fruition in Walras's work.

13 '[L]'objet principal de l'économique appliquée est donc d'indiquer les cas où l'intérêt social permet d'abandonner les entreprises à l'initiative individuelle et ceux où il commande de les réserver à l'initiative de l'Etat ou de les faire organiser ou réglementer par l'Etat' (*EPA*, p. 267).

14 In this sense, Walras differed from Cournot, who had proceeded in the opposite direction: from monopoly through duopoly to perfect competition.

15 Although, for instance, the issuance of paper money can nowadays hardly be considered as 'of exclusive private interest', a salient point is that Walras also questioned the proper organization of production for these kinds of products.

16 *EPE*, §372; emphasis in original.

17 *EPE*, §373.

18 A maximum price, as in our own contemporary terminology, implies an upper limit to the selling price level which is presumably lower than the price level that would have obtained in the case of free competition. A minimum price implies the opposite situation in which a lower bound to the selling price is set which is presumably higher than the free competition price level.

19 It is assumed that the cost of production is the same for all entrepreneurs.

20 Strangely enough, Walras does not discuss new entry of entrepreneurs in the presence of persisting profits.

21 This discussion can be found in lesson 34 of the *Elements* and in the article '*Théorie du libre échange*' (*EPA*, pp. 286–304). The article '*La paix par la justice sociale et le libre-échange*' (*MEPS*, pp. 467–503) contains a restatement of the same idea.

22 '[L]e libre échange n'est autre chose que l'extension au monde entier du régime de la libre concurrence en matière économique' (*EPA*, p. 299).

23 See in particular *EPE*, appendix I, §8, n. 1 and *CLW*, Letter 1027(7), to L. von Bortkiewicz, 18 September 1891.

24 *EPE*, appendix I, §8, n. 1; emphasis in original.

25 Walras mentions the case of an inventor who, by virtue of his inventions, obtains a monopoly. In this case the individual would be wronged if, in the name of social interest, the State were to prohibit that monopoly.

26 As we shall see in Chapter 8, when we come to discuss the monetary policy in Walras's theory, his conclusion that the issuance of paper money should be prohibited goes hand in hand with State intervention in monetary matters in general.

27 'Conclut pour des raisons théoriques d'intérêt économique à l'intervention de l'Etat en matière de monnaie et de monopoles, mais à la liberté de l'initiative individuelle en matière d'agriculture, d'industrie, de commerce, de crédit et de spéculation' (*CLW*, Letter 1288, to Numa Droz, 29 December 1896).

28 *Revue socialiste*, 15 June and 15 July 1898, reprinted in the *EES*, pp. 205-39.

29 *EPE*, §8.

30 *CLW*, Letter 1274, to Georges Weulersee, 1 December 1896.

31 *EPE*, §33.

32 'Ma théorie de la propriété vient de l'Ecole normale' (*CLW*, Letter 1274 and 1274(3), to Georges Weulersee, 1 December 1896; Auguste Walras had been a student at the Ecole Normale).

33 See *CLW*, Letter 1289, to Henri Adrien Naville, 5 January 1897.

34 '*Le droit de propriété d'une personne sur une chose est le droit, pour cette personne, d'appliquer cette chose à la satisfaction d'un besoin, même en la consommant*' (*EES*, p. 205; emphasis in original).

35 At this stage, persons could still be considered either individually (individuals, families, associations) or collectively (townships, provinces, States). This followed from the definition of 'person' we reviewed in Chapter 3 above (see pages 40–1.). The 'things' a person could consequently use to satisfy his needs could according to Walras's classification of social wealth, be divided into capital and income. Capital, comprising either land, personal faculties or capital goods proper, distinguished itself from income in that it can be used more than once in the production process. Income, then, comprised mainly the capital-services and commodities, which can only be used once.

36 'Le propriétaire d'une chose est propriétaire du service de cette chose' (*EES*, p. 206).

37 'Le propriétaire d'une chose est propriétaire du prix de cette chose' (*EES*, p. 207).

38 'Il faut donc ici démontrer que la libre concurrence ne favorise pas les acheteurs au détriment des vendeurs, ou réciproquement . . . . [J]'y vois d'ailleurs le *nœud* de la théorie scientifique de la propriété' (*EES*, p. 207; emphasis added).

39 Two publications by Walras resulted from this conference: *Théorie critique de l'impôt* and *De l'impôt dans le Canton de Vaud*.

40 *EPE*, §392.

41 'Si l'Etat était en possession du sol et vivait des fermages que lui paieraient les entrepreneurs ou consommateurs locataires des terres, il aurait un certain revenu à dépenser' (*EES*, pp. 435–6).

42 As explained by Walras, the State could consider a land tax as well as the expropriation of the land together with a compensation for the landowners. In the case of a land tax, the State would tax the income of the landowners, who in return would try to pass the tax burden on to the consumers. Referring to Ricardo indirectly, and to Destutt de Tracy directly, Walras argued that the landowner is ultimately unable to pass the tax onto anyone else. Hence, when land is taxed over a longer period of time the value of the capital is affected by the tax and this, according to Walras, is equivalent to the confiscation of a part of the land by the State.

Walras's efforts to analyse the effects of taxation of this kind do not seem to be consistent with his general belief in the abolition of all taxes. It transpires, however, that the analysis was merely of theoretical interest and not intended for any practical application. In any case, the system of taxation which would bring the land into the State ownership was seen by Walras as a strictly instrumental and temporary arrangement. Similarly, the other alternative would comprise the (rightful) repurchase of the land by the State. As explained by Walras, such a repurchasing scheme could take place over a longer period of time before, ultimately, the State became the sole owner of the land.

43 'Dans une société où l'on a laissé tomber les terres dans le domaine de la propriété individuelle, et qui serait une société progressive, comme, par exemple, une société en voie de passer du régime agricole au régime industriel et commercial, "il serait possible à l'Etat, tout en rachetant les terres au prix courant, de les payer sans bourse délier, grâce à la plus-value"' (*MEPS*, p. 458).

44 It is interesting in this respect to compare the wording of this topic of both father and son Walras in which a striking similarity seems to appear.

45 'A chaque augmentation du taux de cette plus-value, le prix des terres, en outre de l'augmentation relative à la plus-value existante, augmente en raison de l'apparition d'une plus-value nouvelle; et c'est ce bénéfice, sur lequel les propriétaires n'ont aucun droit de propriété, parce qu'il n'a été ni prévu ni calculé et qu'ils ne l'ont pas payé en achetant les terres, qu'il faut réserver à l'Etat et qui lui permettra d'effectuer l'amortissement du prix d'achat des terres au moyen du fermage' (*EES*, pp. 341–2).

## 8 ECONOMICS OF TRANSITION

1 'Fort du témoignage de l'histoire, je dis que notre prétendue organisation sociale n'est autre chose qu'un état transitoire entre une ancienne société qui s'est décomposé et une société nouvelle qui se

recompose' ('Exposition et conciliation des doctrines sociales', Part II (Doctrines scientifiques des temps modernes), 1873).

2 In '*La bourse et le développement du capital*' it was expressed as follows: 'only savings gives a rigorous explanation of the material prosperity of nations' ('l'épargne seule explique à la rigueur la prospérité matérielle des nations') (*MEPS*, p. 113).

3 1898, in *EPA*, pp. 307–36.

4 1880, in *EPA*, pp. 401–45.

5 'La transformation des épargnes en capital se fait soit en capital circulant, c'est-à-dire en matières premières et produits fabriqués en vente à l'étalage, soit en capital fixe, c'est-à-dire en constructions, machines, instruments, outils de toute nature' (*EPA*, pp. 423–4).

6 Large-scale public works initiated by the State were excluded from the exchange of capital and the determination of prices.

7 '[U]ne partie s'emploie en achat de capitaux neufs à louer en nature à un certain *taux du revenu*; une partie se prête en monnaie comme capital fixe à un certain *taux de l'intérêt*; une partie se prête en monnaie comme capital circulant à un certain *taux de l'escompte*' (*EPA*, p. 316; emphasis in original).

8 '[L]a capitalisation est le but, la spéculation est le moyen' (*EPA*, p. 404). 'Spéculation', in this respect, is considered by Walras simply as the activity undertaken at the Stock Exchange.

9 It should be noted that equation (1) abstracts from the velocity of the circulation of money. As such, it ignores the total value of money necessary for all transactions during the period in question. In other words, the individual's perception of this velocity is expressed implicitly in the amount $H_a$.

10 The expression 'money savings' is rather ambiguous in this respect, since it does not represent total savings. Instead, it represents the amount of cash to buy the shares which will represent the new capital in the model. During the period in question, the capitalist may well generate additional savings which are not taken into account in the expression 'money savings'.

11 It is noted once again that this extension was not integrated by Walras into his general equilibrium model but merely advanced the idea of a partial money model. See also van Daal and Jolink (1993, Part II).

12 The money savings are not actually transformed into money for transaction purposes. Instead, the money savings decrease simultaneously with an increase in the amount of money for transaction purposes, thereby giving credence to the idea of a 'transformation'.

13 '[O]n pourrait exactement comparer ce *circulus* par lequel la monnaie va de la circulation à l'épargne et de l'épargne à la circulation, à celui par lequel l'eau de pluie va des mers aux nuages et des nuages à la mer (*EPA*, p. 331; emphasis in original).

14 'Le rôle de la monnaie est aussi important dans l'économie du corps social que celui du sang dans l'économie du corps humain, et peut-être l'étude des microbes de la circulation monétaire . . . n'est-elle pas moins difficile ni moins urgente que celle des microbes de la circulation du sang' (*EPA*, p. 395).

15 *EPA*, pp. 307–36.

16 This 'peculiarity' in Walras's theory was also observed by Schumpeter (1954, p. 1126); the idea also seems to anticipate the work in this field of the 1930s.

17 'Cette production des capitaux neufs, qui constitue le fait de la capitalisation, ne s'opère pas d'une façon régulière. . . . Ce mouvement est analogue à celui de la mer: il comporte un flux, une marée haute, un reflux, une marée basse' (*EPA*, p. 31).

18 This analysis was carried out by Walras in 'Mesure et régularisation des variations de valeurs de la monnaie' (*EPA*, pp. 20–61).

19 See Jevons (1863).

20 These observations were made in a course on applied economics, in particular in section X entitled '*Des Crises*'. Presumably, this draft was written during the early 1880s when Walras concerned himself with monetary matters. This draft is preserved at the Fonds Walras (Lausanne) and will be further referred to as 'Des Crises'. The observations made in this section X are purely of a theoretical nature and do not seem to be supported by statistical evidence.

21 Walras's quantity theory of money rests on the inverse relationship between *rareté* and the quantity consumed as reflected in the desired cash balance. By adopting a restrictive assumption which identifies a 'mean *rareté*', he was able to declare that these ratios define the prices.

22 'Lorsqu'un certain nombre de spéculateurs ont des raisons de croire que certain produits . . . vont hausser de prix, c'est assez ordinairement sur de bons renseignements . . . Ils achètent et font hausser les prix. Mais la hausse est un fait public qui révèle à tout le monde la spéculation engagée. Alors beaucoup de gens sont attirés qui achètent aussi et font encore la hausse par cela même' ('Des Crises').

23 *EPE*, §322.

24 *EPE*, §335.

25 See Chapter 6.

26 Economic progress, in Walras's terminology, thus implies a more 'capital-intensive' use of the land without changing the technology, as expressed by a production function. One can think of the mechanization of farming, for instance. Once the production technology or production function changes, Walras speaks of 'technical progress', in which previously unused factors of production may replace existing ones.

27 Once again we stress that these results in a progressive economy were meant to be based on the hypothetical outcomes of the static model of Chapter 6. In fact, the final conclusions pertaining to the progressive economy can already be found in the *EPJ*. The underpinning of the conclusions in the mathematical model, however, was only achieved at a much later date.

28 See J.-B. Say (1841: Book II, Chapters 2 and 3).

29 'Le progrès de la production économique s'efforce d'amener et amène effectivement la réduction de plus en plus considérable des intensités des derniers besoins satisfaits, ou des raretés, des produits;

il aura atteint ses dernières limites lorsque nous aurons tous de tout à discrétion' (*EPA*, p. 10).

30 '[L]a solution complète du problème de la circulation consiste à corriger, d'une part, les variations lentes et persistantes de la valeur de la monnaie qui atteignent la propriété en troublant l'équilibre économique général, et à laisser subsister, d'autre part, les variations plus ou moins subites et éphémères qui sont des moyens de rétablissement des divers équilibres speciaux dont l'ensemble constitue l'équilibre général' (*EPA*, p. 396).

31 Third part: 'desiderata statistiques' (*EPA*, pp. 127–51).

32 In particular by James Mill, H.-H. Gossen, H. George, P.-J. Proudhon and, notably, A.-A. Walras.

33 'Or cette augmentation [du fermage] a pour effet inévitable et constant d'enrichir le propriétaire sans que celui-ci aît eu le moindre besoin de se mettre en frais de prévoyence et de calcul, sans qu'il aît été obligé de faire des économies sur son revenu, sans qu'il aît eu à s'imposer la moindre privation' (A. Walras 1948: Chapter III, p. 10).

34 See e.g. A. Smith (1976).

35 'Exposition et Conciliation des Doctrines Sociales' [p. 24].

36 'Laisser les terres aux mains des propriétaires, c'est perpétuer au sein de la société l'enrichissement indéfini d'une classe parasite; les remettre aux mains de l'Etat, c'est faire bénéficier la communauté des resultats du progrès social' (*EES*, p. 446). Text dates from 1896.

37 'L'agriculture doit se transformer complètement, devenir d'extensive intensive, s'exercer en grand et sur le pied d'un large emploi de capital, double condition, technique et économique' (*EES*, p. 221). Text dates from 1896.

38 'Je crois . . . que l'humanité accomplit actuellement une évolution économique considérable. . . . Je crois que cette évolution, qui aura pour résultat une plus-value nouvelle de la rente . . . n'a pu encore être escomptée par les propriétaires. Je crois donc que si l'Etat rachetait les terres avant l'évolution . . . il trouverait amplement dans la plus-value nouvelle le moyen d'amortir le prix d'achat' (*EES*, pp. 368–9).

39 'Ainsi, nous effectuerons pacifiquement l'évolution sociale qu'exige notre évolution économique en établissement rationnellement et expérimentalement à la fois le système de propriété qui convient au régime non seulement agricole, mais industriel et commercial' (*MEPS*, p. 459).

## 9 FROM ROMANTICISM TO LOGICAL POSITIVISM

1 'L'homme est une planète qui, dans le monde moral, fait elle-même sa trajectoire. Cela a lieu par le moyen d'un double effort et d'un double progrès: l'effort de la raison humaine qui cherche l'idéal social, et l'effort de la volonté humaine qui réalise cet idéal' (*EES*, p. 169).

2 See A.O. Lovejoy (1941).

3 F.L. Baumer (1973).

4 See Chapter 6.
5 See Chapter 7.
6 'S'il est vrai, comme le dit Alfred de Vigny, qu'une belle vie soit "une pensée de la jeunesse réalisée dans l'âge mûr", aucune vie n'aura été plus belle que la mienne. A 24 ans je suis entré dans ma voie, (à 30 je la voyais) l'apercevant distinctement tracée devant moi; et pendant 40 ans, j'y ai marché sans hésitation, sinon sans difficultés, jusqu'au bout' (*CLW*, Letter 1369, to Charles Gide, 4 October 1898).
7 'Dans le progrès des sociétés, je distingue deux choses: le progrès des idées sociales et le progrès des faits sociaux' (*EES*, p. 16).
8 'La réalité sociale étant donnée, il convient que cette réalité se modifie spontanément et se rapproche autant que possible de l'idéal' (*EES*, p. 13).
9 Walras believed that the concept of natural selection was one of the major discoveries of his century.
10 'Au point de vue de l'intérêt, il importe que les facultés personnelles . . . appartient à l'individu . . . parce qu' [ainsi] on laisse s'exercer . . . la force de selection . . . grâce auquel l'humanité reële tend à se rapprocher de son idéal actuel et peut-être à concevoir un autre idéal ultérieur' (*EES*, pp. 222–3).
11 'Les idées que la science émet viennent engendrer des faits nouveaux qui constituent le progrès de la pratique; mais ces faits engendrent à leur tour des idées nouvelles qui constituent le progrès de la théorie' ('Discours d'installation' *MEPS*, p. 363).
12 See pages 30–1.
13 'Mon idéal social n'est pas "un idéal invariable"' (*CLW*, Letter 1322, to Maurice Millioud, 19 August 1897).
14 See Figure 1.1.
15 'En ce qui concerne la perfectibilité social, il apparaitrait comme logiquement nécessaire: [q]ue l'idée de perfectibilité social, impliquant celle d'un idéal social théorique et scientifique, dégagé par l'intelligence de la réalité sociale que fournit l'expérience, implique par cela même l'idée de perfection' (*EES*, p. 11).
16 'Ainsi, élaborer d'abord l'économie politique pure en vue de l'économie politique appliquée, et élaborer ensuite l'économie politique appliquée en vue des réformes économiques' (*EPA*, p. 69).
17 'L'idée dominante de mon introduction consiste en ceci que le socialisme doit être une œuvre méthodique de raison et non de sentiment, ou que la théorie de la société doit être constituée comme une science rigoureuse. J'essaye d'établir cette thèse *a priori*; je m'efforce aussi de la démontrer *a posteriori* en prouvant d'une part que la méthode empirique a égaré le socialisme contemporain, et d'autre part que, faute tout à la fois d'une bonne économie politique et d'une saine morale, l'école économiste n'a pas élaboré scientifiquement le problème social ou la question de la Distribution des richesses' (*CLW*, Letter 25, to Louis Jourdan, 23 March 1860).
18 'En présence des plaies de la société, l'économiste doit savoir rester calme, faire taire ses émotions au profit du succès de ses études, enfin

quitter . . . le champ de la réalité impressionante, pour s'élever jusqu'au domaine de la froide abstraction qui est aussi celui de la science' (*EPJ*, p. ii).

19 'Beaucoup d'hommes de ma génération avaient espéré voir se dessiner en Europe cette évolution du régime agricole au régime industriel et commercial par le socialisme scientifique' (*EPA*, p. 487).

20 'L'etat doit être la personification du peuple' (*CLW*, Letter 530, from L.G. von Winterfeld, 4 March 1882).

21 See Chapter 7.

22 *MEPS*, pp. 504–14.

23 'Tel est le socialisme auquel je suis arrivé. C'est un socialisme scientifique, libéral et humanitaire' (*MEPS*, p. 511).

24 See for instance P. Alexander (1964).

25 'J'ai pensé qu'au début de toute spéculation mathématique il y a des hypothèses, et que, pour cette spéculation soit fructueuse, il faut, (comme dans les applications à la physique d'ailleurs) qu'on se rende compte de ces hypothèses. C'est si on oubliait cette condition qu'on franchirait les justes limites.

Par exemple, en mécanique, on néglige souvant le frottement et on regarde les corps comme infiniment polis. Vous, vous regardez les hommes comme infiniment égoïstes et infiniment clairvoyants. La première hypothèse peut être admise dans une première approximation, mais la deuxième nécessiterait peut-être quelques réserves' (*CLW*, Letter 1496, from H. Poincaré, postdated by Walras, 30 September 1901).

# BIBLIOGRAPHY


Alexander, P. 1964. 'The philosophy of science 1850–1910' in: *A Critical History of Western Philosophy*, D.J. O'Connor (ed.), Macmillan, London.

Antonelli, E. 1910. 'Léon Walras'. *Revue d'Histoire Economique et Sociale*, 3(2).

—— 1923. 'Un économiste de 1830: Auguste Walras'. *Revue d'Histoire Economique et Sociale*, 11(4).

—— 1934. De l'unité de valeur (correspondance entre Léon Walras et Henri Laurent)'. *Revue d'Economie Politique*, 48(July).

—— 1935. 'Léon Walras et sa correspondance avec Augustin Cournot et Stanley Jevons'. *Econometrica*, 3(1).

—— 1953. 'Léon Walras et Carl Menger à travers leur correspondance'. *Économie Appliquée*, 6(2/3).

Barrault, H.-E. 1922. 'L'idée d'évolution dans la science économique'. *Revue d'Histoire Économique et Sociale*, 10(1).

—— 1923. 'L'idée d'évolution dans la science économique'. *Revue d'Histoire Economique et Sociale*, 11(3).

Baumer, F.L. 1973. 'Romanticism (ca. 1780–ca. 1830)' in: *Dictionary of the History of Ideas*, P.-P. Wiener (ed.), vol. 4, Scribner's, New York.

Baumol, W.J. 1955. 'Elements of pure economics. By Léon Walras'. *Journal of Political Economy*, 63(1).

Beaujon, A. 1889. 'Wiskunde in de economie'. *De Economist*, 6(9).

Blaug, M. 1985. *Economic Theory in Retrospect*. Cambridge University Press, Cambridge, 5th edition.

—— 1986. *Great Economists before Keynes: An Introduction to the Lives and Works of One Hundred Great Economists of the Past*. Wheatsheaf, Brighton.

Bompaire, F. 1931. *Du principe de liberté économique dans l'oeuvre de Cournot et dans celle de l'Ecole de Lausanne* (*Walras, Pareto*). Librairie du Receuil Sirey, Paris.

—— 1932. L'économie mathématique d'après l'œuvre comparée de ses représentants les plus typiques: A.-A. Cournot, L. Walras, V. Pareto'. *Revue d'Economie Politique*, 46(4).

Bortkevitch, L. 1890. 'Léon Walras. Eléments d'économie politique pure, ou théorie de la richesse sociale'. *Revue d'Economie Politique*, 4 (January/February).

Boson, M. 1951. *Léon Walras, fondateur de la politique économique scientifique.* Librairie Générale de Droit et de Jurisprudence, Paris.

—— 1963. *La pensée sociale et cooperative de Léon Walras.* Institut des Etudes Cooperatives, Paris.

Bousquet, G. H. 1928. *Vilfredo Pareto: sa vie et son oeuvre.* Payot, Paris.

—— 1963. 'Le systeme mathématique de l'équilibre économique selon Léon Walras, et ses origines'. *Revue d'Economie Politique*, 73(November/December).

—— 1964. 'L'autobibliographie inédite de Léon Walras'. *Revue Economique*, 15(2).

—— 1971. 'Les deux fonds Walras (de Lausanne et de Lyon)'. *Revue d'Economie Politique*, 81(3).

Bouvier, E. 1901. 'La méthode mathématique en économique politique'. *Revue d'Economie Politique*, 15(August/September).

Brems, H. 1974. 'A centennial: the Walras vision'. *De Economist*, 122(3).

Brown, V. 1987. 'Value and property in the history of economic thought: an analysis of the emergence of scarcity'. *Oeconomica/Economies et Société*, 11(7).

Busino, G. and Bridel, P. 1987. *L'Ecole de Lausanne de Léon Walras à Pasquale Boninsegni.* Université de Lausanne, Lausanne.

Charléty, S. 1964. *Histoire du Saint-Simonisme (1825–1864).* Gonthier, Paris.

Chirichiello, G. 1982. 'La teoria della capitalizzazione di L. Walras. Aspetti controversi e condizione per la coerenza analitica'. *Giornale degli Economisti e Annali di Economia*, 41(5-6).

Cirillo, R. 1976. 'The true significance of Walras' general equilibrium theory'. *Cahiers Vilfredo Pareto*, 14(37).

—— 1977. 'J. S. Mill's influence on Léon Walras'. *Cahiers Vilfredo Pareto*, 15(40).

—— 1980. 'The "Socialism" of Léon Walras and his economic thinking'. *American Journal of Economics and Sociology*, 39(3).

—— 1981. 'The influence of Auguste Walras on Léon Walras'. *American Journal of Economics and Sociology*, 40(3).

—— 1982. 'Léon Walras and J. M. Keynes'. *Cahiers Vilfredo Pareto*, 20(62).

—— 1984a. 'Léon Walras and social justice'. *American Journal of Economics and Sociology*, 43(1).

—— 1984b. 'Economists and social reformers on land ownership and economic rents'. *Rivista Internazionale di Scienze Economiche e Commerciale*, 31(3).

—— 1986. 'Léon Walras' theory of money'. *American Journal of Economics and Sociology*, 45(2).

Clément, A. 1850. 'Théorie de la richesse sociale par M. Walras'. *Journal des Economistes*, 27(August).

Clerc, J. O. 1942. 'Walras and Pareto: their approach to applied economics and social economics'. *The Canadian Journal of Economics and Political Science*, 8(November).

Collard, D. 1966. 'Walras, Patinkin and the money tâtonnement'. *The Economic Journal*, 76(303).

—— 1973. 'Léon Walras and the Cambridge caricature'. *The Economic Journal*, 83(June).

Cournot, A.-A. 1838. *Recherches sur les principes mathématiques de la théorie des richesses.* (Reprint by Riviere (Paris), 1938), Hachette, Paris.

—— 1872. *Considération sur la marche des idées et des évènements dans les temps modernes.* Hachette, Paris.

—— 1875. *Matérialisme, vitalisme, rationalisme.* (Reprint by Vrin (Paris), 1979), Hachette, Paris.

—— 1877. *Revue sommaire des doctrines économiques.* (Reprint by A.M. Kelly (New York), 1968), Hachette, Paris.

Cousin, V. 1842. *Leçons sur la philosophie de Kant.* Librairie philosophique de Ladgrange, Paris.

Creedy, J. and O'Brien, D. P. 1984. *Economic Analysis in Historical Perspective.* Butterworths, London.

Crossley, C. 1993. *French Historians and Romanticism.* Routledge, London.

d'Aulnis de Bourrouill, J. 1874. *Het inkomen der maatschappij.* S. C. van Doesburgh, Leiden.

de Gijsel, P. 1985. 'Von Léon Walras (1834–1910) zur neoklassik oder: die Verkuerzung der Walrasschen Politischen Oekonomie durch die Neoklassik und das Walrassche Gerechtigkeitsproblem'. Regensburger diskussionsbeitrage zur wirtschaftswissenschaft, nr.181, University of Regensburg.

—— 1987. 'On the Role of General Equilibrium Theory in Walras's System of Political Economy'. Conference paper, presented at the annual History of Economics Society Meeting.

de Villers, Charles-F.-D. 1801. *Philosophie de Kant ou Principes fondamentaux de la philosophie transcendentale.* Collignon, Metz.

De Vivo, G. 1976. 'Sul sistema di equilibrio economico generale di Walras'. *Economia Internazionale*, 29(3-4).

Denizet, J. 1981. 'Equilibre économique et social chez Walras'. *Economie Appliquée*, 34(1).

Dockès, P. (ed.). 1994. *Walras*, special issue of *Economies et Sociétés*, vol. 28, no. 10-11 (PE no. 20-21).

Dockès, P. and Servet, J. M. 1988. 'Notes on the History of Publications and Reserves of the Walras Archives'. Conference paper, presented at the annual History of Economics Society Meeting.

Droz, J. 1983. *Histoire des doctrines politiques.* Vol. 304 of *Que sais-je?*, 8th ed., Presses Universitaires de France, Paris.

Dumez, H. 1985a. *L'Économiste, la Science et le Pouvoir: le cas Walras.* Presses Universitaires de France, Paris.

—— 1985b. 'Walras, Marshall: stratégies scientifiques comparées'. *Revue d'Economie Politique*, 95(2).

Eatwell, J., Milgate, M. and Newman, P. (eds). 1987. *The New Palgrave Dictionary of Economics.* Stockton Press, New York.

Edgeworth, F. Y. 1889. 'The mathematical theory of political economy'. *Nature*, (September).

—— 1891. 'La théorie mathématique de l'offre et de la demande et le coût de production'. *Revue d'Economie Politique*, 5(January).

Einarsen, E. 1890. 'Walras, Léon: Etudes d'Economie Sociale'. *Zeitschrift fuer Volkswirtschaft, Socialpolitik und Verwaltung*, 6(December).

Falise, M. 1971. 'Portée contemporaine des encaisses desirées'. *Revue d'Economie Politique*, 81(3).

Fishburn, P. C. 1976. 'Cardinal utility: an interpretive essay'. *Rivista Internazionale di Scienze Economiche e Commerciali*, 23(12).

Floss, L. 1957. Some notes on Léon Walras' theory of capitalization and credit'. *Metroeconomica*, 9(April).

Friedman, M. 1955. 'Léon Walras and his economic system'. *The American Economic Review*, 45(December).

Giddings, F. H. 1896. *The Principles of Sociology*. MacMillan, New York, 3rd edition.

Gide, C. 1897. 'Léon Walras, études d'économie sociale'. *Revue d'Economie Politique*, 11(March).

Gide, C. and Rist, C. 1926. *Histoire des doctrines économiques depuis les physiocrates jusqu'a nos jours*. Librairie de Recueil Sirey, Paris, 5th edition.

Golay, J. *et al.* 1948. 'Léon Walras à Lausanne'. *Revue économique et sociale*, 6(October).

Gossen, H.-H. 1854. *Entwickelung der Gesetze der Menschlichen Verkehrs*. F. Vieweg und Sohn, Braunschweig.

Guitton, H. 1938. *Economie rationnelle, économie positive, économie synthètique de Walras à Moore*. Librairie du Recueil Sirey, Paris.

Hall, S. G. 1983. 'Money and the Walrasian utility function'. *Oxford Economic Papers*, 35(2).

Hansot, E. 1974. *Perfection and Progress: Two Modes of Utopian Thought*. MIT Press, Cambridge, MA.

Harrod, R. F. 1956. 'Walras: a re-appraisal'. *The Economic Journal*, 66(June).

Heber, E. A. 1910. 'Die sogenannte Lausanner Schule der politische Oekonomie'. *Zeitschrift fuer Socialwissenschaft*, 1(8).

Hecht, L. 1930. *A. Cournot und L. Walras, ein formaler und materialer Vergleich wirtschaftstheoretischer Ableitungen*. Vol. 1 of *Heidelberger Studien*, Verlag der weiss'schen Universitätsbuchhandlung, Heidelberg.

Heertje, A. 1982. 'An important letter from W. S. Jevons to L. Walras'. *The Manchester School of Economics and Social Studies*, 50(4).

Howey, R. S. 1972. 'The origins of marginalism'. *History of Political Economy*, 4(2).

Howitt, P. W. 1973. 'Walras and monetary theory'. *Western Economic Journal*, 11(4).

Hutchison, T. W. 1953. *A Review of Economic Doctrines 1870-1929*. Clarendon Press, Oxford.

—— 1988. 'Walras: mélanges d'économie'. *The Economic Journal*, 98(June).

Ingrao, B. 1989. 'From Walras' general equilibrium to Hick's temporary equilibrium'. *Recherches Economiques de Louvain*, 55(4).

Ingrao, B. and Israel, G. 1985. 'General economic equilibrium theory. A history of ineffectual paradigmatic shifts'. *Fundamenta Scientiae*, 6(1+2).

Jaffé, W. 1935. 'Unpublished papers and letters of Léon Walras'. *Journal of Political Economy*, 43(April).

—— 1951a. 'Walrasiana: the *Eléments* and its critics'. *Econometrica*, 19(3).

—— 1951b. 'La correspondance complète de Cournot et Walras'. *Economie Appliquée*, 5(1).

Jaffé, W. 1953. 'La théorie de la capitalisation chez Walras dans le cadre de sa théorie de l'équilibre général'. *Economie Appliquée*, 6(2/3).
—— 1960. 'Léon Walras and his relations with American economists'. *Revue Economique et Sociale*, 18(April).
—— (ed.). 1965. *Correspondence of Léon Walras and Related Papers.* North Holland, Amsterdam.
—— 1968. 'Walras, Léon'. In *International Encyclopedia of the Social Sciences*, Macmillan and The Free Press.
—— 1971. 'Reflections on the importance of Léon Walras'. In A. Heertje *et al.*, (eds), *Schaarste en Welvaart*, Stenfert Kroese, Amsterdam.
—— 1975. 'Léon Walras, an economic adviser manqué'. *The Economic Journal*, 85(December).
—— 1977a. 'A centenarian on a bicentenarian'. *Canadian Journal of Economics*, 10(February).
—— 1977b. 'The birth of Léon Walras's *Elements*'. *History of Political Economy*, 9(Summer).
—— 1977c. 'The Walras–Poincaré correspondence on the cardinal measureability of utility'. *Canadian Journal of Economics*, 10(2).
—— 1980. 'Walras's economics as others see it'. *Journal of Economic Literature*, 18(June).
—— 1983. 'Léon Walras and his conception of economics'. In D.A. Walker, (ed.), *William Jaffé's Essays on Walras*, Cambridge University Press.
—— 1984. 'The antecedents and early life of Léon Walras'. *History of Political Economy*, 16(1).
Jevons, W. S. 1863. *A Serious Fall in the Value of Gold ascertained and its Social Effects Set Forth.* Edward Stanford, London.
—— 1871. *The Theory of Political Economy.* (Reprint of the 4th edition by Penguin Books (Harmondsworth), 1970), Macmillan, London, 4th edition.
—— 1874. 'The mathematical theory of political economy'. *Journal of the Statistical Society*, 37(December).
—— 1878. 'Bibliography of works on the mathematical theory of political economy'. *Journal of the Statistical Society*, 41(June).
Jolink, A. and van Daal, J. 1989a. 'Léon Walras' latest book: Mélanges d'économie politique et sociale'. *De Economist*, 137(3).
—— 1989b. 'Léon Walras' mathematical economics and the mechanical analogies'. *History of Economics Society Bulletin*, 11(1).
Jouffroy, T. 1833. *Mélanges Philosophiques.* (Reprint by Slatkine (Paris), 1979), Paris.
Kauder, E. 1953. 'Genesis of the marginal utility theory'. *The Economic Journal*, 63(September).
Keynes, J. N. 1904. *The Scope and Method of Political Economy.* Macmillan, London, 3rd edition.
Kolm, S.-C. 1968. 'Léon Walras' correspondence and related papers: the birth of mathematical economics'. *American Economic Review*, 58(December).
Kuenne, R. E. 1954. 'Walras, Leontief, and the interdependence of economic activities'. *The Quarterly Journal of Economics*, 68(3).

Kuenne, R. E. 1956. 'The architectonics of Léon Walras'. *Kyklos*, 4(2).
—— 1961. 'The Walrasian theory of money: an interpretation and reconstruction'. *Metroeconomica*, 13(August).
Laurent, H. 1900. 'Note sur les principes de l'Ecole de Lausanne'. *Bulletin Trimestriel de l'Institut des Actuaires Français*, 10(December).
—— 1901. 'Communication de M. H. Laurent, membre agrégé, sur les analogies qui existent entre la chrématistique et la mécanique'. *Bulletin Trimestriel de l'Institut des Actuaires Français*, 11(March).
Le Van-Lemeste, L. 1988. 'Origins of Social Economics in France: E. Antonelli as intermediary between Walras and social security (1879-1971)'. Conference paper, presented at the annual History of Economics Society Meeting.
Leduc, G. 1953. 'Léon Walras et ses devanciers'. *Economie Appliquée*, 6(2/3).
—— 1967. 'Léon Walras et sa correspondance'. *Revue d'Economie Politique*, 77(1).
—— 1971. 'Aux origines de l'Ecole de Lausanne'. *Revue d'Economie Politique*, 81(3).
Leone, E. 1911. 'Léon Walras und die hedonistisch-mathematische "Schule von Lausanne"'. *Archiv fuer Sozialwissenschaft und Sozialpolitik*, 32(1).
Leroy, L.-M. 1923. *Auguste Walras, economiste; sa vie, son oeuvre*. Librairie générale de droit et de jurisprudence, Paris.
Letort, C. 1874. 'De l'application des mathématiques à l'étude de l'économie politique'. *L'Economiste Français*, 3(44).
Lévy, J.-P. 1972. *Histoire de la propriété*. Vol. 36 of *Que sais-je?*, Presses Universitaires de France, Paris.
Lewontin, R. C. 1968. 'Evolution: the concept of evolution'. in: *International Encyclopedia of the Social Sciences*, David L. Sills (ed.). Macmillan and The Free Press.
Lhuillier, V. 1992. *Léon Walras, Lecteur de Kant*. Mémoire pour le D.E.A, Université de Paris I.
Lotka, A. J. 1956. *Elements of Mathematical Biology*. Dover, New York.
Lotter, F. 1985. 'Léon Walras: de la mesure observée à la mesure imaginée'. *Economies et Sociétés*, 19(3).
Lovejoy, A. O. 1941. 'The meaning of romanticism for the historian of ideas'. *Journal of the History of Ideas*, 2, 3.
McCreery Hart, A. J. 1985. 'The translation of Léon Walras's correspondence with American economists'. *Atlantic Economic Journal*, 13(2).
Maks, J. A. H. 1986. 'Walras: understood or misunderstood?'. Research memorandum, RU Limburg.
Marget, A. W. 1931. 'Léon Walras and the "cash-balance approach" to the problem of the value of money'. *The Journal of Political Economy*, 39(5).
—— 1935. 'The monetary aspects of the Walrasian system'. *The Journal of Political Economy*, 43(2).
Meek, R. L. 1971. 'Smith, Turgot, and the "four stages" theory'. *History of Political Economy*, 3(1).
Meek, R. L. 1976. *Social Science and the Ignoble Savage*. Cambridge University Press, Cambridge.

Ménard, C. 1980. 'Three forms of resistence to statistics: Say, Cournot, Walras'. *History of Political Economy*, 12(4).

Mirowski, P. 1984. 'Physics and the Marginalist Revolution'. *Cambridge Journal of Economics*, 8(4).

—— 1989. *More Heat than Light*. Cambridge University Press, Cambridge.

Montgomery, W. D. 1971. 'An interpretation of Walras' theory of capital as a model of economic growth'. *History of Political Economy*, 3(2).

Morishima, M. 1977. *Walras' Economics: A Pure Theory of Capital and Money*. Cambridge University Press, Cambridge.

—— 1980. 'W. Jaffé on Léon Walras: a comment'. *Journal of Economic literature*, 18(June).

Oulès, F. 1950. *L'école de Lausanne; textes choisis de L. Walras et V. Pareto*. Librairie Dalloz, Paris.

Page, A. N. 1980. 'Marshall's graphs and Walras' equations: a textbook anomaly'. *Economic Inquiry*, 18(1).

Pareto, V. 1910. 'L'opera scientifica di Léone Walras'. *Giornale degli Economisti e Annali di Economia*, 39(January).

Pesciarelli, E. 1978. 'The Italian contribution to the four-stages theory' *History of Political Economy*, 1978, 10, 4, pp. 597–607.

Pic, P. 1902. 'Eléments d'économie politique pure, ou théorie de la richesse'. *Questions Pratiques de Législation Ouvrière et d'Economie Sociale*, 3(March).

Pirou, G. 1946. *Les théories de l'equilibre économique: Walras et Pareto*. Domat Montchrestien, Paris, 3rd edition.

Pokorný, D. 1978. 'Smith and Walras: two theories of science'. *Canadian Journal of Economics*, 11(3).

Potestio, P. 1987. 'Investment and social categories in Walrasian analysis'. *Economie Appliquée*, 40(1).

Potier, J. P. 1988. 'Léon Walras, critique de l'école libérale orthodoxe française'. In *Les Cahiers de l'A.C.G.E.P.E., volume 2: Walras*.

Potier, J. P. and Hébert, C. 1989. 'The Cooperativist Ideas of Léon Walras'. Conference paper, presented at the annual History of Economics Society Meeting.

Rotheim, R. J. 1987. 'Equilibrium in Walras's and Marx's theories of capital accumulation'. *International Journal of Social Economics*, 14(7/8/9).

Rugina, A. N. 1982. 'Léon Walras: the pure scientist versus the social reformer'. *International Journal of Social Economics*, 9(3).

—— 1988. 'The unending search for universals and lasting peace: from Léon Walras to Jan Tinbergen and beyond'. *Review of Social Economy*, 46(3).

Say, J.-B. 1841. *Traité d'économie politique*. Guillaumin, Paris, 6th edition.

Say, L. and Walras, L. 1866. *Les obligations populaires*. Guillaumin/Dentu, Paris.

Schaller, F. 1971. 'Réflexions sur la pensée politique et sociale de Léon Walras'. *Revue d'Economie Politique*, 81(3).

Schultz, H. 1932. 'Marginal productivity and the Lausanne School'. *Economica*, 12(August).

Schumpeter, J. A. 1910. 'Marie Esprit Léon Walras'. *Zeitschrift fuer Volkswirtschaft, Sozialpolitik und Verwaltung*, 19.

Schumpeter, J. A. 1951. *Ten Great Economists: from Marx to Keynes.* Oxford University Press, New York.

—— 1952. 'Marie Esprit Léon Walras: 1834-1910'. In *Ten Great Economists from Marx to Keynes,* Allen & Unwin, London.

—— 1954. *History of Economic Analysis.* Allen & Unwin, London.

Sée, H. 1926. 'L'idée d'évolution en histoire'. *Revue Philosophique,* 102(July).

Shackle, G. L. S. 1955. '*Elements of Pure Economics*; or, *The Theory of Social Wealth.* By Léon Walras'. *Economica,* 22(November).

Skouras, A. 1980. 'Land and its taxation as issues in economic theory'. *American Journal of Economics and Sociology,* 39(4).

Smith, A. 1976. *An Inquiry into the Nature and Causes of the Wealth of Nations.* Clarendon Press, Oxford, Glasgow edition.

Solow, R. 1956. 'Elements of pure economics. By Léon Walras'. *Econometrica,* 24(1).

Spengler, J. J. 1969. 'The Marginal Revolution and concern with economic growth'. *History of Political Economy,* 4(2).

Tarascio, V. J. 1967. 'Léon Walras: on the occasion of the publication of his correspondence and related papers'. *Southern Economic Journal,* 34(July).

—— 1981. 'William Jaffé, 1898–1980'. *History of Political Economy,* 13(2).

Thio, B. 1988. 'De inkonsistentie van de walrasiaanse theorie van de kapitaalakkumulatie'. *Tijdschrift voor Politieke Ekonomie,* 11(3).

Turgot, A. R. J. 1844 *Oeuvres de Turgot.* Guillaumin, Paris.

Uzawa, H. 1960. 'Walras' Tâtonnement in the theory of exchange'. *Review of Economic Studies,* 27(74).

Vacherot, E. 1858. *La métaphysique et la science.* Chamerot, Paris, 2nd edition.

van Daal, J. 1989. 'On production in Walras' theory of general economic equilibrium'. In F. Muller and W.J. Zwezerijnen, (eds) *The Role of Economic Policy in Society,* Universitaire Pers Rotterdam.

—— 1990. 'On Walras's Theory of Money and Circulating Capital'. Conference paper, presented at the annual History of Economics Society Meeting.

van Daal, J. *et al.* 1985. 'On Walras' model of general economic equilibrium'. *Zeitschrift fur Nationaloekonomie,* 45(3).

van Daal, J. and Jolink, A. 1990. 'L'article "économique et mécanique" de Léon Walras: une note'. *Economie Appliquée,* 43(2).

—— 1993. *The Equilibrium Economics of Léon Walras.* Routledge, London.

van Daal, J. and Walker, D. A. 1990. 'The problem of aggregation in Walras' general equilibrium theory'. *History of Political Economy,* 22(3).

van Parijs, P. 1981. *Evolutionary Explanation in the Social Sciences: An Emerging Paradigm.* Tavistock, London.

van Witteloostijn, A. and Maks, J. A. H. 1989. 'Walras: A Hicksian *avant la lettre*'. *Economie Appliquée,* 41(3).

—— 1990. 'Walras on temporary equilibrium and dynamics'. *History of Political Economy,* 22(2).

Walker, D. A. 1970. 'Léon Walras in the light of his correspondence and related papers'. *Journal of Political Economy,* 78(July/August).

Walker, D. A. 1972. 'Competitive tâtonnement exchange markets'. *Kyklos*, 25(2).

—— 1980. 'Walras' economics: a pure theory of capital and money. By Michio Morishima'. *History of Political Economy*, 12(1).

—— 1981. 'William Jaffé, historian of economic thought, 1898–1980'. *The American Economic Review*, 71(5).

—— (ed.) 1983a. *William Jaffé's Essays on Walras*. Cambridge University Press, Cambridge.

—— 1983b. 'William Jaffé, *Officier de Liaison Intellectuel*'. *Research in the History of Economic Thought and Methodology*, 1.

—— 1983c. 'Biography and the study of the history of economic thought'. *Research in the History of Economic Thought and Methodology*, 1.

—— 1984a. 'Is Walras's theory of general equilibrium a normative scheme?'. *History of Political Economy*, 16(3).

—— 1984b. 'Walras and his critics on the maximum utility of new capital goods'. *History of Political Economy*, 16(4).

—— 1985. 'Keynes as a historian of economic thought: the biographical essays on neoclassical economists'. *History of Political Economy*, 17(2).

—— 1986. 'Walras's theory of the entrepreneur'. *De Economist*, 134(1).

—— 1987. 'Bibliography of the writings of Léon Walras'. *History of Political Economy*, 19(4).

—— 1988. 'Iteration in Walras's theory of tâtonnement'. *De Economist*, 136(3).

—— 1989. 'A primer on Walrasian theories of economic behaviour'. *History of Economics Society Bulletin*, 11(1).

Walras, A.-A. 1831. *De la nature de la richesse et de l'origine de la valeur.* (Reprint by Alcan (Paris), 1938), Johanneau, Paris.

—— 1833. 'De la Nature de la loi'. *Recueil de la Société Libre d'Agriculture, Sciences, Arts et Belles- Lettres du département de l'Eure*, 4(April).

—— 1835. *Réfutation de la doctrine de Hobbes sur le droit naturel de l'individu.* Ancelle fils, Evreux.

—— 1848. 'La Vérité Sociale par un travailleur, Avril 1848'. Unpublished manuscript preserved at the Fonds Walras (Lausanne).

—— 1849a. *Mémoire sur l'origine de la valeur d'échange ou exposition critique et réfutation des opinions les plus accréditées, chez les économistes, sur cette question.* Pankoucke, Paris.

—— 1849b. *Théorie de la richesse sociale, ou résumé des principes fondamentaux de l'économie politique.* Guillaumin, Paris.

—— 1912. 'Lettres inédites de et à Léon Walras'. *La Révolution de 1848*, 9(51/54).

—— 1913. 'Lettres inédites de et à Léon Walras'. *La Révolution de 1848*, 10(56/57).

—— 1914. 'Lettres inédites de et à Léon Walras'. *La Révolution de 1848*, 11(58/60).

—— 1990. *Richesse, Liberté et Société*. vol. 1 of the *Oeuvres économiques complètes*. Economica, Paris.

Walras, L. 1858a. *Francis Sauveur.* E. Dentu, Paris.

—— 1858b. 'Philosophie de l'art'. Unpublished manuscript preserved at the Fonds Walras (Lausanne).

Walras, L. 1859a. 'Du sens esthétique; de l'art; et des opinions en matière d'art'. Unpublished manuscript preserved at the Fonds Walras (Lausanne).

—— 1859b. 'De la propriété intellectuelle; position de la question economique'. *Journal des Economistes*, 24(December).

—— 1860a. *L'économie politique et la justice. Examen critique et réfutation des doctrines économiques de M. P.-J. Proudhon précédés d'un introduction à l'étude de la question sociale.* Guillaumin, Paris.

—— 1860b. 'Philosophie des sciences économiques'. *Journal des Economistes*, 25(February).

—— 1860c. *Théorie critique de l'impôt, précedée de souvenirs du congrès de Lausanne.* Guillaumin, Paris.

—— 1860d. 'Application des mathématiques à l'économie politique (1ère tentative 1860)'. Unpublished manuscript preserved at the Fonds Walras (Lausanne).

—— 1860e. 'Paradoxes économiques. Que le sens commun n'est point le criterium de la science en générale, ni en particulier celui de l'économie politique'. *Journal des Economistes*, 27(December).

—— 1860f. 'Paradoxes économiques II: Que le point de vue économique est le point de vue social par excellence'. Unpublished manuscript preserved at the Fonds Walras (Lausanne).

—— 1861a. *De l'impôt dans le Canton de Vaud.* Imprimerie de Louis Vincent, Lausanne.

—— 1861b. 'Paradoxes économiques III: De la richesse naturelle ou gratuite – De la richesse sociale ou économique – De la richesse intellectuelle'. Unpublished manuscript preserved at the Fonds Walras (Lausanne).

—— 1863. 'Principes de la théorie des richesses par M. Cournot'. *Independant de la Moselle*, (13 July).

—— 1865a. 'Projet de loi sur les sociétés à responsabilité proportionnelle'. *Moniteur Financier*, (5 March).

—— 1865b. 'De l'organisation financière et de la constitution légale des associations populaires'. *Journal des Economistes*, 45(March).

—— 1865c. *Les associations populaires de consommation, production et de crédit.* Dentu, Paris.

—— 1865d. 'Le crédit et les finances, par Victor Bonnet'. *Journal des Economistes*, 48(December).

—— 1866. 'Des réformes économiques'. *Le Travail*, 1, 1, July.

—— 1868. *Recherche de l'idéal social.* Guillaumin, Paris.

—— 1870. 'Application des mathématiques à l'économie politique (2e tentative 1869–1870)'. Unpublished manuscript preserved at the Fonds Walras (Lausanne).

—— 1871a. 'Des billets de banque en Suisse'. *Bibliothèque Universelle et Revue Suisse*, 41(July).

—— 1871b. *Discours d'installation, seance académique du 20 octobre.* Académie de Lausanne, Lausanne.

—— 1871c. 'Application des mathématiques analytiques à l'économie politique (1871) 3e tentative'. Unpublished manuscript preserved at the Fonds Walras (Lausanne).

Walras, L. 1873a. 'Exposition et conciliation des doctrines sociales'. Unpublished manuscript preserved at the Fonds Walras (Lausanne).

—— 1873b. 'Le cadastre et l'impôt foncier'. *Bibliothèque Universelle et Revue Suisse*, 43(November/December).

—— 1874/77. *Eléments d'économie politique pure ou théorie de la richesse sociale.* Guillaumin/Corbaz/Georg, Paris/Lausanne/Basel.

—— 1874a. 'Principe d'une théorie mathématique de l'échange'. *Seances et Travaux de l'Academie des Sciences Morales et Politiques*, 1(January).

—— 1874b. 'Principe d'une théorie mathématique de l'échange'. *Journal des Economistes*, 34(April).

—— 1874c. 'Théorie mathématique de l'échange – question de priorité'. *Journal des Economistes*, 34(June).

—— 1874d. 'De l'influence de la communication des marchés sur la situation des populations agricoles'. *Journal de la Société Vaudoise d'Utilité Publique*, (5/6).

—— 1874e. 'L'Italia Industriale, studi del prof. Alberto Errera'. *Journal des Economistes*, 36(November/ December).

—— 1876a. 'Un nuovo rama della matematica dell'applicazione delle matematiche all'economia politica'. *Giornali degli Economisti*, 3(1).

—— 1876b. 'Note sur le 15 1/2 legal'. *Journal des Economistes*, 44(December).

—— 1877. *Théorie mathématique de la richesse sociale.* Guillaumin, Paris.

—— 1878a. 'Bibliographie des ouvrages relatifs à l'application des mathématiques à l'économie politique'. *Journal des Economistes*, 4(12).

—— 1878b. 'De l'assurance sur la vie'. *Almanach pour 1879 (La Suisse, Société d'Assurance sur la Vie).*

—— 1879a. 'De la culture et de l'enseignement des sciences morales et politiques'. *Bibliothèque Universelle et Revue Suisse*, 3(7/8).

—— 1879b. 'Théorie mathématique du billet de banque'. *Etudes d'économie politique appliquée* (1898), 339–75.

—— 1880a. 'La bourse, la spéculation et l'agiotage'. *Bibliothèque Universelle et Revue Suisse*, 5(March).

—— 1880b. 'La bourse, la spéculation et l'agiotage (deuxième partie)'. *Bibliothèque Universelle et Revue Suisse*, 6(April).

—— 1880c. 'La Question Sociale'. *Gazette de Lausanne*, (22 July).

—— 1880d. 'Théorie mathématique du prix des terres et leur rachat par l'Etat'. *Bulletin de la Société Vaudoise des Sciences Naturelles*, 17(November).

—— 1881a. *Mathematische Theorie der Preisbestimmung der Wirtschaftlicher Guter.* Enke, Stuttgart.

—— 1881b. 'Théorie mathématique du bimétallisme'. *Journal des Economistes*, 14(May).

—— 1882. 'De la fixité de valeur de l'étalon monétaire'. *Journal des Economistes*, 20(October).

—— 1883. *Théorie mathématique de la richesse sociale.* Corbaz, Lausanne.

—— 1884. 'Monnaie d'or avec billon d'argent régulateur'. *Revue de Droit International et de Législation Comparée*, 16(6).

—— 1885a. 'Un économiste inconnu. Hermann-Henri Gossen'. *Journal des Economistes*, 30(April–June).

Walras, L. 1885b. 'A Monsieur le Rédacteur du Figaro'. *Journal des Debats*, (18 June).

—— 1885c. 'Primi elementi di economia politica, di Luigi Cossa'. *Bibliothèque Universelle et Revue Suisse*, 27(8).

—— 1886a. *Théorie de la monnaie*. Corbaz, Lausanne.

—— 1886b. 'Théorie de la monnaie'. *Revue Scientifique (Revue Rose)*, 23(15/16).

—— 1887. 'Note sur la solution du problème monétaire anglo-indien'. *Revue d'Economie Politique*, 1(December).

—— 1889a. 'Théorème de l'utilité maxima des capitaux neufs'. *Revue d'Economie Politique*, 3(May/June).

—— 1889b. *Eléments d'économie politique pure ou théorie de la richesse sociale*. Guillaumin/ Rouge/ Duncker & Humblot, Paris/ Lausanne/ Leipzig, 2nd edition.

—— 1890. 'Observation sur le principe de la théorie du prix de MM. Auspitz et Lieben'. *Revue d'Economie Politique*, 4(May/June).

—— 1891. 'De l'échange de plusieur marchandises entre elles'. *Mémoires et Comptes Rendu des Travaux de la Société des Ingenieurs Civils*, 44(January).

—— 1892. 'Geometrical Theory of the Determination of Prices'. *The Annals of the American Academy of Political and Social Science*, (July).

—— 1895. 'Le péril bimétalliste'. *La Revue Socialiste*, 22(July).

—— 1896a. *Etudes d'économie sociale. Théorie de la répartition de la richesse sociale*. Pichon/Rouge, Paris/Lausanne, 1st edition.

—— 1896b. *Eléments d'économie politique pure ou théorie de la richesse sociale*. Pichon/Rouge, Paris/Lausanne, 3rd edition.

—— 1896c. 'Méthode de la conciliation ou de synthèse'. *La Revue Socialiste*, 23(April).

—— 1896d. 'Théorie de la propriété'. *La Revue Socialiste*, 23(June).

—— 1896e. 'Théorie de la propriété (suite et fin)'. *La Revue Socialiste*, 24(July).

—— 1896f. 'Le problème fiscal'. *La Revue Socialiste*, 24(October/November).

—— 1897a. 'L'état et les chemins de fer (1)'. *Revue du Droit Public et de la Science Politique*, 7(May).

—— 1897b. 'Théorie du libre échange'. *Revue d'Economie Politique*, 11(July).

—— 1897c. 'L'état et les chemins de fer (suite et fin)'. *Revue du Droit Public et de la Science Politique*, 8(August).

—— 1897d. 'L'économique appliquée et la défense des salaires'. *Revue d'Economie Politique*, 11(December).

—— 1898a. *Etudes d'économie politique appliquée. Théorie de la production de la richesse sociale*. Pichon/ Rouge, Paris/ Lausanne.

—— 1898b. 'Théorie du crédit'. *Revue d'Economie Politique*, 12(February).

—— 1898c. 'La caisse d'épargne postale de Vienne et le comptabilisme sociale'. *Revue d'Economie Politique*, 12(March).

—— 1898d. 'Esquisse d'une doctrine économique et sociale'. *Revue des Questions Sociales et Ouvrières*, 46(December).

—— 1900a. *Eléments d'économie politique pure ou théorie de la richesse sociale*. Pichon/ Rouge, Paris/ Lausanne, 4th edition.

Walras, L. 1900b. 'Note sur l'Equation du taux du revenu net'. *Bulletin Trimestriel de l'Institut des Actuaires Français*, 10(December).

—— 1902. 'Lettre de M. L. Walras en réponse à l'étude bibliographique de M. P. Pic'. *Questions Pratiques de Législation et d'Economie Sociale*, 3(April).

—— 1905. 'Cournot et l'économique mathématique'. *Gazette de Lausanne*, 107(163).

—— 1906a. 'Bibliographie économique'. Unpublished manuscript preserved at the Fonds Walras (Lausanne).

—— 1906b. 'Bibliographie littéraire'. Unpublished manuscript preserved at the Fonds Walras (Lausanne).

—— 1907. 'La paix par la justice sociale et le libre échange'. *Questions Pratiques de Législation Ouvrière et d'Economie Sociale*, 8(6).

—— 1908a. 'Un initiateur en économique politique: A.A. Walras'. *Revue du Mois*, 6(2).

—— 1908b. 'Léone Walras, autobiografia'. *Giornale degli Economisti*, 37(6).

—— 1909a. 'Ruchonnet et le Socialisme scientifique'. *La Revue Socialiste*, 50(295).

—— 1909b. 'Economique et mécanique'. *Bulletin de la Société Vaudoise des Sciences Naturelles*, 45(166).

—— 1918. 'Le Socialisme scientifique'. *La Clairière*, 1(18).

—— 1926. *Eléments d'économie politique pure, ou théorie de la richesse sociale.* Pichon & Durand-Auzias/Rouge, Paris/Lausanne, definitive edition.

—— 1938. *Abregé des éléments d'économie politique pure.* Pichon & Durand-Auzias/Rouge, Paris/Lausanne.

—— 1952. 'Trois lettres de Léon Walras'. *Revue Economique*, 3(4).

—— 1954. *Elements of pure economics.* (Translated by W. Jaffé. Reprint by Orion (Philadelphia), 1984), Allen and Unwin, London, 4th edition.

—— 1960. 'Economique et mécanique'. *Metroeconomica*, 12(1).

—— 1962. 'Cournot et l'économie mathématique'. *Revue d'Economie Politique*, 72(1).

—— 1967. 'Pensées et reflexions'. *Cahiers Vilfredo Pareto*, 11.

—— 1987. *Mélanges d'économie politique et sociale.* Economica, Paris.

—— 1988. *Eléments d'économie politique pure ou théorie de la richesse sociale.* Economica, Paris, variorum edition.

—— (forthcoming). *Cours d'économie politique et sociale.* Economica, Paris.

—— undated. 'Des crises'. Section X of an unpublished manuscript on applied economics, preserved at the Fonds Walras (Lausanne).

Whitaker, J. K. and Kymn, K. O. 1976. 'Did Walras communicate with Marshall in 1873?'. *Rivista Internazionale di Scienze Economiche e Commerciali*, 23(4).

Zylberberg, A. 1987. 'The French Disciples of Léon Walras before 1814'. Conference paper, presented at the annual History of Economics Society Meeting.

—— 1990. *L'économie mathématique en France, 1870–1914.* Economica, Paris.

# INDEX

abstraction 31, 40, 44, 47, 75, 98, 146, 148, 168, 178
Adam, J. 152
adaptation 9, 22, 63, 158
agrarian reform 27, 146; and society 28, 59
agriculture 10, 12, 14, 17–19, 57, 77, 114, 137, 163, 172, 176
Aristotle 154
art 29, 30, 36–9, 41–3, 45, 73, 77, 79, 98, 105, 106, 154, 156, 164, 170
assumption 86, 107, 144, 147
authority 101, 102, 108

Balzac, H. de 37
Baranzini, R. 4
Barrault, H.-E. 62, 161
Bastiat, F. 43, 68
Baudrillart, H. 157
Baumer, F.L. 140, 141, 177
belief 29, 139, 142
Berkeley, G. 154
Blaug, M. 2
Bonaparte, L. 28, 152
Boson, M. 2, 152
Bossuet, J.-B. 12, 13
Bridel, P. 5
Byron, G.N.G. 140

Cabanis, P.-J.G. 154
capital 7, 15, 18, 59, 82, 88–90, 92–6, 116–20, 123–8, 130–3, 136, 137, 164, 167, 168, 172–6; formation of 7, 89, 92, 93, 95, 123–8, 130, 167, 168
capitalist 109, 126, 136, 174
categories 12, 22, 23, 40, 44, 69, 88, 119, 120, 129
causality 48
cause 12, 17, 41, 47, 62, 74, 77, 85, 86, 88, 95, 109, 128, 129, 133, 135, 167
classification 45, 57, 70, 72, 88, 98, 119, 172
Comte, A. 62
Condillac, E. de 154
Condorcet, A.N. de 55, 62
co-ordination 70, 75, 78, 100, 114, 120
Cournot, A.-A. 28, 62, 152, 161, 168, 171
Cousin, V. 157
credit 77, 92, 113, 114, 124, 127–130, 163, 172

Daal, J. van 4, 167, 174
definition 11, 15, 22, 23, 70, 78, 88, 94, 98, 99, 116
Delacroix, E. 140
Descartes, R. 154
Destutt de Tracy, A.L.C. 173
development 11, 15, 18, 29, 32, 58
dichotomy 32, 38
Droz, N. 151, 161, 172
Duhem, P. 148
Du Camps 55, 159

Du Mesnil-Marigny, J. 76, 163
Du Pont de Nemours, P.S. 13, 17

economic perspective 48, 58, 68–70, 74, 76
economics: applied 2–4, 7, 59, 67, 76–8, 80, 97, 103, 106–9, 114–16, 118–19, 123, 141, 145, 175; pure 1, 3, 4, 25, 55, 77, 79, 80, 82, 96, 97, 103, 106, 114, 121, 130, 145, 156, 166
employment 26
Enfantin, B.P. 53
entrepreneur 59, 65, 126, 138
equality 15, 22, 37, 60, 84, 96, 100–3, 111, 118, 140, 147, 161
equilibrium 2, 4, 6, 37, 84, 90–2, 94–6, 109, 131, 132, 134, 141, 171, 174
evolution 6, 9–12, 14, 15, 22, 23, 62, 63, 115, 121, 123, 131, 135, 138, 142, 144, 147, 151, 161, 176, 178
evolutionist 1, 7, 9, 11, 16, 19–22, 25, 62, 63, 96, 105, 123, 139, 141, 142, 144, 145
existence 38–40, 43, 140, 155, 156

facts 32, 36, 41, 44, 57, 58, 64, 65, 70, 72, 76, 142–4, 156
Fontenelle, B. Le Bovier de 13
Fouquier, H. 53–5, 158, 159
France 6, 13, 16, 17, 26–9, 37, 60–3, 118, 123, 136, 139, 142, 151, 154, 161
free competition 63, 64, 81–3, 89, 90, 92, 94–6, 105–7, 109–13, 117, 125, 171
free trade 43, 111
freedom 16, 22, 50, 60, 63, 101, 106, 114

Gassendi, P. 154
George, H. 176
Giddings, F.H. 97, 168
Gide, Ch. 167, 177
Gossen, H.H. 121, 176
government 14, 15, 19, 57, 68, 100
Greef, G. de 170
Gresham, T. 135
Grotius, H. 12
growth 77, 122
Guéroult, A. 26, 31, 76, 152, 155, 163
Guillaumin, U.G. 151, 156, 158, 162, 175

Habenack 54, 55, 158, 159
Hansot, E. 22, 23, 151
Herder, J.G. 55
Hertz, H. 148
Hicks, J.R. 2
history 5–6, 9–13, 20, 33, 55–8, 60, 62–5, 72–3, 106, 123, 139–42, 144, 147; of economic thought 2
Hobbes, T. 116
hypothesis 47, 48, 148, 149

induction 47, 157
industrial revolution 28
industry 10, 63, 73, 75, 77, 106 114
information 82, 83, 129
institution 19–20, 83, 99, 124–5, 140, 143
interdependence 3

Jaffé, W. 3, 25–9, 33, 39, 47, 54, 55, 61, 79, 97, 102, 103, 114, 116, 142, 144, 146, 147, 149, 152, 156, 161, 163, 165–7
Jevons, W.S. 127, 128, 175
Jouffroy, Th. 38, 43, 45, 100, 154
Jourdan, L. 146, 177

Kant, E. 55, 154, 157
Keynes, J.N. 156, 163, 170

labour 14, 30, 64, 90, 96, 117–19, 121, 131, 132; division of 15, 26, 49, 50, 68, 69, 74, 98, 137; theory of value 146
Lambert, Ch.-J. (alias Lambert-Bey) 53, 158
Laurent, H. 165, 166
laws 9, 12, 14, 16, 18, 47, 76–8, 80, 81, 94–6, 144, 145, 148, 149
Le Roy, G. 54, 55, 158, 159

Lewontin, R.C. 151
Lhuillier, V. 5
liberalism 7, 31, 32, 153, 168, 169
liberals 32
liberty 17, 21, 22, 32, 45, 57, 100–2, 117, 140, 145
Locke, J. 12
logic 48, 83
Lotka, A.J. 151

Macé, J. 157
Mach, E. 148
Maks, J.A.H. 3
Malebranche, N. 154
marginal productivity 132
market 3, 65, 81–4, 86, 90–4, 111–13, 128, 131, 165; asymmetry 107; regulated 96
Marx, K. 147
materialism 39, 67, 155, 168, 169
mathematics 35, 72, 83, 95
Maugin, G. 54, 158, 159
mechanism 3, 20, 63, 64, 82–4, 88–90, 92–5, 124–6, 130, 134
Meek, R.L. 12, 13, 15, 17, 151
metaphysics 30, 38, 39, 60, 168, 169
methodology 42, 43, 67, 71, 72, 80, 94, 99, 146
Mill, J. 176
Mill, J.S. 170
Millioud, M. 177
model 2, 6, 88–95, 124, 125, 130, 136, 141, 148, 149, 167, 168, 174, 175
money 88–90, 92–4, 110, 113, 114, 117, 124–30, 133–5, 167, 168, 171, 172, 174, 175
monopoly 109, 112, 113, 171, 172
Morishima, M. 2, 3
Musset, A. de 140

nationalization 2, 121, 136, 147, 149
Naville, H.A. 172
natural selection 9, 11, 143, 144, 177
nature 47–50, 76, 81, 83–4, 95, 97, 116
Nefftzer, A. 26
organism 140, 145

Pareto, V. 4, 154, 164
Parijs, Ph. van 151
Patinkin, D. 2
peace 57
Pesciarelli, E. 13, 151
Pezzo, P. del 151
Pfeiffer, E. 152
physics 20, 56, 72, 148, 160
Piccard, P. 167
Plato 154
Poincaré, H. 148, 165, 166, 178
politics 31–3, 73
population 14, 28, 57, 61, 86, 96, 131, 132, 137, 159, 161
positivism 6, 30, 139, 145, 149, 176
positivist 30
Potier, J.-P. 4
poverty 43, 61, 121
premises 122, 149
production, cost of 109, 111–13, 117, 132, 171
profit 91–2, 107, 111–13, 122, 138, 171
Proudhon, P.-J. 27, 136, 146, 152, 161, 176
Pufendorf, S. von 12

quality 13, 41, 163
Quesnay, F. 16, 151

rational 30, 39, 43, 51, 60
reality 7, 15, 20, 30–2, 36, 38–45, 48, 60, 89, 98, 99, 123, 143–6, 152, 156, 157
reform 2, 3, 15, 27, 30, 33, 60, 62, 63, 119, 122, 131, 135, 138, 140, 141, 143–6
research programme 67
revolution 28, 29, 36, 152; French 60, 100, 121, 136, 141
Ricardo, D. 173
romanticism 37, 139–41, 149, 158, 176
Ruchonnet, L. 148, 161

Saint-Simon, C.H. 54, 55, 62, 80, 164
Sainte Beuve, L.A. de 153

Sarcey, F. 153
Say, J.-B. 22, 26, 27, 50, 68, 70, 105, 116, 133, 146, 175
scarcity 26, 74, 86, 128, 129, 131, 132
Scherer, E. 31, 153
Schumpeter, J.A. 2, 102, 169, 175
Senior, N. 170
Smith, A. 12–22, 57, 146, 176
social ideal 50, 139, 144, 145
social order 7, 16, 26
social question 28, 46, 47, 50, 60–3, 68–70, 72, 73, 76, 79, 80, 105, 122, 123, 142, 147, 153
'socialistes' 27, 30, 153, 157
socialists 32, 46, 47, 50, 146, 153, 161
spiritualism 39, 67, 155, 168, 169
State, the: as agent 99, 120, 130, 135, 145, 147
static 3, 6, 7, 9, 18, 94, 95, 123, 130, 131, 167, 175
Stock exchange 82, 125, 165, 174
substance 39, 40, 155, 156
synthesis 39, 47, 89, 101, 105

tâtonnement 94–6
tax reform 119, 173; system 26, 118
Thiers, A. 54, 158
Thulié, dr 54, 55, 158, 159
transition 6–7, 55, 62, 97, 123, 130, 139, 144, 149
truth 48, 57, 99, 140
Turgot, A.R.J. 12–16, 18–22, 55, 57, 151

universals 44, 156
utility 26, 58, 84–7, 90–2, 106, 165–7; marginal 2, 132, 171
utility curve 171
utopia 22, 23
Vacherot, E. 30, 38, 39, 41, 152, 155
value in exchange 70, 74, 76, 77, 81–3, 85, 87; cause of 88, 167; consequences of 94
verification 48
Vico, G. 13, 55
Vigny, A. de 140, 141, 177
Villers, C.-F. 157

Walker, D.A. 3, 5
Walras, A.-A. 7, 25–7, 35, 37, 40, 42, 54, 56–8, 63, 73–4, 102, 116, 136, 146, 151–2, 160, 170, 172
Winterfeld, L.G. von 178
Witteloostuijn, A. van 3
Wuelersee, G. 172